BLACK EDUCATION

BLACK EDUCATION

A Quest for Equity and Excellence

Edited by
Willy DeMarcell Smith and Eva Wells Chunn

Transaction Publishers
New Brunswick (U.S.A.) and Oxford (U.K.)

Copyright © 1989 by Transaction Publishers, New Brunswick, New Jersey 08903. Originally published as a special issue of the *Urban League Review*, Summer 1987, Winter 1987-88, copyright © 1988 by the National Urban League, Inc. Research Department.

Library of Congress Catalog Number: 88-13831
ISBN: 0-88738-781-0
Printed in the United States of America

Library of Congress Cataloging-in-Publication Data

Black education : a quest for equity and excellence / edited by Willy
  DeMarcell Smith.
    p.   cm.
    "Originally published as a special issue of the Urban League
review, summer 1987, winter 1987-88"—T.p. verso.
   ISBN 0-88738-781-0
   1. Afro-Americans—Education.   2. School integration—United
States.   3. Educational equalization—United States.   I. Smith,
Willy DeMarcell.
LC2717.B54   1989
370.19′342—dc 19
                                                          88-13831
                                                             CIP

CONTENTS

BLACK EDUCATION

Black Education:
A Quest for Equity and Excellence

Willy DeMarcell Smith and Eva Wells Chunn

John Stuart Mills once wrote, "[w]hen society requires to be rebuilt, there is no use in attempting to rebuild it on . . . old plan[s]." From time to time, changes (or the lack thereof) in society raise challenges that call for a change of the plans, policies, and programs by which the less fortunate in our society are assisted in maintaining their survival and ensuring their well-being—be it political, socioeconomic or educational. Indeed, the last decade, particularly for persons who are black or members of other minority groups and poor, has been a period of transition. During this time, we have witnessed a change from federal responsibility to authority and autonomy at the local government level. In addition, many institutions that once worked quite well no longer do so. Many progressive social programs and public policies, which originally promised much, have been forsaken, failed, or just faded away.

Pivotal to these times and changes is the question of the extent the American educational system—its policies, its plans, and its practices—has been and is capable of being responsive to, incorporating, and even instigating equity and excellence for black Americans. If, as it has been remarked, the American educational system is uniquely designed for maintenance, we are compelled to ask maintenance of what: the basic values and policies upon which it was/is structured or the dissemination of knowledge and the distribution of resources as it appears currently? When maintenance of one comes into conflict with maintenance of the other, what happens, especially to blacks, other minorities and the poor? What types of educational policies and strategies must be developed to mitigate against this conflict of maintenance? Under what circumstances does one type of educational policy and practice conflict with other types, thereby calling for a national and scholarly soul-searching of priorities? Answering these questions calls for a reassessment of what has and has not been accomplished; it calls for a realignment of agendas and new, imaginative, innovative analyses and strategies for structuring a more equitable and quality educational system.

The questions posed above, if unanswerable empirically, should at least be answerable heuristically. These authors contend that the prerequisite steps for promoting educational equity and excellence must include the following:

1. enacting and interpreting laws that represent an unconditional commitment to equality, equity, and excellence, specifying the means and directions by which state and local governments must achieve these goals, and establishing specific time frames in which they must be achieved;
2. energetic administrative enforcement and implementation coupled with a sympathetic and empathetic understanding of the ramifications of the beneficiaries' problems and needs;
3. a synchronized effort by socially responsible groups to encourage and facilitate potential beneficiaries to take advantage of progressive educational programs, as well as to participate in and make practical demands and suggestions to improve the educational system.

These conditions, in turn, must occur within a context of balanced analyses to impart the sense of urgency necessary for their execution.

Although these conditions for acquiring educational equity and excellence reflect an ideal state, they can be used as benchmarks by which to assess efforts toward such goals for they reveal what should be self-evident: that the acquisition of educational equity and excellence does not involve isolated efforts either inside or outside the system, regardless of the intentions or resources of those making such efforts. Rather, it involves a dynamic-holistic approach of reciprocal influences whose effects are determined by their mutual relationships and analyses. This, in turn, suggests that it is myopic to view the American educational system as limited to entrenched policies and established traditions. Such a view ignores the process by which new ideas, new methods, and even new channels can serve as means to influence and create equity and excellence within an educational system currently and widely believed to be ineffective.

Viewed in this context, this collection presents some analytic, yet timely, treatises that offer incisive and systematic discussions of those educational issues that have an acute and enduring effect on the lives of black Americans. These writings offer a wide variety of perspectives, including policy-political, research, and pragmatic viewpoints. By approaching critical educational issues from multiple perspectives, the end result should be the emergence of a global and timeless picture that could not otherwise be obtained. This thought-provoking blend of scholarly and practical writings, it is hoped, will promote a fuller acquaintance with the issues at hand, as well as avoid the atomization of knowledge.

Instead of avoiding controversial topics and issues, this volume includes selections written by authors who are passionately but professionally devoted to educational equity and excellence. The book aims to encourage an objective appraisal of ideas and proposals with an eye toward developing a critical appreciation among readers for educational issues that need immediate attention. The writings for this volume were selected on the basis of the assistance they offer in understanding and developing specific effective educational programs and curricula for black Americans, the poor, and other minorities.

Our odyssey in unraveling the elements of educational equity and excellence begins with a set of commentaries by John Jacob, President of the National Urban League, and James Cheek, President of Howard University. Both authors offer a rich agenda of ideas and strategies wrought by the world today and changes taking place in society. In his commentary, "Taking the Initiative in Education: The National Urban League Agenda," Mr. Jacob discusses the pivotal role that the National Urban League has long played in black education. Jacob delineates the ongoing educational initiatives of the National Urban League and its 112 affiliates in advancing educational equity and excellence for black Americans. Cheek's commentary, "A Leadership Blueprint for Equity and Excellence in Black Higher Education," describes the crucial role played by college presidents, noting that black college presidents serve as one of the chief instruments of progress for black Americans. The author identifies three fundamental areas in the pursuit of academic equity and excellence: curriculum development, financial stability, and community involvement.

In the first article of this volume, "Equity in Education: A Low Priority in the School Reform Movement" Faustine Jones-Wilson provides an overarching perspective on the school reform movement and its attendant issues. Jones-Wilson argues that educational reform movements are cyclical and that the present call for excellence can be seen in previous cycles. Noting the absence of a concern for equity in the many recent reports and studies on education reform such as *Equality and Excellence: The Educational Status of Black Americans*, the author discusses the concepts of equity, equality, and excellence. Jones-Wilson proposes several alternative reform measures to enhance equity for blacks, the poor, and other minorities.

In "Educational Policy Trends in a Neoconservative Era," Marguerite Barnett traces and describes the shifts in national educational priorities. Barnett argues that the current administration's efforts are clearly toward reduced federal guidance in the area of public education and greater federal support of private schooling. Such efforts, Barnett contends, are primarily ideological choices clothed in unsubstantiated claims of economic efficiency.

John Smith's article, "Legislating for Effective Schools and Academic Excellence," provides a short but powerful portrait of how the federal government can create progressive legislation (i.e., H. R. 5, The School Improvement Act of 1987) for promoting and supporting public schools that can teach students to excel. This bill has been passed in the House of Representatives but, at the time of this writing, has not yet been implemented. Smith soberly points out that although this legislative action was sorely needed, much more remains to be done by the federal government to strengthen the public school system.

Perhaps no single factor threatens to weaken the very foundation of black education more than the decreasing number of black teachers. Mary Dilworth, in the article "Black Teachers: A Vanishing Tradition," offers a capsule view of the historic, social, and political forces that have drained the supply of blacks and other minority teachers. Dilworth notes that poor salaries and working conditions combined with better career options have diminished the attractiveness of the profession. The author further posits that newly-imposed certification requirements and assessment criteria in teacher education have had an even greater impact on the participation of blacks and other minorities than all other deterrents combined. Dilworth concludes by offering several recommendations to mitigate against the vanishing presence of black teachers.

Diana Slaughter and Valerie Kuehne examine the major assumptions on which the practice of parental involvement in schools is based in "Improving Black Education: Perspectives on Parent Involvement." The authors begin by analyzing theories about the role of parental involvement as based on Project Head Start and end with the recently-emerging view of the importance of an ecological perspective on parental involvement. This latter perspective, the authors contend, is necessary to balance the dual aspects of involvement—parental enpowerment and parental education. Moreover, such an ecological perspective gives rise to policy, programs, and research goals that can be directly applied to the lives of black families and the education of their children.

Few issues have commanded more attention from policymakers, educational specialists, and practitioners, and laypersons than that of intelligence and aptitude testing. Sylvia Johnson's article, "Test Fairness and Bias: Measuring Academic Achievement Among Black Youth," reviews and examines this sensitive topic. The author writes that "tests" must be cast in proper perspective to remove the measurement mystique among the general public and professional test users. This can be done, the author notes, by improving the extent and quality of measurement training provided for teachers, counselors, and other professionals who use and interpert standardized tests. Johnson argues that tests must be viewed only as part of the picture when examining and appraising abilities and achievement, especially as it relates to black Americans. Mindful of this situation, the author concludes that educators must broaden the purpose of test-taking and use varied approaches to measuring important attributes, if such measurements are to continue to play such a pivotal role in determining the rewards and positions within society. Johnson closes by recommending that if measurements and testing of black academic achievement are to be continued, more black professionals must be included in the process to bring a broader and more sensitive perspective.

In a similar vein, the article, "Sorting Black Students for Success and Failure: The Inequity of Ability Grouping and Tracking," warns of the dangers involved in selective academic categorization based on ability grouping and tracking. Eva Chunn reviews the determinants and selected consequences of such practices and concludes that black and low-income students are disproportionately affected by stereotyping them as less intelligent and/or less able to learn and excel. Ability grouping and tracking, the author underscores, reinforces such stereotypes by way of teachers' expectations and ultimately results in self-fulfilling prophecies about black students' academic performance. Chunn offers some practical recommendations and cites specific strategies to counter the practice of ability grouping and tracking.

In the "The Eroding Status of Blacks in Higher Education: An Issue of Financial Aid," Mary Carter-Williams treats the problem of educational access and the choices faced by blacks and the Historically Black Colleges (HBCs) from the perspective of student financial aid. The author traces the evolution of student financial aid vis-a-vis higher education from the early 1970s to the mid-1980s. In doing so, Carter-Williams examines the gains and losses of black students at all levels of higher education. She examines how HBCs are currently losing ground because of financial instability wrought by federal cutbacks in education. As a result, HBCs are increasingly stymied in their efforts to provide academic equity and excellence to predominantly black student populations. The author also provides a detailed analysis, backed by voluminous data, on the way in which federal financial retrenchment on student aid has contributed to the decline in the number of blacks in higher education. The article concludes by suggesting various actions necessary to renew the federal student financial aid system.

One of the most divisive, yet searching issues that reaches the core of the quest for educational equity and excellence is school desegregation—its purpose, its strategy, and its usefulness. Indeed, much acrimony surrounds the debate about how best to desegregate public education at the elementary, secondary, and postsecondary levels. Over the last thirty-three years, competing legal and nonlegal arguments have been proffered to resolve this issue. This volume presents four articles that address various aspects of school desegregation. However, because of the extreme importance of this topic, we believe it is appropriate to provide some in-depth discussion in this preamble of the origin and evolution of school desegregation efforts.

In 1954, the Supreme Court in *Brown v. Board of Education of Topeka et al.,* 347 U.S. 483 (1954), struck down the racially-segregated school system that had been previously mandated by state law in much of the South. The Court ruled that separate schools for white and nonwhite students are inherently unequal. In the year following the *Brown* decision, many of the legally-segregated school districts were forced to replace their dual school systems with a single school system for all students.

The *Brown* decision, however, did not address the segregation that existed within school districts, caused either by residential housing patterns or by gerrymandering school attendance zones. Stated differently, the 1954 decision was addressed to *de jure*, but not *de facto* segregation. Because of the migration of the white middle class (and increasingly the white working class as well) into the suburbs that grew around the cities, racial ghettos developed in many of the nation's urban schools, and *de facto* segregation became increasingly prevalent. In 1971, the Court decided *Swann v. Charlotte-Macklenburg Board of Education,* 402 U.S. 1 (1971), where it attempted to deal with the issue of *de facto* segregation for the first time. In that case, the Court held that the school district in and around Charlotte, North Carolina, had to integrate its schools, even if it required the busing of children. In the subsequent decision of *Millikan v. Bradley,* 418 U.S. 717 (1974), the Court overruled a lower court decision that had ordered a region-wide desegregation plan. The district court found that various actions of the Detroit Board of Education, the State Board of Education, and the Michigan legislature (such as barring the use of state funds for busing) had resulted in *de jure* segregation in the city of Detroit. This situation, the court said, could only be remedied through a plan encompassing fifty-three school districts (Detroit and its suburbs). In its reversal, the Supreme Court held that Detroit and its suburbs did not have to maintain a system of cross-busing between central city and suburban school districts to facilitate desegregation. In so ruling, it stated that

> [b]efore the boundaries of separate and autonomous school districts may be set aside by consolidating the separate units for remedial purposes or by imposing a cross-district remedy, it must first be shown that there has been a constitutional violation within one district that produces a significant segregation effect in another district.

Thus, because Detroit's schools were not segregated as a result of the actions of Oakland and Macomb counties, "[those counties] were under no constitutional duty to make provisions for [Detroit's] Negro students."

These decisions revealed judicial recognition of two separate but not entirely disparate concepts. First, to desegregate schools within a school district, children could be assigned to schools outside their neighborhood. However, cross-district school assignment is not an acceptable method of eliminating *de facto* segregation unless the other districts were responsible in some way for the segregation of the predominantely non-white district.

The alleged purpose of sending children to schools outside their neighborhood (which often requires busing) is to provide racial integration, and by extension, to enhance social class integration. Moreover, it is intended to provide more equitable educational opportunities for inner-city, largely black students vis-a-vis the more affluent, often white suburban children. Indeed, blacks are more likely to attend inner-city schools, which are generally believed to be academically inferior and less well-funded than middle-class city or suburban schools that many white children attend. Consequently, busing within or between districts to achieve racial balance is seen as a possible solution to educational inequity.

There is certainly no shortage of arguments and data to support the conflicting views regarding the effectiveness or lack thereof of both voluntary desegregation (such as the use of magnet schools) and compulsory integration (usually accomplished through busing). The articles in this volume cover many of such arguments.

In the article, "The Intended and Unintended Benefits of School Desegregation," Charles Willie reveals a striking finding about the unanticipated consequences of desegregation. The author states that:

> [t]he school desegregation movement has had a greater impact on the white population than on the black population ... it has enhanced the self-concepts of individuals in both racial populations by enabling blacks in predominantly white settings to overcome a false sense of inferiority and whites in predominantly black settings to overcome a false sense of superiority. These outcomes of school desegregation equip students in both racial populations with the kinds of attitudes ... needed for adult living.

Given the frequent inability of urban school systems to meet educational needs and the difficulties that such schools face in dealing with racial imbalance, some observers contend that the black community can better serve its black students by creating an independent and separate school system. Derrick Bell proposes such a controversial action in the article, "The Case for a Separate Black School System." Bell's reasoning stems from the increasing number of black inner-city parents frustrated with the poor quality of urban schools and who as a result want greater control over the schools their children attend. These parents and other concerned persons are demanding community control over their schools and their children's education. As Bell writes:

> [C]ritics [of a separate Black school system] fail to recognize that the New District's [Milwaukee district school system] emphasis will be control, not color. Black parents seeking to transfer from the new district will be able to do so. Whites seeking to enroll their children will be welcomed. And if the new district succeeds in implementing the programs that have been effective in improving the academic performance of inner-city black children in several schools around the country, experience indicates that whites will enroll their children in the new school system.

In many ways, Bell's advocacy of a separate black school system mirrors what white middle-class parents have demanded and sought for years. What the outcome of such demands for community control of an inner-city school will be cannot be determined. Such uncertainty is related not only to the politics of education, but to the character of urban succession patterns.

As with Bell's article, Alvin Thorton and Eva Chunn, in the article "Desegregating with Magnet and One-Race Elementary and Secondary Schools," address ways to improve the quality of black education—particularly that of blacks who reside in suburban communities. It can be argued, these authors imply, that suburban community control of schools is less problematic because it provides a neat fit into the funding unit—that is, the school district.

Desegregation at the higher-education level is examined by James and Jewel Prestage in the article, "The Consent Decree as a Tool for Desegregation in Higher Education." These authors note that the consent decree is a legal mechanism that constitutes an official policy response to the lingering problem of racial segregation and gross resource distribution inequities in a state-sponsored system of higher education institutions. The Prestages point out that the consent decree is somewhat akin to other desegregation efforts such as busing and the use of magnet schools: it is a remedy utilized at the level of secondary schools that includes efforts to equalize resources across all educational units affected, and attempts to selectively offer specialized programs at certain institutions in order to encourage a racial mix across those schools.

Examining the various strategies for promoting academic excellence is similar to viewing a painting under strobe lights. At the same time that the viewer sees the painting as exciting and even revealing, the juxtaposition of scenes often confuses and disrupts the consistency of the presentations. Thus, to increase the clarity of the image, one must view the painting as a whole, even though constant illumination reveals some flaws in the parts. This analogy underscores the need to incorporate the best elements of diverse strategies to promote academic excellence for black students. For this reason, five articles are presented collectively that offer divergent yet complementary approaches for promoting and enhancing educational equity and excellence.

In "Elements of Effective Black Schools," Charles and Christella Moody, review the emergence of the effective school movement as conceived by the late educator Ron Edmonds. These authors provide a descriptive analysis of the components that make schools effective. They include (a) a principal who is a strong instructional leader; (b) a climate of high expectations in which no student is allowed to fall below minimal levels, in an atmosphere that is orderly without being rigid or oppressive; (c) an emphasis on the teaching of basic skills in a well-prepared classroom where students spend most of their time on clearly-defined tasks; and (d) frequent monitoring of students' progress. The Moodys conclude by proffering four elements that are essential for any equity-based education: access, process, achievement, and transfer.

The second article dealing with strategies toward achieving academic excellence, "School Power: A Model for Improving Black Student Achievement," is authored by James Comer, Norris Haynes, and Muriel Hamilton-Lee. These authors acknowledge both the strengths and weaknesses of the Effective School approach as outlined by the Moodys. Comer et al. argue, however, that the significant flaw of the effective schools movement is in the limited value attached to parental involvement in the schools. In developing an alternative approach, the authors present a model wherein parental involvement is a key factor. Comer and his associates provide an in-depth description of their School Development Program, which includes the following major components: (1) School Planning and Management Team, (2) Mental Health Team, (3) Parent Participation Program, and (4) Curriculum and Staff Development. Their program, the authors state, is based on the assumption that educational improvement can be achieved most efficiently and effectively at an institutional level. Of particular interest is the research study based on empirical data presented by the authors to validate the conceptual-descriptive elements of the School Development Program.

Asa Hilliard writes in the article "Reintegration for Education: Black Community Involvement with Black Students in Schools," that the primary responsibility for educating black students lies with the black community. The author stresses the two most important elements in the educational process: (1) the academic/college preparatory curriculum for the masses of black children, and (2) socialization goals, including outlook, values, and behaviors. The socialization process, Hilliard declares, provides black children with a sense of coherence about their experience and a sense of time and space; a location on the map of human history; an orientation, a set of values, and a place in the larger, cohesive community to which the child belongs. Hilliard says that the black community has a concept of itself, with roots in a true (African) cultural reality and an historical foundation. The existence of this community is manifest through institutional structures that have continuity, focus, and purpose. This black community, Hilliard points out, must take the initiative in setting educational goals and in providing models for children's behavior, monitoring the progress of the masses of black children, providing activities that express the community's beliefs about legitimacy, and offering fiscal support for the socialization and educational processes. With these elements, Hilliard concludes, major inroads will occur to help effectively educate all black students.

The final two articles on academic strategies to enhance the quality of education among black students are "Memphis Inner-City Schools Improvement Project: A Holistic Approach For Developing Academic Excellence," written by Willie W. Herenton, Superintendent of the Memphis Public School System, and "A Community Initiative Making a Difference in the Quality of Black Education," authored by William A. Johnson Jr., Betty Dwyer, and Joan Z. Spade of the Rochester Urban league. Both articles are exemplary of how concerned communities, working cooperatively with sectors that include businesses, educational institutions, and human service agencies, can together create a resourceful and practical strategy to enhance the educational achievement of the entire student population.

Our odyssey in search of equity and excellence ends with two articles on two unquestionably timely concerns: school dropouts/pushouts and teen pregnancy. In the article "Black School Pushouts and Dropouts: Strategies for Reduction," Antoine Garibaldi and Melinda Bartley focus on several successful ongoing efforts designed to abate the early departure of students from America's public schools. Indeed, there is an alarming rate of black students who either drop out or are pushed out of school through suspensions or expulsions before they obtain a high school diploma. Garibaldi and Bartley reason that the best strategy to combat black student dropouts and pushouts is to ensure that black students learn the necessary academic and cognitive skills to proceed to the next grade level. These authors concede, however, that these problems are multi-faceted, require complex solutions, and demand the complete cooperation of the entire community.

Joyce Ladner's article "Black Teenage Pregnancy: A Challenge for Educators," analyzes one of the most urgent problems in education—the impact of pregnancy on the education of black adolescents. Ladner examines black teen pregnancy's scope, social context, and consequences. The author further discusses effective approaches to teenage pregnancy prevention, including sex and family life education, school-based health clinics, life skills, school retention, and self-esteem. The author notes that today's pregnant teens have health problems, inadequate or nonexistent child care and become school drop-outs with no job skills or employment opportunities. Ladner concludes that teen pregnancy is a national problem that transcends racial and class boundaries. Nonetheless, it takes a far greater toll on the lives of blacks and the poor than on other groups. Finally, the author recommends that due to the decreases in federal social programs, black organizations must provide much of the leadership efforts to bring about solutions to black teen pregnancy.

Certainly, many of the challenges and problems relating to educational equity and excellence have yet to be solved. What is clear, however, is that the contributors to this volume of writings collectively believe that education provides an unassailable opportunity by which blacks, the poor, and other minorities can move into the mainstream of American society. As long as this belief in the value of education exists as a prevailing goal, the quest for equity and excellence will remain a viable challenge for the black community.

Let us close with a few reflective words that further buttress the rationale for this book. Two rival concepts of education have long existed: that the purpose of education is to form a person's mind and that the purpose of education is to free a person's mind. A key aim of this volume is to free the minds of black Americans. Indeed, no policy, no institution, and no method of education would work with the notion of equity and excellence or with the ideal of a free mind if such a proposal were governed by the principle that a person's mind should be formed and trained to accept the status quo as is—without question.

Our quest for educational equity and excellence in black education is, so to speak, a mission for freedom. There is, of course, no true freedom without personal liberty and socioeconomic opportunity. To be sure, the source of all true freedom is the freedom of the mind. In tandem with this belief, we fully ascribe to the motto of the United Negro College Fund, "A mind is a terrible thing to waste."

2

Taking the Initiative in Education: The National Urban League Agenda

John E. Jacob

Throughout its history, the National Urban League has consistently emphasized the importance of a high-quality education in promoting the advancement of black Americans. Thus, the League has vigorously advocated initiatives and reforms to open the doors of educational opportunity and to secure equitable treatment of black students in the nation's educational institutions. These advocacy efforts have been supplemented by the development and delivery of a range of education-oriented services such as early childhood education, tutorial assistance, and career counseling.

The League's longstanding commitment to education has been driven by its recognition that educational achievement is key to the economic well-being of blacks, the poor, and other minorities. This fact is no less compelling now than it has ever been. Indeed, as we approach the year 2000, a growing number of black youth face a perilous economic future precisely because they are not being adequately equipped to participate in an economy that is undergoing fundamental structural change. The goods-producing, manufacturing sector, traditionally the major source of employment opportunity for blacks, is in severe decline, while high tech and service industries are on the ascendancy. This transformation is having a profound impact on the education and skills requirements of the working population.

Increasingly, only those who have acquired technical and professional skills in such fields as engineering, computer technology, communications, and business management will have access to the better-paying, high-demand jobs the new economy generates. Others will be relegated to the less secure and rewarding positions, while still others are apt to find themselves out of the labor market altogether. Given their pronounced educational disadvantages, the prospects for black Americans are bleak. The dimensions of this problem have been underscored by several incisive reports.[1]

THE PLIGHT OF BLACK STUDENTS

Black students are graduating from high school at rates well below those of white students. By age 18 or 19, a student is usually expected to complete high school.

However, only 62.8% of black 18 to 19 year-olds graduated from high school in 1985, compared to 76.7% of white students of this age.[2] Despite improvements in standardized test scores of black students, they still lag well behind white students in the critical areas of reading, science, and math. Black students are underrepresented in higher-level academic courses in mathematics, science, and language arts.[3] By the same token, black students are overrepresented in classes for the educable mentally retarded. Although they comprised just 16% of total school enrollment in 1984, black students accounted for 37% of all placements in classes for the educable mentally retarded.[4] The dropout rate for black students is alarming. In 1985, black 18 to 19 year-olds dropped out of school at a rate of 17.3% nationally. In some urban areas, the dropout rate for blacks has reached epidemic proportions.[5]

The picture is no better in the area of higher education. The enrollment rates for blacks in 4-year and 2-year institutions in 1984 were 5.0% and 3.8% respectively, compared with 51.5% and 28.8% respectively for whites. Not surprisingly, the number of black students who continue their education to the terminal degree is very small—in 1980-81, 1,265 doctoral degrees were received by blacks, compared with 25,908 earned by whites. Most of the doctorates received by black students were in the areas of education and the social sciences; the fewest were in engineering and the physical sciences.[6]

Such data document a crisis of menacing proportions. It is all too easy to lay the blame for such a situation on black Americans themselves—to blame black students for being unmotivated and unresponsive to instruction; to blame black families for not providing sufficient support of their children's education; or to blame the black community as a whole for fostering or condoning social conditions that militate against educational achievement. Such views, however, amount to blaming the victims for institutional failures. The real responsibility rests with a federal government whose actions to ensure a quality education for all Americans have fallen far short of its rhetoric. The real responsibility rests with school systems that accord preferential treatment to nonminority school districts. The real responsibility rests with teachers who fail to engage black students in the kind of challenging educational experiences that tap their full potential.

THE GOVERNMENT'S POSITION

Of course, the Urban League is aware of the growing public concern about the state of American education in general. Various commissions have examined the subject and addressed the need for improvement in curriculum development, school finance, teacher training, educational administration, and other areas.[7] The nation is indeed "at risk," as weaknesses in its educational system limit its ability to meet the serious challenges posed by an increasingly competitive world marketplace. Nonetheless, the general preoccupation with school reform is biased against the special educational needs of blacks and other disadvantaged minorities. This bias is cogently evidenced by the pattern of expenditures at the state level vis-a-vis education reform. States allocated some $2 billion in the 1985-86 school year to implement a range of reform proposals.

Only 13 of 47 states studied earmarked funds for "at risk" youth, and the total amount set aside was a mere $67.3 million. Based on these findings, the Children's Defense Fund probably understates the case in observing that "[t]he state education reform movement . . . has yet to develop an agenda designed to provide disadvantaged students with the resources and attention they need."[8]

At the national level, the Reagan administration, despite its bold pronouncements about achieving educational excellence, has shown meager appreciation of what is required. To the contrary, the administration's budget initiatives have seriously undermined educational opportunity, especially for the disadvantaged. Thus, the federal government's share of financing for elementary and secondary schools dropped from 9.2% in 1979-80 to 6.4% in 1985-86.[9] Adjusting for inflation, funding for Chapter I of the Education Consolidation and Improvement Act has declined by more than 7% since 1981. Chapter I supports remedial education and other programs that have greatly benefited black and other disadvantaged students. The impact of the real reduction in funding is aggravated by the fact that the number of eligible students has increased substantially during this time. The federal retrenchment has not been limited to elementary and secondary education. Funding for the Work-Study Program, for example, which helps disadvantaged students to complete college, has been slashed by 22%. Moreover, the administration's budget for the 1988 fiscal year would discontinue suport for this program altogether.

The insensitivity exhibited by the national government and the states is antithetical to the principle of equal educational opportunity embodied in the *Brown* decision. However, much more is at stake here than the society's moral rectitude; the nation's economic future is also jeopardized. By the next century, one out of every three persons entering the labor force will be a black or a member of another minority group. This demographic change dictates that a quality education be provided to these groups; otherwise, the nation will find itself lacking the skilled human resources required for further technological advancement and will be hard pressed to maintain its competitive position on the world scene.

The National Urban League will continue to demand the policy responses and fiscal resources necessary to deal effectively with the educational crisis confronting black youth. It will continue to protest measures that compromise or disregard their well-being. At the same time, the gravity of the situation compels black Americans themselves to take more aggressive initiatives on behalf of our children. In large part, such collective action must occur at the local level and concentrate on rectifying the under-education of black youth in the elementary and secondary grades. The effort must be multifaceted, recognizing that multiple factors impinge upon the educational achievement of black students. It must make optimal use of the available institutional and personal resources. Above all, the effort must be a sustained one, for this shared problem does not lend itself to quick solutions.

THE NATIONAL URBAN LEAGUE INITIATIVE

Responding to the imperative, the National Urban League has mounted an unprecedented, movement-wide campaign to improve the education of black students in the public schools of the cities it serves. Launched in September 1986 after a year-long period of planning and development, the League's Education Initiative contains the essential components of an effective community-based strategy.

First, the Education Initiative stresses maximum involvement on the part of black parents, local civic organizations, professional groups, business and industry leaders, and concerned citizens. Through intensive mobilization and coalition-building activity, the objective is to ensure that school systems are held accountable for their performance in meeting the educational needs of black students. Such accountability can only be effected through organized vigilance and broad participation in the educational process. This does not mean that the League is promoting an adversarial approach to school officials. To the contrary, it seeks a partnership, wherever possible, to develop and implement necessary remedial measures. The experience of the Rochester Urban League, described elsewhere in this volume, is a prominent example of such a mobilization and coalition-building thrust.

Second, the Initiative is results-oriented. Thus, Urban League affiliates have designated specific target groups and defined concrete measurable outcomes they want to achieve. These outcomes include reducing the dropout rate among black students, increasing the number of black students in college-bound classes and in math and science courses, and raising black students' scores on scholastic aptitude tests. In Harrisburg, Pennsylvania, a group of students participating in the Urban League's academic support program have been helped to improve their test scores in math, science, and language skills by 70-100 points. Emphasis on such concrete outcomes is necessary to keep the process of change in perspective. The process can be modified, whereas the results we seek should remain fixed until they are achieved. Further, a focus on specific, measurable outcomes is critical to effectuating the system accountability to which I have alluded.

Third, the Education Initiative encompasses the provision of direct services to black students and their parents as well as advocacy activity on their behalf. This two-pronged methodology is consistent with the League's historical approach to solving pressing social and economic problems and is vital in the present instance. A strong advocacy function influences institutional change, while service-giving addresses the immediate needs of individuals.

Finally, the Education Initiative is a long-term undertaking, carried out as a priority endeavor over a five-year period. This time frame is consistent with the program's objectives.

The Urban League's Education Initiative, then, is the cornerstone of its agenda to brighten the social and economic future of black youth. We have no illusion about the task before us and the black community as a whole; it is immense and formidable. However, the league also has no illusion about the consequences of inaction. If we do not act with forthrightness and perseverance, black youth will continue to populate the wasteland of discarded human resources in disproportionate numbers. This prospect is wholly unacceptable.

It has been more than three decades since the historic *Brown* decision that was intended to equalize educational opportunity for all citizens. Significant progress has been achieved. Nevertheless, the nation has thus far made only partial payment on its commitment. As the black community acts to safeguard its interests, we of the National Urban League must make it clear to the larger society that we will not be satisfied until the account is fully settled. We will not be satisfied until every black child is able to realize his or her full potential. We will not be satisfied until equity and excellence in education becomes a reality throughout black America. Thus, we will not be satisfied until the League's agenda becomes the nation's agenda.

NOTES

1. *Barriers to Excellence: Our Children at Risk* (Boston, Ma: National Coalition of Advocates for Students, 1985); *Equality and Excellence: The Education Status of Black Americans* (New York: The College Board, 1985); *Saving the African-American Child* (Washington, DC: National Alliance of Black School Educators, 1984.)

2. Center for Education Statistics; *The Condition of Education: A Statistical Report.* (Washington, DC: Office of Educational Research, U.S. Department of Education, 1987), p. 26.

3. The College Board, *Equality and Excellence.*

4. *1984 Elementary and Secondary School Survey* (Washington, DC: U.S. Dept. of Education, Office of Civil Rights, 1986).

5. Center for Education Statistics, *Digest of Education Statistics*, (Washington, DC: Office of Education Research, U.S. Dept. of Education, 1987) p. 86.

6. Center, *Digest,* pp. 15, 199, 212.

7. *A Nation at Risk,* (Washington, DC: The National Commission on Excellence in Education, 1983); *A Nation Prepared: Teachers for the 21st Century* (New York, NY: The Carnegie Corporation, 1986); *Time of Results: The Governors' 1991 Report on Education,* (Washington, DC: National Governors' Association, 1986).

8. *A Children's Defense Budget* (Washington, DC: The Children's Defense Fund, 1987), p. 141.

9. Children's Defense Fund, p. 145.

3
A Leadership Blueprint for Equity and Excellence in Black Higher Education

James E. Cheek

There are potentially as many leadership agendas in higher education as there are constituency groups—faculties, students, staff, alumni, private benefactors, and other supporters including, in some cases, governmental entities at the state and federal levels and the publics they represent. The existence of so many constituencies in higher education creates the need for leadership that can forge constructive harmonies out of diversity.

Notwithstanding the direct yet divergent responsibilities and obligations black leaders in higher education have to the diverse groups involved, a critical concern exists, not with leadership per se, but with leadership as it relates to ensuring educational equity and excellence for black Americans. Indeed, this topic urgently invites assessment of the leadership agendas, both actual and ideal, of blacks in the context of the unique historical mission of predominantly black institutions of higher education, setting aside a consideration of the leadership role of blacks in predominantly white institutions. This does not deny a role for blacks in such schools; rather, it is a measure of progress of blacks in American society that such a role exists.[1] This paper provides some prescriptions regarding leadership in black higher education as it strives to provide both equity and excellence.

HISTORICALLY BLACK COLLEGES

Within the past decade, nearly 90% of the 113 historically black colleges and universities (HBCs) have undergone a leadership change. This situation may be a sign that such colleges and universities are seeking different kinds of solutions to persistent problems as well as reassessing their mission in the light of present realities.[2]

It must be noted straight away that no two HBCs are alike though they have much in common with each other as well as with predominantly white institutions of higher

Originally published in the *Urban League Review,* Vol. 9, no. 1 (1985) and entitled "Leadership Agenda In Higher Education."

education. All such institutions subscribe to the three-fold mission of education, research, and public service. Beyond that, however, predominantly black colleges and universities were founded as "the chief instruments of racial progress for black Americans."[3] The rationale for their continued existence is embedded in this as yet unfulfilled purpose, in the light of which both black leaders and the institutions they serve are to be judged.

Collectively, HBCs enroll only one-fifth of all blacks enrolled in higher educational institutions, yet they graduate thirty-eight percent of the baccalaureates awarded to blacks by all degree-granting institutions. Moreover, they contribute a disproportionately higher percentage of blacks who go on to earn Ph.D.s, as Mary Carter-Williams' article reveals in this collection. While such degree-granting by HBCs is an impressive achievement, it is not enough, because the total number of black graduates with first as well as higher degrees is well below parity.[4] Increasing the number of college-educated blacks should be a number-one priority of black leaders in higher education.

An African proverb states to the effect that if you do not know where you want to go, any road will take you there. The characterization of leadership as knowing where to go and of management as knowing how to get there cannot be as readily applied to academic institutions as to the corporate world from which it is derived. Both identifying and achieving goals are responsibilities of leadership in higher education.[5] But knowing where to go presupposes awareness of where you are as well as where you want to go. And so the question arises, Where is black America and where does it want to go?

THE ROLE OF EDUCATION

Measurable disparities characterize the status of blacks and whites in American society: disparities in rates of unemployment, income, housing conditions, access to and quality of health care, and educational opportunity, to name but a few. For example, historically the overall rate of unemployment of blacks has beeen twice that of whites, and since 1960 the median black family income has only once been as high as 62% of white family income. For example, it was 55% in 1982, the same percentage as back in 1960.[6] Progress of blacks in American society means closing and eventually eliminating these and other inequities. If the American dream is to come true for black Americans, we must assume that at some point it will no longer be possible to differentiate black and white Americans by such disparities. What black leaders in higher education can do to help close these gaps, then, is the issue.

A persistent theme in black America has been that education, or more generally, self-improvement, can by itself equalize the status of blacks and whites in American society. Thus, in 1884 the great Frederick Douglass wrote that full citizenship would be enjoyed by blacks if only they developed "industry, sobriety, honesty, and intelligence."[7] Self-improvement includes the development of intelligence as well as what the late Dr. Martin Luther King, Jr. referred to as "the content . . . of character" in his famous "I Have A Dream" speech. While there is general agreement that developing intelligence is the responsibility of educational institutions, there are differing views about the responsibility for developing character, a responsibility shared with families and religious institutions.

But education in today's world is likely to mean fulfilling the requirements of accredited educational institutions, and so conceived and executed, it has not been the panacea many black Americans hoped it would be. Such blind faith in education reveals a lack of understanding that blacks have been rejected, and still are rejected by some whites, "primarily because of their racial identity, not because they did not measure up to certain social and economic conditions," as has been pointed out.[8]

If, on the other hand, education is taken as preparation for living in a pluralistic world, as well as for working there, then faith in education as a panacea is well-founded. Education in this sense takes into account massive evidence from anthropology and other disciplines pointing to equality of races. By this view of education, it is necessary to stress the need for education of whites as well as of blacks in order to further racial progress in America.[9]

Whatever the outcome of the current debate on the means to achieve equity and excellence in education, it is the single most important key to racial progress in America. Indeed, it would be a grave error for blacks to forego acquiring the best education they can get until such time as racism is eliminated from American society. As Professor Charles Asbury has put it, "We must continue to fight the battle of racism in American society," but in the meantime, "black children and youth must be taught to make a distinction between their potential as individuals on the one hand and the present condition of American Blacks as a group on the other."[10]

To forfeit the development of one's potential is a form of suicide, which, if it were to become widespread among blacks, could lead to a form of self-inflicted genocide. Moreover, it is of vital interest to our nation, not merely to blacks, to make full use of untapped black resources.[11] Therefore, ensuring that there is equal educational opportunity for blacks and that blacks take full advantage of such opportunities represents the best hope for continuing racial progress in America. In this light, the dropout rate of black high school students, although recently declining,[12] is a matter of grave alarm and serious consequence for black America. A similar point may be made with regard to blacks at the postsecondary level.

That education plays an important role in the mobility of blacks is not merely a matter of conventional wisdom. According to a recent author, "One of the most replicated, central findings from research on stratification and occupational mobility is that the number of years of education completed is the primary determinant of occupational success"—more important than family background, measured intelligence, or school grade point average.[13]

The same author confirmed for his sample that dropouts had higher I.Q.'s than those who remained in school, and that their decision to leave school was based on their perceptions, first of all, that the occupational system was closed and second, that there was racial discrimination in the schools in question.[14] Such dropouts are sacrifices on the altar of racism, if indeed their perceptions are correct. But these students should not be abandoned by the system.

Dr. Stephen C. Wright, distinguished educator and president emeritus of Fisk University, has connected the dropout problem with higher education in the following way:

> [T]he enormous waste of the black mind and talent occurs at every level of education—and the higher the level, the more serious the problem. Approximately 27% of the black students . . . are casualties of drop-outs and "pushouts" at the high school level. This proportion is nearly double the rate (15 percent) for whites. And while blacks constitute roughly 12 percent of the nation's population and 10 perent of the undergraduate enrollment, they receive only 6.38 percent of the baccalaureate degrees—only about half the number they should be receiving. This low percentage indicates a very disproportionately high attrition rate at the college level. Blacks represent only 6.25 percent of the graduate school enrollment and receive only about 3 percent of the degrees. Again, the enrollment is only about half of what it should be and the graduate rate . . . indicates a very disproportionately high attrition rate. The enrollment of blacks in the professional schools is equally dismal. In medicine, for example, blacks constitute only 5.93 percent of the enrollment—about half of what it should be; in dentistry, 4.04 percent—about a third of what it should be; and in law, only 4.60 percent—again about a third of what it should be.[15]

One black leader, asked to identify the most critical problems involving the higher education of blacks in America, pointed to the inadequate basic preparation of young people, including both educational and personal development. Another leader described the plight of black youth in the big ghettos as "the worst problem not only for the black community but for the whole American community."[16]

CURRICULUM DEVELOPMENT

Of seventeen black leaders responding to the same question, all listed two basic concerns: (1) the black colleges and universities—their survival and further development; and (2) the black students in higher education and the special problems that adversely affect their access, choice, survival, and optimum development.[17] Moreover, a number of black college presidents have published articles expressing related concerns regarding the status of higher education for blacks. Two are cited here.

Dr. Andrew Billingsley, a sociologist writing in 1982 while president of Morgan State University, stressed the need to strengthen faculties in black colleges, observing that for black colleges, as for other institutions with a distinct cultural heritage, "the character of the faculty must match the character of the student body if maximum effect is to be realized." Black college professors, he pointed out, are "approaching the status of an endangered species."[18]

Whereas black college enrollment doubled from 1965 to 1981, there was no comparable increase in the number of black college professors. Noting that fewer than 1% of the
faculties of the more than 3,000 predominantly white institutions are black, Billingsley
stressed that "the historically black colleges . . . remain the only significant academic
home for interracial faculties."[19] Among various obstacles to strengthening black faculties are the high black dropout rate at the pre-college level, the high attrition rates of
black college students, negative counseling of black students, and the dearth of and
inequitable distribution of graduate and professional fellowships for blacks from public
and private sources.[20]

The president of the College of the City of New York, Dr. Bernard Harleston, has
lamented a distorted sense of priorities "with respect to the nature, origins, and worth
of our resources, human and material," in commenting on what he called "the crisis of
higher education." Remarking that "educational access without a commitment to excellence is a fraud," he enumerated a number of challenges faced by urban institutions
of higher education, challenges that stem, in part, from the inadequate preparation of
students.[21]

Moreover, the black community, when consulted about educational priorities in a
national survey, indicated that its greatest concern was for student achievement and
career education for blacks.[22] These findings are remarkably consistent in suggesting
where black America needs, if not wants, to go; the question now is how to get there. In
this survey, directors of education of 105 Urban League Centers across the country
encompassing some 59% of the American black population were asked to rank educational priorities for their areas. "Priority," for the purpose of the survey, was given a
precise definition as follows: "If you had the time and money, what areas would you feel
are most in need of the attention of Urban League efforts?"[23]

FINANCIAL STABILITY

Because inadequate finances have always plagued black institutions of higher education, and still do so today (some privately controlled institutions having reached the
critical stage), it may be instructive to formulate a similar question for black leaders in
higher education. Otherwise—and quite understandably—getting more money is likely
to be first, second, and third on the list of our agendas.

The question, therefore, is posed, "If money and time were no obstacles, what would,
and should, black leaders in predominantly black institutions of higher education do to
remedy the problems we have been discussing?"

It seems that a serious response to the question cannot avoid the need to maintain
and increase enrollment (with the attendant need for increased student financial aid),
strengthen faculties, and make capital improvements, including renovation of out-
moded facilities and provision of up-to-date equipment. Such a response, however,
undoubtedly would be forthcoming from any one of the leaders of the more than 3,000
institutions of higher education in this country, the overwhelming majority of whom, it
goes without saying, are white. Such a response, therefore, is forgetful of the urgent

obligation historically black colleges and universities have to further the progress of black Americans toward equity and excellence.

If it is added that the students would be, for the most part, drawn from the black population traditionally served by HBCs, it is not clear that the response yet suffices. Certainly, little evidence exists to suggest that blacks who drop out of high school or those who graduate but do not attend college are frustrated in their desire to attend HBCs and would do so, if they were given sufficient financial aid.[24] Furthermore, even if such students would attend HBCs, these colleges would have to accomplish extensive remediation because of students' poor preparation. (It should be reiterated that dropouts have been found to have higher I.Q.s than those remaining in school, including both college students and those who graduate but do not attend college.)

The point, as may be obvious at this juncture, is that money alone will not curb the waste of talent about which Dr. Wright has effectively spoken. Rather, academic and counseling programs are needed—effective programs that promote both educational and personal development of black youths, including the necessary motivation. Thus, black colleges and universities need to develop programs to redeem talented black dropouts and push-outs; having developed the programs, which admittedly requires money, attention can then be turned toward securing the financial resources necessary for implementation.

HISTORICAL SIGNIFICANCE

To further buttress the forgoing comments, it is useful to reflect on the early history of most HBCs. Founded on shoestrings just before and after the Civil War, HBCs opened their doors to freed slaves and their descendants at a time when only a few of the four million blacks in the U.S. population could read or write. In tandem with the custom of the times, these institutions were called colleges and universities, notwithstanding that most of the students required extensive preparation before they could undertake college-level work. The academies and preparatory schools made good the deficiencies that were the legacy of deprivations far more severe and comprehensive than those that the present generation of dropouts have known. These "high schools," including the one at Howard University, fed these colleges until well into the present century.[25]

It is not necessary for HBCs to reopen their academies. Indeed, in the case of some public HBCs, there may be legal barriers to their doing so. Nevertheless, HBCs should give serious consideration to establishing relationships with local school boards in black communities with a view toward helping to motivate, counsel, and prepare black youths for college work. It is encouraging to note that Florida A & M University has begun such a program and that it has been copied throughout the state.[26] Moreover, it should be mentioned that Howard University has "adopted" a model academic high school that has shown impressive results in its first three years of operation.[27]

HBCs have a special expertise and sensitivity needed to unlock talented but dormant black minds. It is their responsibility, given the urgent need, to share that expertise with the black community to a greater extent than is done at present. Clearly, "universities can play an important role in advancing equality of opportunity since they wield influence over the process of learning itself, over institutions and attitudes, and they play an important role in determining the status and life chances of individuals."[28]

Black leaders in higher education must be concerned not only with remedying the waste of black talent, but also with ensuring that blacks are trained for high-tech careers needed in today's economy. As we have seen, black leaders in higher education are increasingly pointing out the dearth of black scientists and engineers. The president of SUNY, Dr. Clifton Wharton, recently stated that scientific and technical knowledge is the "main jumping off point to power" for blacks in the future.[29]

On the other hand, a recent national report deplored the decline of humanities programs at U.S. colleges and universities over the past two decades and cited specialization and marketing as contributing to the decline. Such pressures may be felt more keenly by blacks than by white students, because the marketplace frequently favors whites. If students in general need to be exposed to the foundations of civilization, black students also need to be exposed to black studies. However, evidence has indicated that many black students are deterred from pursuing an interest in black studies because they have been led to believe that a degree in black studies has no marketability.[30] Wharton's suggestion that blacks strive to have the black viewpoint incorporated into the general college curriculum may have merit, especially in context of the growing debate about balancing college curricula between the humanities and sciences.[31]

Billingsley and Harleston emphasized the importance of comprehensive basic studies and revitalized liberal arts. Harleston reasoned that it is a function of educational leadership to maintain "clarity about what the purposes of education are, particularly liberal education." Pointing to directions society will take over the next two decades, he has argued that "to respond to these new directions we must reaffirm the centrality of reading, writing, and quantitative skills; we must teach for a global perspective and an international focus; and we must teach for technological literacy and intelligence, including critical thinking."[32]

The quintessential aim of liberal education is that the student is exposed to a wide variety of learning experiences—in the humanities, social sciences, and natural sciences—that will enable him or her to better understand society, and the world. It cannot be overemphasized that there is no royal road to knowledge and understanding. A lot of hard work—and some talent—are requisites.

CONCLUSION: AM I MY BROTHER'S KEEPER?

The forgoing comments have identified a progammatic thrust for black leaders in higher education to pusue. This thrust has two aims to promote equity and academic excellence of blacks in American society, and to provide these goals, to both current college students and to those who should be, but are not presently, enrolled. It also has been suggested that money will be needed to accomplish these objectives. Because leaders are obliged to manage resources in relationship to avowed goals, the question arises, Where does the money come from for such extra efforts?

The answer is that the money must come from those who have it, rather than from those who do not, including government and private sources, such as foundations, corporations, and individuals. The government's interest in racial progress is abundantly clear when a cost/benefits analysis that points out the alternatives in social costs is considered. A study by L. Dean Webb entitled "Race, Education, and the New Economics," offers a compelling discussion of these points. The corporate interest is clear when long-term economic prosperity is viewed in its domestic and global dimensions. An investment in education is an investment in human capital, a point upon which some corporations act out of enlightened self-interest.

Our society currently places a high value on individualism. A recent paper noted that black students in predominantly white institutions of higher education tended to espouse personal career goals, such as becoming financially well-off or succeeding in business, to the exclusion of helping fellow blacks; black students in predominantly black institutions, on the contrary, reflected societal goals such as aiding the community or influencing policies, consonant with the mission of HBCs.

The question is often asked, "Am I my brother's keeper?" Often, those asking it fail to realize that it was Cain who first asked it—right after he slew Abel—in response to God's query as to Abel's whereabouts. This Biblical story gives rise to an encouraging example of what individuals can do to academically motivate black youths. The *Washington Post* reported the story of a black couple who receive 20 high school youth into their $300,000 home 4 evenings a week; the couple gives the students dinner (financed jointly by the couple and the major corporation for which they work) and then supervise the students' homework. This couple has been doing this for four years, the article indicated, and most of their "graduates" have gone on to college. These adults are leaders in education although they may not think of themselves as educators.

In conclusion, black leaders in higher education must stress quality. Since everyone subscribes to quality, there is no need to argue this point. But as John Ruskin has observed, "Quality is never an accident. It is always the result of intelligent effort. There must be the will to produce a superior thing."

NOTES

1. A recent publication presents a model, based on case studies, for black student development in the context of predominantly white colleges and universities. See C. Scully Stikes, *Black Students in Higher Education* (Carbondale and Edwardsville: Southern Univ. Press, 1984). According to Professor Mary Berry, in 1982, only 4.3% of the total higher education faculty at predominantly white institutions (451,000) were black. See Mary Berry, "Black in Predominantly White Institutions of Higher Learning," *State of Black America 1983* p. 311.

2. Report of Wingspread Conference of Pesidents and Chancellors of Historically Black Colleges and Universities and Foundation Executives, "In Search of Partnerships: Black Colleges and Universities/Private Philanthropy," (The Johnson Foundation; The Charles Stewart Mott Foundation; The Council on Foundations; and The National Association for Equal Opportunity in Higher Education (NAFEO), Jan. 4-6, 1984.

3. Cheek, James E., "If We Do Not, Then Who Will? The Continuing Burden to Undo the Yoke of Bondage," Convocation Address, Washington, DC, Howard Univ., Sept. 26, 1980.

4. Some figures are given below.

5. Dressel, *Administrative Leadership*, (San Francisco, Washington, London: Jossey-Bass Publishers, 1981) for example, affirms this (see p. 182).

6. Vaugn-Cooke, Denys, "The Economic Status of Black America—Is There a Recovery?" *The State of Black America 1984*, (New York: National Urban League, Inc., Jan. 19, 1984), p. 15.

7. Douglass, Frederick, *The North Star* (July 14, 1884), cited by Daniel Thompson in *Sociology of the Black Experience* (Westport, Ct. and London: Greenwood Press, 1974), p. 15.

8. Thompson, Sociology, p. 14. It should be noted that Thompson directed this remark at black leaders of the approximately 250,000 blacks who were free before the Civil War.

9. The issue of the content of undergraduate education is currently being debated.

10. Asbury, Charles "Black Expectancy: Implications as a Variable for Research," *Journal of Negro Education* 51, no. 4 (Fall 1982), p. 370.

11. Cheek, "If We Do Not."

12. Jones-Wilson, Faustine C., in "The State of Urban Education," *The State of Black America 1984*, p. 96.

13. Felice, Lawrence G., "Black Student Dropout Behavior: Disengagement from School Rejection and Racial Discrimination," *Journal of Negro Education*, 50, no. 4 (Fall 1981) pp. 415-16.

14. Ibid., pp. 421-22.

15. Wright, Stephen J., "The Tragic Waste of the Black Mind and Talent," Lecture, Charles H. Thompson Lecture/Colloquium, Howard Univ., Washinton, DC, Nov. 5, 1980. The citation is from the version published in the *Journal of Negro Education* no. 2 (Spring 1981) on p. 102. Wright enumerated four cases contributing to the waste of the black-mind: (1) the relatively poor quality of public education that the great majority of blacks receive, (2) the inadequate counseling provided for black children from homes where the educational level of the parents is low, (3) the barriers to access to higher education (especially financial), and (4) the limitations of choice of institutions of higher learning for blacks, p. 103.

16. Ibid., p. 101.

17. Ibid.

18. Billingsley, "Building Strong Faculties in Black Colleges," *Journal of Negro Education*, 51, no.1 (Winter 1982), p. 5.

19. Ibid.

20. Ibid., p. 9.

21. Harleston, Bernard H., "Higher Education for Minorities: The Challenge of the 1980s," Charles Thompson lecture, Washington, DC, Howard Univ. Nov. 3, 1982. The citation is from the version pubished in the *Journal of Negro Education*, 52, no. 2 (Spring 1983), p. 97. According to Harreston, to meet the challenge of urban institutions of higher education, a commitment to "excellence as an academic value" is necessary he also cited a need to revitalize liberal arts, to participate in outreach programs to ensure basic math, science and writing experiences, to be actively involved in the preparation of teachers for primary and secondary schools, and to formulate and make a commitment to an urban mission for the urban university.

22. Bickel, William, Lloyd Bond, and Alice Carter, "Educational Priorities Among Urban Black Populations," *Journal of Negro Education* 50, no. 1 (Winter 1981), pp. 3-8.

23. Ibid., p. 6.

24. It must be noted, however, that financial assistance is a desideratum that cannot be ignored if the number of black college graduates is to be improved significantly at all levels.

25. See Rayford/Logan, *Howard University: The First Hundred Years, 1867-1967* (New York: New York Univ. Press, 1969), especially at p. 166, where it is noted that Howard's Academy "continued to graduate students through 1920."

26. A brief description of the program is to be found in Wingspread Conference, "In Search of Partnership."

27. The suggestion for the Howard Univ. School of Education to adopt a high school is found in Wright, "Tragic Waste."

28. Cheek, James E., "Higher Education's Responsibility for Advancing Equality of Opportunity and Justice," ISEP 1, (Howard Univ. Institute for the Study of Educational Policy, 1977), p. 13.

29. Wharton, Jr., Clifton R., "Toward an Agenda for Black Intellectuals in the 1980s," Mordecai Wyatt Johnson Memorial Lecture, Howard Univ. Washington, DC Nov. 16, 1984.

30. Speaking mainly about departments at predominantly white institutions, David Riesman has written that "the black studies departments and cultural centers served many black students as decompression chambers where they could find like-minded people and work to counter patronizing, if not bigoted, attitudes on the larger campus. These enclaves allowed them to venture forth into the wider unversity with the support, sometimes including the academic 'soft' options, provided by even peripheral involvement in the balck studies departments or programs." *On Higher Education* (San Francisco, Washington, London: Jossey-Bass Publishers, 1980, p. 144.) The report referred to is entitled "To Reclaim a Legacy," written by the chairman of the National Endowment for the Humanities, the full text of which is published in *The Chronicle for Higher Education* XXIX, no. 14 (Nov. 28, 1984).

31. If the black viewpoint was incorporated into existing courses in the humanities and social studies, all students would be exposed to it without having to enroll in separate courses, Wharton argued. There is a vast and growing volume of material supporting this view; see *Journal of Negro Education* 53, (no. 3) for an extensive discussion of black studies programs.

32. Harleston, "Higher Eduation," p. 100.

33. Webb, L. Dean, "Race, Education, and the New Economics" *Journal of Negro Education* 51, no. 4 (Fall 1982) pp. 372-91.
34. Berry, "Black in White Institutions," p. 301.
35. "Couple Gives Thanks by Sharing," The District Weekly, *Washington Post,* November 22, 1984

4

Equity in Education: A Low Priority in the School Reform Movement

Faustine C. Jones-Wilson

Educational reform movements occur in cyclical fashion, often in response to crisis—real or perceived. In his analysis of the reform reports of the 1980s, A. Harry Passow[1] pointed out that the deplorable state of American education has been a recurring theme over the last ninety years or so. Passow and Tyack et al.[2] liken the current reform movement to the Sputnik era of 1957. At that time, it was the charge that the American public school system had failed to educate scientists and engineers of sufficient quality and quantity to outpace the Russians in the space race that provided an impetus to reform our schools. In the fall of 1982, the most recent of the recurring reform movements was initiated with *The Paideia Proposal: An Educational Manifesto*[3].

However, it was with the publication of *A Nation at Risk*[4] in the spring of 1983 that public attention was focused on schools. This report proclaimed that mediocrity pervaded the American educational system, and that once again we were losing out to foreign competition—this time to the Japanese, whose economy had grown more rapidly and exhibited more stability than our own, and whose children scored higher on tests.

"EXCELLENCE" IN EDUCATION

The cure for mediocrity, as well as the core of the present reform movement, has been a full dose of "excellence." Of very low priority now, as in the 1957 period, is an emphasis on equity for those individuals and groups who are underprivileged and underachieving in comparison with majority-group persons. The educational needs of children and youth who have not had the economic, social, environmental opportunities, or advantages enjoyed by the dominant group receive minimal attention in most of the school reform reports. It is those advantages that prepare fortunate children to be ready, able, and motivated to master learning at the expected rate of development.

Originally published in *Urban Review*, Vol. 9, no. 1 (1986).

Less fortunate children will continue to need additional help at school through policies and programs that will enable them to overcome the shortcomings of their life circumstances.

The school reform reports focus on what they see as the improvement of education in general. Most of them make recommendations such as the school day, week, and year; raising standards for graduation from high school and admission to college; increasing requirements in mathematics and science; increasing the number of units required for high school graduation; and greater reliance on standardized testing for students and teachers. School improvement is signified by the use of the term *"excellence,"* which often is not defined. In fact, it appears that many authors permit the reader to supply the interpretation.[5] In general, the excellence movement not only focuses on superior performance, but stresses the highest standards of performance for all students, teachers, and schools. It does not tell us how to attain those standards or where the funding will come from to do so. A fundamental error is the failure to link "excellence" to the public purposes of public schooling.

Public schooling has been provided and institutionalized in our society to produce an informed citizenry; good citizens are considered to be essential to the preservation and maintenance of our democratic state. Thus, democracy has made education a mass phenomenon, and education is designed to preserve democratic government. Schooling and democracy complement and reinforce each other; neither is mutually exclusive. The democratic ideal of equality of opportunity translates into equality of educational opportunity with respect to formal schooling. At the same time, the school is expected to meet the diverse needs of individual children and youth as it prepares them to become employable and functional for the rest of their lives. The public schools are expected to provide a literate labor force for a changing economy, and to keep America economically competitive with foreign countries—the latter goal obviously being beyond the power of the school to accomplish. If the school cannot meet all of the expectations imposed upon it by such a changing and diverse society, then the current school reform movement opts for raising standards and ignoring equity, or merely giving lip service to the concept.

THE CONCEPT OF EQUITY

What is equity, and how might it differ from equality? Equity emphasizes justness and fairness and makes judgments that might bypass strict law in the interest of conscience or the spirit of the law.[6] Equality suggests sameness; equity takes individual circumstances into consideration. Herbert J. Gans holds that

> Equity requires some degree of equality, for inequality is unfair. Conversely, more equality would itself bring about greater equity, and once major inequalities were removed, individual cases that might require some new inequalities in the name of equity could then be dealt with more easily.[7]

If the schools are to meet the often-expressed ideal of educating all the children of all the people to the utmost of the children's individual capabilities so that they become contributing members of a democratic society, providing ably for themselves and their future families, equity and equality must not be excised from the school reform movement in the name of "excellence." If our society dares to be authentic, we will use the school reform movement to create a system of public education that does, in fact, educate all children.[8] *Excellence* will not be permitted to become the new code word for exclusion of some and selection of others in the institution that is designed to ensure the continued existence of our society via the transmission of its heritage and the organized learning of the human race to our young. Children from all low-income families, migrant-stream situations, minority group origins, the handicapped, and/or recent immigrants must benefit from equity in educational arrangements if they are to succeed in school and in life. As Thomas Toch said in *Phi Delta Kappan:*

> If the U.S. fails to insure [sic] that the excellence movement reaches every student, the current calls for school reform may do nothing more than widen the gulf between the educational haves and the have nots, leaving those citizens who lack adequate training increasingly less able to manage in an increasingly complicated world.[9]

We must recall that it has been only thirty-two years since the 1954 *Brown* decision mandated an end to the separate and unequal institutional discrimination in education that had been legal for the fifty-eight years since 1896. More than that, it was only twenty-two years ago, with the passage of the 1964 Civil Rights Act and enforcement of its Section VII that denied federal funds to the discriminating school district that the school desegregation authorized by *Brown* began to become a reality. Thus it can be Brown made equity possible, and the 1964 legislation initiated its beginning. Educational literature was flooded with information about disadvantaged children and urban education in the 1960s, but by 1972 disillusionment with the idea of equity and other liberal ideas of the 1960s had set in.[10,11] Educational discussions among leading scholars recommended that declining expectations should prevail, that minorities and women were asking too much, and that genetic differences accounted for the test-score gap between blacks and whites[12] This brief flirtation with the concept and policies of equity ended with a mere eight years of uneven efforts at formulating and implementing programs designed to attain equity for disadvantaged children and youth.

Donald Vandenberg argues persuasively that

> The Brown Case should have been understood through the language of human rights, rather than through the spurious shift in the concept of equal educational opportunity. . . . It should have focused upon the human right to education, which is the right to use one's developmental time as a child and youth productively so that one can assume a position in society as a morally responsible, free citizen, i.e., as a moral agent. Although the amount of time allocated to development is

relative to a particular society, equity requires that everyone be granted the resources that will enable them to use that educational time most productively.[13]

It is indeed ironic that at the same time equity was mandated and initiated in schools, our public schools were flooded with children of the post-World War II baby boom. This situation resulted in overcrowded schools, half-day attendance sessions, use of portable buildings, and shortages of books and other materials for almost a decade. In many urban communities, the result was that children received a substandard education. In spite of an expressed belief in equity, these unfortunate youth were passed from grade to grade because of permissive grading policies instituted to move each wave ahead as a response to the press of large numbers of youth behind them, needing their seats and the attention of teachers. It is no wonder that equity never really was instituted—due to continuing resistance that can be attributed to racial and/or social class differences, overcrowded schools, and lack of commitment from policymakers, intellectuals, school officials, and local school boards.

LACK OF EQUITY IN CURRENT SCHOOL REFORMS

In what ways does the current school reform movement show a lack of commitment to equity? Some of the recommendations are clearly of high cost—the longer school day, week, and year, for example. The reports do not tell us where funds will come from to implement such recommendation or to ensure equity among school districts even if time allocations remain as they are at present. It is obvious that affluent school districts now offer more educational options and higher quality than do poor school districts. The educational achievement gap will widen if affluent districts are able to offer summer school advancement, remedial programs, or after-school programs that poorer districts cannot consider. Even big-city school districts with large budgets cannot initiate "extra-help" programs for most of their underachieving students because there are so many youth who need remedial work to meet established, accepted standards—to say nothing of achieving excellence. The reports usually do not recommend smaller class sizes, which of course also would require more funds to employ additional teachers or teacher aides. But smaller classes would permit each student to have more of the teacher's time and should increase learning possibilities. As it stands, the recommendations for time differentials will not produce the excellence that is desired but probably would increase inequity among school districts. All children will not have a fair chance to meet the new standards of excellence unless their districts can afford the cost. Smaller classes for underachievers would be equitable in terms of increasing their opportunity to learn.

Most of the reports contain recommendations to reduce electives and concentrate on the customary college-bound program, perhaps with more science and mathematics added. This type of plan does not permit adaptation of the curriculum to the diverse needs, interests, and learning levels of the nation's youth. It fails to relate learning to community needs or to problem-solving relationships that would stimulate students' motivation to apply themselves to their studies.

Several of the reports recommend the abolition of tracking in schools. Not only are students in lower tracks stigmatized, but they usually receive a different kind of instruction and less interest from teachers—the result of which is inequitable knowledge. Jeannie Oakes, in *Keeping Track: How Schools Structure Inequality* provides evidence that the assigment of students to different tracks is usually not made on objective grounds and leads to different and markedly unequal educational experience. Tracking thus both reflects the class and racial inequalities of the larger society and helps to perpetuate them.[14] If the reform reports were implemented, they would help achieve equity by ending a practice that is discriminatory in intent and effect.

The excellence movement fails to give equitable attention to creative and artistic students. The emphasis is generally on superiority in academic achievement in reading, mathematics, science, and writing—all subject matter skills. Creative and artistic students' talents and needs are given short shrift.

It is strange that the education of gifted and talented students is not given much space in the reports. These "special" learners deserve special arrangements. However, school systems must take care to ensure that poor and minority group children have the opportunity to show that they may be gifted or talented. In many systems, the assumption is that all poor and/or minority children are disadvantaged and deprived and therefore cannot possibly qualify for gifted and talented status.

On the other hand, poor and minority children saturate the vocational training classes. It is common for these children to be told that they need to learn to work with their hands, and in the process, they may receive less academic study. Job training and work-study arrangements, in tandem with sound academic study, can be desirable for many youth. Equal access to knowledge is the concern of both parents and communities, so that these youth will have an equal chance in the society in their adult lives.

A major threat to equity is the racial gap in test performance. Our society is well aware of the economic, social, environmental, and educational insufficiencies that were foisted on minority groups for most of America's history. In spite of that knowledge, we have moved in rapid fashion to assess student and now teacher competencies by their scores on standardized tests. If such testing is to become the norm for the future, it is mandatory that minority persons be taught more test-taking skills and receive more practice in test taking, that minority persons participate in writing test items and evaluating tests for bias, and that norms for these tests include large numbers of minorities in the samples. Further, performance indicators of mastery and success should be included in evaluations of students and teachers—if equity is to be real. Some of these students must continue to receive bilingual education in order to reach a level of language competence that would enable them to score high on pencil-and-paper tests.

In a recent College Board report, "Equity and Excellence: The Educational Status of Black Americans," the fear is expressed that the increased requirements for graduation, coupled with uniform educational requirements administered without flexibility and sensitivity, might exacerbate dropout rates.[15] Those rates already are higher for blacks and Hispanics than for white or Asian youth.

A shortage of qualified teachers is expected to be upon us within the next five years, created by the retirement of many incumbent teachers and because fewer young people are majoring in teacher education. Even now, shortages exist in the areas of science and mathematics. It can be predicted that a supply shortage of teachers will result in serious staffing problems in schools populated by minority and poor children, thereby affecting the quality of their education. Neither equity nor excellence is possible without an ample supply of well-educated, caring teachers. Urban schools experienced times in the late 1950s and early 1960s when teachers were assigned to classes outside their areas of competence on a "temporary" or "emergency" basis, with disastrous results for the youth enrolled in those classes.

The Reagan administration's cutbacks in federal funding for compensatory education in elementary and secondary schools, as well as of financial assistance for college work or graduate study, have adversely affected arrangements that were making opportunities more equitable for blacks and the poor. Yet this is the same administration that finds our nation at risk because of the "mediocrity" of its educational system. This inconsistency between policies and rhetoric is not lost on most individuals who support the concept of equity.

We face a future in which minority persons will constitute ever-larger proportions of the population in this country. In addition, there are increasingly larger proportions of young people among the minorities than in the majority white group, which means that these youth need to be educated in order to provide the able work force our nation will need in the next century. These will be the people who must contribute to a social security system for older citizens, and who will be expected to maintain our democratic system. None of these needs can be met with a conglomerate of poorly-educated Americans who have been victimized by the politics of the moment in education.

RECOMMENDATIONS FOR THE PRESENT AND FUTURE

Educational policies must not be used to deprive children of equal access to equal opportunity. Equity ought to be part and parcel of a "Bill of Rights" for elementary and secondary school students—not a codicil to the excellence reform movement.

We are a diverse society, a pluralistic culture whose varied elements come together in a mosaiclike arrangement. Equitable formal schooling is the mortar that can hold these varied elements together. There is no shortage of ideas to improve schools so that education can be more effective. For example, Colman McCarthy[16] reported the views of twenty high school teachers who were part of the Teacher Renaissance Initiative, a national program sponsored by the Education Commission of the States. Among their recommendations to improve high schools were (1) smaller classes; (2) flexible school days; (3) drug and alcohol programs; (4) requirements for administrators to return to the classroom every five years; (5) better instructional materials; (6) courses for interpersonal relationships; and (7) basic skills to be taught before high school. Education reforms must respect the views of these and other teachers who want schools to improve, and who want schooling to be more equitable for all.[17]

With respect to the successful education of low-income and/or minority children, we know that early childhood education programs of high quality make a difference in their achievement levels. Such programs as Head Start, Homestart, Follow Through, Upward Bound, and the like should be strengthened and continued. They provide a learning support system that reduces the inequities attendant on low-income and minority status. The beneficial effects of early childhood intervention programs have been demonstrated through the longitudinal Perry Preschool Project,[18] which showed increased motivation, value placed on schooling, school achievement, fewer dropouts, fewer placements in special education classes, decrease in deviant behavior, increase in adult success, fewer teenage pregnancies, and a projected increase in lifetime earnings.

Testing should be diagnostic and prescriptive, with follow-up instruction, not used as punitive instruments for eliminating people from jobs or access to educational options.

Concrete recommendations for improving public secondary education made by James B. Conant in *The American High School Today*[19] have not been implemented. Some of these recommendations would be useful today to obtain equity. For example, starting counseling in the elementary school would give more individual, personalized attention to students; individualized programs would meet human needs; English composition and writing time needs to be increased—and so on—just as was recommended in 1959. Many of these twenty-one recommendations would not be financially expensive to implement but would make schools more effective and more equitable.

In a similar manner, a publication of the Public Education Information Network[20] made recommendations for equity and excellence, hoping to reform schools so that they provide education for a democratic future. This group offers equitable options and alternatives for reforming the curriculum and school structure and governance and for increasing teacher effectiveness, testing and evaluation, pedagogy, and school discipline. This pithy, easy-to-read publication urges the building of national and local coalitions working for schools that will educate all children.

Although our country has made progress toward equity by abolishing the inequitable separate and unequal system of legally segregated schools, it still has a long way to go to realize equity in the schoolrooms. Low-income students, recent immigrants, minority children, and the handicapped all need an equal chance to learn. That means equity in financing schools and programs; providing competent, caring teachers; retaining compensatory programs that demonstrably work; relating the subject matter of the curriculum to real-life situations and problem solving; creating and using appropriate achievement and evaluation measures; providing enrichment trips and learning opportunities supplemental to classroom work; meeting individual needs; and allowing for individual differences. While equity is not a high priority in the school reform movement, we who care about our youth and our democratic society must stand together to ensure that the concept is not lost in the bedlam of the moment. It is time to end the negative interrelationships of social, economic, and educational inequities on behalf of all youth and in the general welfare.

NOTES

1. Passow, A. H., "Tackling the reform reports of the 1980's"; *Phi Delta Kappan* 65, (1984), pp. 644-83.

2. Tyack, D., Lowe, R., and Hansot, E., *Public Schools in Hard Times: The Great Depression and Recent Years.* (Cambridge: Harvard University Press, 1984).

3. Adler, M., *The Paideia Proposal: An Educational Manifesto.* (New York: Macmillan, 1982).

4. National Commission on Excellence in Education, *A Nation at Risk* (Washington, D.C.: U.S. Government Printing Office, 1983).

5. Glenn, B. C., "Excellence and equity: Implications for effective schools", *Journal of Negro Education* 54: (1985), pp. 289-300.

6. Wiener, P., "Equity in law and ethics," in *Dictionary of the History of Ideas: Studies of Selected Pivotal Ideas* (New York: Charles Scribner's Sons, 1973).

7. Gans, H.J., *More Equality* (New York: Pantheon Books, 1973).

8. Willie, C.V., "Educating students who are good enough: Is excellence an excuse to exclude?" *Change* 14, (1982), pp. 16-20.

9. Toch, T., "The dark side of the excellence movement," *Phi Delta Kappan* 66, (1984), pp. 173-76.

10. Daniel, W.G., "Problems of disadvantaged youth, urban and rural," *Journal of Negro Education* 33, (1964), pp. 218-24.

11. Smiley, M.B., and Miller, H.L. (eds.), *Policy Issues in Urban Education* (New York: Free Press, 1968).

12. Jones, F.C., *The Changing Mood in America: Eroding Commitment* (Washington, D.C.: Howard University Press, 1977).

13. Vandenberg, D., *Human Rights in Education* (New York: Philosophical Library, 1983).

14. Oakes, J., *Keeping Track: How Schools Structure Inequality* (New Haven: Yale University Press, 1985).

15. College Board, *Equality and Excellence: The Educational Status of Black Americans* (New York: College Board, 1985).

16. McCarthy, C., "Ask the teachers," *Washington Post* (March 22, 1986), pp. 277.

17. Ohanian, S., "Huffing and puffing and blowing schools excellent," *Phi Delta Kappan* 66, (1985), pp. 316-21.

18. Schweinhart, L.J., and Weikart, D.P., *Young Children Grow Up: The Effects of the Perry Preschool Program on Youth Through Age 15* (Ypsilanti, Mich.: High/Scope Press, 1980).

19. Conant, J.B., *The American High School Today: A First Report to Interested Citizens* (New York: McGraw-Hill, 1959).

20. Public Education Information Nettwork, *Equity and Excellence: Toward an Agenda for School Reform* (St. Louis: Public Education Information Network, 1985).

5
Educational Policy Trends
in a Neoconservative Era

Marguerite Ross Barnett

Few would deny that public policies can have multiple purposes and be understood and interpreted at various levels of analysis. This article presents an encompassing explanatory framework that integrates major current thrusts of educational policy and shows their relationship both to the development of educational public policy over the past twenty years and to economic and technological transformations in society. Certain policies may also simultaneously fill a number of different kinds of needs. The Reagan administration's opposition to affirmative action and to busing may reflect a nationwide majority consensus against these policies. Approval of IRS tax exemptions for schools that discriminate may serve political needs and also reflect deeply-held emotional beliefs. Tuition tax credits, in addition to growing out of an individualistic, privatized, triage perspective may also be useful as a policy to win the support of middle- and upper-class voters. The point is, whatever their other purposes, none of the major education policies of the Reagan administration violates or contradicts the overarching themes of contraction, triage, and individualism, and most such policies reflect the interrelatedness of all three.

All current major educational policies constitute a clear break with the policy trend (rooted in the *Brown* case and realized in the mid-1960s with ESEA as well as other education reform policies) toward equal educational opportunity. Further, the overall shift in policy and ideology is consistent with the structural change currently underway in the economy. A labor market in which advanced computer technology and sophisticated robotics has altered the kinds of laborers needed for the future has also altered the kind of education those workers need. Early predictions suggest that much more manpower will be needed in highly skilled occupations—those held by scientists, mathematicians, computer engineers, software developers, and so on—and much less in blue-collar and lower-level white-collar positions.

Originally published in the *Urban League Review* 8, no. 2 (1984) under the title "Equity, Technology and Educational Policy."

EDUCATIONAL REFORM IN THE 1950s: "WHY CAN'T JOHNNY READ?"

In the later 1950s, concern with the supposedly low quality of public education in the U.S. led many scholars to ask rhetorically: "Why Can't Johnny Read?" Emphasis on improving U.S. education reflected the perceived exigencies of military competition (the launching of the Soviet satellite Sputnik was a key triggering factor in evoking fear) and commercial considerations—a general uneasiness about the United States losing its commercial advantage or even falling behind other Western nations in advanced technology.[1] However, a critical third factor was the *Brown* v. *Board of Education* decision. *Brown* set the stage for a generation of policies aimed at achieving equal educational opportunity. Some of those efforts involved school desegregation, busing, and integration, while other efforts involved improving on-site education for low-income minority children. The term "disadvantaged" came into common use as a descriptor for these children.

The line between the findings in the *Brown* case and the emergence of a general policy of federally-sponsored education programs for the disadvantaged was inherent in the social science appendix and other material prepared by Kenneth and Mamie Clark for the plaintiff's brief in the *Brown* case. Clark argued that officially-sanctioned segregation by a state or local government caused personality damage to children of both minority and majority groups. Minority group children, Clark believed, became aware of their subordinate status and often reacted with feelings of inferiority and a sense of personal humiliation.[2] Extending Clark's argument, various education theorists made the case that segregation caused behavioral patterns that led to crime and violence among lower-income blacks and frustration and withdrawal among middle- and upper-income blacks.

By extending Kenneth Clark's argument in the *Brown* case, social scientists developed the idea of a culture of poverty as it related to educational aspirations. Segregation and racial discrimination were said to lead to lowered educational aspirations and performance. In order to improve educational performance on the part of low-income minorities, the reason went, an educational war on poverty was needed. Such an educational war on poverty was rationalized by the same ideas of equal educational opportunity that were embedded in the *Brown* decision. Head Start centers, the Elementary and Secondary Education Act of 1965 with its special programs for the disadvantaged, and the Title IV technical assistance programs all flourished during the 1960s and 70s, and barely survived into the 1980s. All such programs were based on the priority given to achieving equal educational opportunity.

Palmer and Sawyer stated: "Federal funding as a percentage of total elementary and secondary school revenues has increased from 2.9 percent in 1949-50 to 4.6 percent in 1959-60 and 9.8 percent in 1980-81."[3] A review of the dollars spent from the 1960s to the present underscores this dramatic increase: in 1960, federal education expenditures were $490 million, in 1970 3.2 billion, and in 1979 up to $6.7 billion. Federal outlays for elementary and secondary education were $5.6 billion in fiscal year 1987; outlays for vocational education were $882 million. Of this spending, $3.9 billion went to compensatory education for disadvantaged students under Title I. The legislative intent of Title I is, of course, to assist schools with large percentages of disadvantaged students, to help the schools with low revenue levels, to provide special services to low-achieving students, and to provide programs that contribute to the cognitive, social, and emotional development of these students.

ASSESSMENTS OF FEDERAL INTERVENTION

As early as the late 1960s and early 1970s, the short-term benefits of early childhood intervention were debated. Although there was rarely sufficient data of acceptable quality to make bottom-line evaluations, the available data often showed varying results. Isolated projects, such as Bereiter and Englemann's program in Teaching Disadvantaged Children in Preschool,[4] or the Perry Preschool Project in Ypsilanti, Michigan,[5] indicated immediate and positive effects on children enrolled in them. But several early reviews of the research, such as those of the Westinghouse Learning Corporation and Ohio University, Bronfenbrenner, and White, Day, and Freeman,[6] fed the widespread belief that early educational intervention was ineffective in reducing the academic failure of disadvantaged children.

More recently, however, the Consortium for Longitudinal Studies has revealed evidence that the same project which aroused pessimism about short-term results, has had beneficial long-range effects. This analysis of 8 follow-up studies of some 3,000 youngsters indicates that in nearly every case the youngsters were found to be performing better in school than peers who did not attend preschool.[7] Neiman and Gastright also report higher reading and math scores for all-day kindergarten graduates.[8] Teachers College IUME research in the early 1970s also showed similar gains for pre-kindergarten experience for reading scores in the fifth and sixth grades for English-speaking students.[9]

In a detailed monograph following Perry Preschool graduates as well as control subjects over eleven years, Schweinhart and Weikart have corroborated and filled in the evidence favoring the positive, long-range effects of preschool intervention. For these authors, preschool has an "interactive" effect: the heightened commitment to schooling created in the youngsters leads to the greater receptivity of teachers, and this in turn leads to better student affective and cognitive performance.[10]

Both direct and indirect evidence indicates that massive federal intervention in the education of black children in the elementary school years can have positive results. Indirect evidence comes from national changes in achievement scores during the 1970s and early 1980s. Burton and Jones summarize recent trends in achievement levels for black and white youths. They report that "typically when achievement for white students has declined, that for Black students has declined less; when Whites have improved, Blacks have improved more. The difference between the races has decreased at both ages (9 to 13) in mathematics, science, reading, writing, and social studies." According to Burton and Jones, "Programs designed to foster equal educational opportunity may be among the factors that have contributed to the reduction in White-Black achievement differences."[11] More directly, the National Assessment of Educational Progress (NAEP) report observed that students in large urban cities have gained slightly more than those in smaller cities between 1975 and 1979. Moreover, "The NAEP reported that the largest gains during the 1970's has been among students where federal money, particularly Title I money, had been concentrated."[12]

Further, research on school improvement and effective schooling has now become more sophisticated. It is now possible to create and implement projects that have measurable results in improving the performance of all children—particularly children from economically deprived backgrounds.[13] These projects and the voluminous amount of literature on instructionally effective schools have focused on several key characteristics of school environments that correlate with educational achievement and are under the schools' control. Strong leadership by the principal, including active participation in decisions on instructional strategies and on organizing and distributing the school's resources; high expectations for all students; a secure, relatively quiet, pleasant school atmosphere; and an instructional program that emphasizes pupil acquisition of reading skills (reinforced by careful and frequent evaluation of pupil progress) have all been identified as examples of school characteristics that are linked to educational achievement. Indeed, a growing amount of literature suggests that controllable school practices have the most significant effect on achievement.[14] This idea differs markedly from earlier works, which encouraged policymakers to believe school failure among minorities and the poor was intractable.

The evidence that school failure among minorities could be ameliorated and that specific organizational and institutional change well within the power of schools could make a difference is significant in light of assessments by the Reagan administration that, federal intervention has been an unmitigated failure.

The emergence of equal educational opportunity as a core goal for the federal government and the subsequent history, growth, and results of an array of projects aimed at improving education for disadvantaged students provide an important part of the backdrop for understanding current education policy and philosophical direction.

TECHNOLOGY AND THE TRANSFORMATION OF AMERICAN SOCIETY

A second important part of understanding the present is the technological and structural transformation occurring in the American economic system particularly, and in society generally. A brief contrast with the 1960s, the period when federal intervention in education was initiated, is appropriate.

During the 1960s, the struggle for the advancement of blacks coincided with American economic interests. The multiple reasons for this congruity of interest reflect the domestic economic circumstances of that time: there was economic prosperity, a demand for labor, and the belief among business persons that blacks represented a new and untapped potential source of semiskilled and skilled labor. In such a tight labor market, big business sought the development of an educated, aggressive black strata willing to accept lower than average wages as the "price" to be paid for absorption into the expanding, technologically advanced economy.[15]

By the time some gains were registered in this area, however, the domestic economy had begun to change. Facing (1) strong competition on the world market from other capitalist countries (particularly Germany and Japan), (2) the decline of the dollar, (3) the increasing independence of nations in the Middle East, Africa, Asia, and Latin America, controlling and setting prices for their own raw materials, and (4) greater demands for higher wages and lower prices from both organized and unorganized workers, the United States slipped into a persistent economic crisis. The resulting economic stagnation resulted in the limited availability of and increased competition for jobs, educational opportunities, and so on, as well as cutbacks in social services. There was less demand and/or space for blacks, minorities, and women in the job market. In short, the nation entered a period of persistent downturn, decremental planning, and truncated expectations.[16]

Despite the economic deterioration, the technological revolution—specifically the introduction of computers and robotics to provide increasingly-automated work environments—has continued. On October 26, 1981, the *Wall Street Journal* reported:

> Industrial robots are rapidly moving into the U.S. labor force as manufacturers accelerate automation in order to hold down costs, boost sagging productivity and compete better in world markets. Today's robots could replace one million workers by 1990 in the automotive, electrical-equipment, machinery and fabricated-metals industries.[17]

An article in the *New York Times* reported on a congressional hearing assessing the impact of the computer revolution, specifically in the new field of robotics: "Senator Lloyd Bentsen [of Texas] told the Congressional Office of Technology Assessment today to stop hedging and come up with some estimates of the magnitude of the convulsion that he predicts will disrupt the American work force as robotics takes over many jobs." Citing predictions that robot sales will rise 35-50% a year, Senator Bentsen, the ranking Democrat on the Joint Economic Committee, said "millions of jobs, conceivably one-quarter of the nation's factor work force, could be lost to robots by 1990."[18] A major concern of industrialists and educators has been the educational preparation of white-collar workers capable of maintaining and expanding U.S. advances in the computer/robotics field. Little attention, however, has been given to issues of equity.

Although data are limited and research findings tentative at best, two kinds of equity problems have emerged with the computer revolution. First is the problem of adequate access for minorities and for women; second is the problem of upgrading the quality of access and exposure minorities and women receive. The first problem is more widely recognized than the second and has been the subject of numerous newspaper and magazine articles. One article highlighted the problem of access in the following way:

> Surveys show that in the number of computers available and the way they are used, students in less affluent schools receive less sophisticated instruction than

students in more affluent schools. Forty-four percent of the schools in which fewer than five percent of the students come from families below the poverty level have computers. An October 1982 survey by Market Data Retrieval found only 18.3 percent of the schools with more than 25 percent of students from lower-income families had computers.[19]

While sheer access is the more immediate problem, quality of access may be the long-range issue. Early research on the impact of the introduction of computers into schools indicates that there is a differential impact by gender and by minority group status. In general, non-minority students, and boys particularly, are able to use computers for enrichment.[20] They learn to program the computer to control and manipulate new technologies, and are, therefore, undergoing preparation for future positions as computer programmers, computer engineers, and developers of innovative software packages.

In contrast, computers have been used, in a disproportionate number of cases, for remedial work for minorities. In some instances, they have taken the place of instructors in providing basic academic preparation. The computer revolution can introduce new inequities resulting from the accumulated impact of a large number of decisions made at the corporate, school, and district level about when computers are to be purchased and how they are to be used within schools and classrooms. It should also be mentioned that inequity is reinforced by the ability of middle-class families to purchase their own microcomputers for home use, again giving a head start to children that are already educationally advantaged.[21]

EQUITY AND CURRENT FEDERAL POLICY TRENDS IN EDUCATION

In reviewing educational trends over the last 30 years, this author has noted the importance of military and commercial factors in creating the 1950s climate of concern about the quality of American education. However, by the end of that decade, the *Brown* case had directed the attention of education policymakers toward equity concerns and educational opportunity for the disadvantaged. Educational opportunity and equity in education remained core symbols for over 15 years (1965-1980). More than symbolic reassurance occurred. Federal intervention was responsible for measurable gains in minority educational achievement. Those gains, however, were not substantial enough to offset the tremendous counterbalancing forces that buttress continued black subordination[22] and the overall pattern of school failure among the disadvantaged. Indeed, it has been argued that schools operate to maintain and reproduce existing structures of disadvantage.[23]

Emphasis on educational equity and on reforms that would improve education for the disadvantaged emerged during the 1960s. During this time the economy was strong and there was a perceived need for large numbers of semiskilled and low-level white-collar workers. With the rapid development of robotics and other advanced forms of computer technology in the larger context of economic downturn, it became clear that the problem is not sheer manpower, but the development of highly skilled manpower. The combination of forces set the stage and context for the Reagan administration in 1980.

Scholars and practitioners have made contradictory statements and comments about current educational policy. On the one hand, we often hear that we are in the midst of a public policy revolution in education; on the other hand, some specialists have asserted that education is unimportant to the current administration and that educational policy is incoherent and unsystematic. In contrast to this latter perspective, careful assessment reveals there is a good deal of coherence and systematic pursuit of an identifiable set of goals in current policy initiatives. Furthermore, education policy is in fact intrinsically related to and well-integrated within the overall ideological and philosophical perspective of the administration.

Though they are seemingly disparate and unrelated, there is an underlying unity of perspective that exists and links such policies as:

- Tuition tax credits;
- Budget reductions;
- Support for IRS granting of tax exemptions to schools that discriminate;
- Opposition to busing for racial balance;
- Transformation of the Department of Education into a foundation;
- Opposition to affirmative action;
- Emphasis on educational excellence and freedom for the educational consumer;
- New federalism.

Three themes seem to be key: (1) contraction of the public sphere and of the definition of what constitutes the legitimate public interest, (2) social triage, and (3) individualism and privatization of the public interest.

A major thrust of the Reagan administration has been the limiting, contraction, and shrinking of the public sphere and of what are considered legitimate subjects for public policy. The administration has redefined the location of the dividing line between what constitutes appropriate action of the government activity and actions of the private citizenry. This can be seen most clearly in the presentation and rationalization of the block grant concept as part of the new federalism. Initially, most of the major educational programs for the disadvantaged were slated for inclusion in block grants—a process that would have left the states to define how much educational funding should go to these programs. Subsequent pressure from a variety of special interest groups was responsible for the administration modifying that proposal.

THE NEW FEDERALISM

Policy Contractions

The major policy thrust of the New Federalism are block grants. When these grants are accompanied, as they have been, by budget reductions, some of the necessary preconditions for contraction of the public sphere are thereby accomplished. The New Federalism summarily serves three purposes. First, it removes debates on many pressing political and social change issues from the federal level—where the press and the public can monitor, mobilize, and organize for national solutions to national problems—to separate states, where attention and mobilization are necessarily fragmented. Second, it lowers our expectations about what the federal government can and should legitimately do. Third, it shifts some political conflict from the federal arena, where a broad array of groups have already mobilized to lobby for public interest issues, to state arenas, where it is more difficult for groups with universalistic, public interest concerns (such as equity in education) and social change goals to mobilize an effective presence.

The proposal to transform the Department of Education into an educational foundation also seems part of the same general effort to delimit the scope of federal policy and public action. An educational foundation would presumably have a very different mandate and set of priorities from those of the present Department of Education. What such an "education foundation" might see as its major priorities is indicated by the current shift in the priorities of the existing department and administration away from educational equity and toward the dual goals of excellence and freedom for the educational consumer.

Social Triage

These goals and the overall concern with shrinkage of the public sphere are further elucidated by a second current ideological theme—social triage. Social triage describes the idea that students can be divided into three groups: those for whom middle- and upper-class status is assured, those for whom it is possible, and those for whom it is virtually impossible. Advocates of social triage believe that because resources spent on the third group are largely wasted (such as programs for the educationally disadvantaged), it makes more sense to help those in the second group, for whom success is at least possible. Perhaps the best current example is tuition tax credits.

To the extent that tuition tax credits will benefit the poor—in contrast to members of the middle and upper classes, who will clearly be helped—the poor children most likely to benefit are those with the best possibility of achieving upward mobility. Administration analysts and conservative thinkers believe it is the more motivated children and parents who are likely to use tax credits to leave ghetto schools. Glazer comments: "Do those who wish to escape have the duty to stay behind with the worst? And does society have an obligation to force them to? I think the answer to both questions is no. To me freedom is a higher value than those advanced by the forced association of the aspiring and achieving with those who create an environment in which they can neither aspire nor achieve."[24] Other examples of social triage include the interpretation of National Commission on Excellence report to mean that federal and local governmental bodies should be selective in educational innovation, focusing on improving math and science and emphasizing programs for the intellectually gifted. Although it is not a conscious federal initiative, the non-policy on computers in the schools will eventually have the effect of reinforcing the educational advantages enjoyed by middle- and upper-income youngsters.

Individualism and Privatization

The third ideological theme is individualism and privatization of public life. So key is this idea of the priority of individualism and of individual choice over group goals and social, collective, or public choices in arenas where individual and private action is possible that individual choice often gets equated with freedom and justice. Because we are ending an era in which justice has often been equated with equity (although sometimes only approximately), in public dialogues on education, the equation of justice with choice sounds innovative, but in actuality, it is a simple restatement of classical economic thought in which freedom is equated with individual choice in the marketplace.

The issues that have evoked the most articulate expressions of the priority of individualism and private choice over public and social goals are those surrounding civil rights. Publicly-stated presidential opposition to busing and to affirmative action, and support of tax exemptions for schools that discriminate have been justified or rationalized through the juxtaposition of individual to group rights. The denial of virtually all group rights and public responsibility to redress group discrimination, deprivation, or exploitation are further examples of ignoring group goals. Instead, efforts to redress these problems are themselves attacked as inimical to the rights and essential freedom of the individual.

CONCLUSION

In viewing the development of public policy in general and educational policy in particular from 1954, the general trend until 1980 and the election of Ronald Reagan had been toward (1) expansion of the definition of the proper realm of public policy; (2) priority placed on the search for equity and the willingness to contemplate and, in some instances, implement and/or redistribute social change policies aimed at assisting low-income groups; and (3) political recognition of issues, problems, and dilemmas of cultural pluralism as appropriate for public policy. In an important sense, the *Brown* decision was a stimulus to the overall era of expansion of the sphere of public policy and of ideas about the public interest.

The expansion of public policy created its own opposition as well as the seeds of its own destruction. The current administration's emphasis on public policy shrinkage, priority for individualistic-private pursuits, and adoption of concepts of triage may well be the ideological antithesis of the revolution in social thinking and social policy that emerged in the 1960s.

The country is currently facing significant political and economic choices, many of which are reflected in educational policy. Such choices must be made within an ideologically informed and historically meaningful context. On an abstract level, values in the human experience are in conflict and can be seen as a set of contradictions including: individual rights and group or collective needs, the need for centralized direction and for decentralized initiatives, excellence—which in any society, including ancient Greece, has meant an emphasis on the few, the elite—and equity and opportunity for the many. On a less abstract level, the key issue is the way in which tax dollars and distributed and the groups that will concretely benefit from public policy decisions.

This analysis suggests not only that there is a danger of losing much of the momentum gained during the 1960s and 1970s in the education of low-income and minority children, but also that changes in the economy and marketplace threaten to introduce and crystallize new forms of socioeconomic inequity throughout the remainder of this century and perhaps beyond.

NOTES

1. Spring, Joel. *The Sorting Machine: National Educational Policy Since 1945* (New York: David McKay Co., 1976).

2. Bell, Derek, Jr., *Race, Racism and Law* (Boston: Little, Brown & Co., 1973).

3. White, S., M.C. Day, P.K. Freeman, S.A. Hartman and K.P. Messenger, *Federal Programs for Young Children: Review and Recommendations.* Publication no. (OS) 74-101 (Washington, D.C.: U.S. Government Printing Office, 1973).

4. Bereiter, Carol, and S. Engelmann, *Teaching Disadvantaged Children in Preschool* (Englewood Cliffs, New Jersey: Prentice Hall, 1966).

5. Weikart, David P., J.T. Bond, and J.T. McNeil, *The Ypsilanti Perry Preschool Project: Preschool Years and Longitudinal Results Through Fourth Grade Curriculum Demonstration Project* (Ypsilanti, Mich.: High/Scope Research Foundation, 1978).

6. Westinghouse Learning Corporation and Ohio University, *The Impact of Headstart Experience on Children's Cognitive and Affective Development*, P.B. 184328 (Springfield, Va.: U.S. Department of Commerce Clearinghouse, 1969).

7. Bronfenbrenner, Urie, *A Report on Longitudinal Programs, Is Early Intervention Effective?* Vol. 20f (DHEW Published Number HD, 74-21, 1974).

8. Nieman, Ronald H., and Joseph F. Gastright, "The Long Term Effects of Title I Preschool and All-Day Kindergarten," *Phi Delta Kappan*, (November 1981), pp. 184-85.

9. Consortium for Longitudinal Studies, 1978.

10. Schweinhart, Laurence S., and David P. Weikart, *Young Children Growing Up: The Effects of the Perry Preschool Program on Youths Through Age 15* (Ypsilanti, Mich.: The High/Scope Press, 1980).

11. Burton, Nancy, and Life V. Torres, "Recent Trends in Achievement Levels of Black Youth," *Educational Researchers* 2, no. 4 (April 1982): pp. 10-14.

12. Passow, A. Harry, "Urban Education for the 1980s: Trends and Issues," *Phi Delta Kappan*, April 1982, pp. 519-22.

13. Clark, Terry A., and Dennis P. McCarthy, "School Improvement in New York City: The Evolution of a Project," *Educational Researchers*, 12, no. 4 (April 1983): pp. 17-24.

14. Edmonds, R.R., "Effective School for the Urban Poor," *Educational Leadership* 37 (1979), pp. 15-27; Edmonds, R.R., "Making Public School Effective," *Social Policy* 12 (1981), pp. 46-60; Edmonds, R.R., "Program of School Improvement: An Overview," *Educational Leadership* 40 (1982), pp. 4-11; Mackenzie, D.E., *Leadership for Learning: What Research Shows About Effective Schools* (Washington, DC: National School Boards Association, 1981).

15. Barnett, Marguerite Ross, and Linda F. Williams, "The Political Economy of Affirmative Action" in Marguerite Barnett and Glenn Pasanen, (eds.), *The Politics of Retrenchment and Block Grants in Education* (forthcoming).

16. Barnett, Marguerite Ross, and Ndora Vincent Vera, "Afro-American Politics and Public Priorities," *The Black Scholar*, (March-April 1980), pp. 9-23.

17. *Wall Street Journal*, October 26, 1981.

18. *New York Times*, March 19, 1983.

19. Euchner, Charlie, *Education Week* 2, no. 23 (March 2, 1983).

20. Johnson, James P., "Can Computers Close the Educational Equity Gap?" *Civil Rights Quarterly Perspectives*, (Fall 1982).

21. Johnson, "Computers."

22. Barnett, Marguerite Ross, "Towards a Theory of School Desegregation: A Revisionist View," in Marguerite Ross Barnett and Charles Harrington, (eds.); *Race, Gender, and National Origin: Desegregation in Public Education*, Vol. 8 of Readings on Equal Education, (New York: AMS, forthcoming).

23. Carnoy, Martin, *Schooling in Corporate America: The Political Economy of Education in America* (New York: David McKay Co., Inc., 1972).

24. Glazer, Nathan, *The Future Under Tuition Tax Credits: The Case for Homogeneity in Schools* (Washington, DC: National School Boards Association, 1981).

6
Legislating for Effective Schools and Academic Excellence

John W. Smith

The late Ron Edmonds once proclaimed that we know more than enough to educate the children of the poor, and if we choose not to, it may be because we do not intend to. This is a rough translation of the wise words of the father of the Effective Schools (ES) movement in this country. But they convey his meaning quite well: that educating our children is not the mystery; the mystery is why we have chosen not to do what we know is well within our ability.

THE EFFECTIVE SCHOOL CONCEPT

Edmonds, a professor at Michigan State and Harvard and a key administrator in the New York City public school system, acted on his research, which had located effective schools in the most economically-deprived communities in this nation. These schools, populated with high-energy black youngsters, featured school principals who were great instructional leaders, teachers who had high expectations for student success, an environment that spoke its articulated mission, a stable (not repressive) school climate, and a consistent system of assessing student progress. The classrooms were exciting laboratories of learning. Moreover, teachers and students worked together to make learning fun and purposeful. The students in these schools were successfully achieving above grade-level norms and above local, regional, state, and national norms on tests for reading, mathematics, language, and other academic subjects. These students were being promoted each and every year, graduating from high school and going on to college.

In the St. Louis public schools, as administered by Dr. Rufus Young, the idea of the Effective School approach has been particularly telling. Since 1980, Dr. Young, Assistant Superintendent for Effective and Efficient Schools in the St. Louis Public Schools, has been the leading advocate for this approach. For a number of years prior to 1980, Dr. Young immersed himself in the concept by meeting with Edmonds and other Effective Schools advocates.

TABLE 1
Stowe Middle School Test-Scores Percentage Passed
Basic Education Skills Test (BEST)—Reading/Language

	Eighth Grade	Seventh Grade
1985 results	93.4	90.7
1986 results	97.6	91.7
1987 objectives	98.0	92.0
1987 results	98.8	90.7
California Achievement Test (CAT) Total Battery		
Eighth Grade		
1985 results	*GE 9.1	
1986 results	GE 10.0	
1987 objectives	GE 9.9	
1987 results	GE 10.0	

*Grade Equivalency

Source: Achievement Test Results Report. Effective and Efficient Schools Division. St. Louis (Mo.) Public Schools. June, 1987.

In 1980, under Dr. Young's supervision, the initial Effective Schools effort in the St. Louis public school system, began at four Chapter I (federally-funded compensatory education program) schools located in severely economically-deprived ghetto neighborhoods: Stowe Middle School, Hempstead Elementary, Arlington Elementary, and Laclede Elementary Schools. The introduction of the ES concept, however, was not without pitfalls. The principals of Stowe Middle School and Laclede Elementary School were opposed to the concept, but today are ardent advocates for the ES principles. From 1981-87, these schools have made remarkable gains with significant numbers of students who perform at or above grade level on nationally standardized achievement tests (see Tables 1 and 2).

The 1980 ES project was entitled SHAL, which represents the first letter in the name of each of the four schools involved. Because of the resounding success of the SHAL program, Dr. Young is now responsible for supervising the school-wide ES program in the St. Louis public schools.

Although the St. Louis schools' ES movement is one of the most successful to date, other U.S. schools have also successfully implemented the ES concept. Indeed, Effective Schools is a concept whose time has come.

LEGISLATIVE INITIATIVES FOR EFFECTIVE EDUCATION

In order to promote this very dramatic concept of school improvement and academic excellence, the U.S. Congress now has House Resolution (H.R.) 5, the School Improvement Act of 1987 for its consideration. This bill, introduced by California, extends practically every federally-supported elementary, secondary, and adult education program through fiscal year 1993. H.R. 5 provides funding for Effective Schools programs because in Congress' view ... "school effectiveness can be increased through effective schools programs to improve student achievement, student behavior, teaching, learn-

TABLE 2
Laclede Elementary School 1983-87
California Achievement Test (Total Battery)*

Grade	April 1984	April 1985	April 1986	April 1987
1	55.6	57.0	59.1	64.9
2	50.5	58.7	62.3	64.0
3	50.2	53.4	59.7	63.4
4	52.4	47.0	56.1	64.5
5	59.6	62.9	59.2	72.3

*Percent of students performing at or above national norms. Baseline year 1983–84.

Source: Achievement Test Results Report. Effective and Efficient Schools Division. St. Louis (Mo.) Public Schools. June, 1987.

ing, and school management." A companion bill in the Senate, S. 373, The Elementary and Secondary Education Amendments of 1987, provides similar Effective Schools language as articulated in H.R. 5.

These two legislative proposals continue a federal education policy that has consistently emphasized academic excellence in education for the nation as a whole, and conforms with the Elementary and Secondary Education Act (ESEA) of 1965 by reaffirming the goals of providing access to high quality education for disadvantaged and other special needs students.

Although the passage of the landmark ESEA in 1965 did not end the debte regarding the appropriate degree of federal involvement in education, it did highlight the need for governmental programs to ensure that quality schooling is available to the nation's educationally-deprived children. A troubling aspect of the Act, however, has always been its focus on a deficit model of education: it rewards (with federal dollars) those state and local educational agencies whose school populations are academically achieving below standardized test levels. Some educators refer to this deficit model as "penalizing success." School districts that increased the achievement levels of their educationally-deprived children would often see their students "test out" of the program, thereby reducing the school's compensatory education allocation.

With the above thoughts in mind, Congressman Hawkins, Chairman of the House Committee on Education and Labor, requested local, state, and national organizations to provide the committee with written statements on ways to improve the federally-funded compensatory education program. The responses and ideas generated were overwhelming, coupled with congressional testimony at committee hearings. Indeed, a great number of suggestions to improve the law were written into H.R. 5. This new language encourages program improvement and thereby attempts to reward success in the following ways:

- annual effectiveness reviews will be conducted by local school districts and be used for program improvement purposes;
- local school districts must modify programs to improve performance of students who show no improvement;

- local school districts can use 5% of the allocation for innovative projects;
- student improvement should occur in more advanced as well as in basic skills;
- students who "test out" of the compensatory education program may remain in them for two more years;
- the U.S. Department of Education may make small grants to study promising educational models;
- schools may conduct educational programs to upgrade an entire school;
- parental involvement is strengthened;
- schools may spend some of their allocated funds for year-round and intensive summer programs.

H.R. 5 represents most of the best ideas in congressional legislation that will help continue the federal presence in education. In his introduction to the House floor debate, Congressman Hawkins contended that H.R. 5 was a "rearmament declaration;" which would supply the tools necessary to attack illiteracy; to stem the tide of educational dropouts; to reverse declining test scores; to close the gap in math, science, and advanced skills; and to achieve equity and excellence. As the bill's report notes, H.R. 5 "is the most far-reaching education bill of the decade. It makes good on the Federal promise to join with States and local school districts in enhancing the quality of our Nation's elementary and secondary schools."[1]

ACTIONS AGAINST RETRENCHMENT

Both the House bill (H.R. 5) and the Senate bill (S. 373), in their attempts to address the need to dramatically improve education, recognize the severity of Reagan admistration budget cuts occurring since 1981. Less was spent on major education, job training, and social service programs in 1985 than was spent in 1980. In more recent years, there have been attempts to stop these funding decreases. Nevertheless, insufficient progress has been made in fully funding such programs.

However, some milestones are being reached. In one most important instance, the Committee for Economic Development (CED) has become involved. The CED is an independent research and educational organization of over two hundred business executives and educators. This organization has recently called for full federal funding of Chapter I (the federally-funded compensatory education program) and Head Start, so that these programs are "brought up to levels sufficient to reach all eligible children." In its report, the CED noted that:

- Effective solutions to the problems of the educationally disadvantaged must include a fundamental restructuring of the school system. But they must also reach beyond the traditional boundaries of schooling to improve the environment of the child. An early and sustained intervention in the lives of disadvantaged children, both in school and out, is our only hope for breaking the cycle of disaffection and despair.

- Any plan for major improvements in the development and education of disadvantaged children that does not recognize the need for additional resources over a sustained period is doomed to failure.[2]

CED further urges corporations to promote polices that can help educate educationally deprived students by encouraging their employees to participate in local school district activities through:

- informing employees of local educational issues and providing opportunities for sustained involvement;
- encouraging participation on school boards by qualified corporate leaders and key managers;
- providing release time and flexible schedules for employees who must attend to their children's educational needs or who want to serve their local school system as volunteers;
- recommending that corporate policies encourage executives experienced in management, research and development, and human resources to apply their talents to the problems of the educationally disadvantaged.[3]

Similarly, the House and Senate have recognized the need to reasonably increase program dollars, as indicated in the selective compilation in Table 3:

TABLE 3
Draft Budget Estimate for Fiscal Year 1988

Program	1987 Appropriation	1988 House	1988 Senate
Budget authority (in thousands of dollars)			
1. Ed. Consolidation Improvement Act—Chapter I	$3,951,163	$4,590,000	$4,477,000
2. Ed. Consolidation Improvement Act—Chapter 2	$ 529,337	$ 529,337	$ 530,137
3. Magnet Schools	$ 75,000	$ 75,000	$ 75,000
4. Bilingual Education (Incl. Immigrant Ed. and Refugee Ed.)	$ 188,981	$ 198,981	$ 196,918
5. Vocational Education	$ 881,967	$ 906,748	$ 949,598
6. Student Financial Aid (Pell Grants)	$4,137,000	$4,450,000	$4,500,000
7. Guaranteed Student Loans	$2,717,000	$2,425,000	$2,935,000
8. Aid for Institutional Development (Higher Ed)	$ 147,208	$ 180,000	$ 138,300
(Historically Black Colleges & Universities)	$ 51,741	$ 84,533	$ 68,300
	(included in "Aid" funding)		
9. Howard University	$ 170,230	$ 179,865	$ 174,230
10. Office for Civil Rights (Department of Education)	$ 43,000	$ 42,333	$ 42,333

Source: U.S. Department of Education: Draft (Budget) Sequester Estimate for Fiscal Year 1988. October 23, 1987

This is an impressive list of programs and it provides intensive insights into the current mood of Congress. Still, even though this list represents a statement of federal commitment to education, there looms the recently-passed Balanced Budget and Emergency Deficit Control Reaffirmation Act. This Act amends the original Gramm-Rudman-Hollings legislation and requires the President and the Congress to enact budgets each year that achieve legally-established deficit targets.

If the deficit target of $144 billion is not met this year, then a "sequestration" (which means setting aside or withdrawing a certain amount of funds) process is automatically triggered. If this happens, approximately $23 billion would be withheld in order to meet the fiscal year target. The initial sequester report was issued on October 20, 1987; this order has resulted in a temporary withholding of funds from obligation. Education's share of this "sequestration" is an 8.5% reduction. The President and congressional leadership have indicated that an agreement has been achieved on the deficit target; now there must be an agreement on where funding cuts will be made in order to reach that target. Negotiations are still in progress on this issue.

THE CONTINUING FEDERAL COMMITMENT

The commitment of the federal government to excellence and to meeting the eductional needs of special populations must remain in force. This commitment must be observed and kept if we are to educate all of our children and especially educationally deprived students.

As Congressman Hawkins noted in a recent presentation:

> It is precisely out of our concern, and even love, as guardians for *all* children, that flows our natural concern for our own children and any group of children suffering injustice as a class. Whether it be economic disadvantage, racial discrimination, or geographic discrimination, no one can deny that Black children have suffered and continue to be the recipients of grave and documented injustice.
>
> It is, therefore, correct from a policy perspective, that we zero in on one of an identifiable group, Black children, as a proxy for all; and even as a means of identifying broader problems in American education and the solutions needed to improve the entire system.
>
> Just as important, and in the final analysis, probably even more important, is what a quality education can do for the individuals who receive it, and for the communities in which they live, and the future direction of all mankind.
>
> Every child deserves, and has a fundamental right to a quality education which will prepare [him or her] to the best of [his or her] individual abilities for the opportunity for advancement and the chance to excel.
>
> Every child should be adequately prepared to be an active, more literate citizen, with a say about his or her environment;
>
> Every child should be able when old enough to vote and participate in our great Democratic way of life;

Every child should be properly educated so that if so talented, [he or she] can conquer scientific mysteries and can achieve medical breakthroughs to rid our earth of disease and human misery;

And every child should experience the dignity and pride that is derived from reaching one's full potential.[4]

NOTES

1. House Committee on Education and Labor Report No. 100-95 on The School Improvement Act of 1987 (H.R. 5), May 15, 1987; p. 1.

2. Children In Need: Investment Strategies For the Educationally Disadvantaged, report of the Committee For Economic Development (CED), (New York: 1987), p. 2, 4.

3. Ibid., p. 78.

4. Congressman Augustus F. Hawkins, Presentation: Congressional Black Caucus Annual Legislative Issues Forum, Washington, D.C., 1987.

7
Black Teachers:
A Vanishing Tradition

Mary E. Dilworth

Black, Hispanic, and other youth have legitimate reasons for choosing professions other than teaching, not the least of which are new certification requirements. Although educational policy makers are aware of such deterrents, very little is being done to correct the situation. This article offers a capsule view of the historic, social, and political conditions that have drained the supply of black and other minority teachers.

A CENTURY-OLD TRADITION

Blacks have a longstanding tradition of excellence in education; for more than a century, teaching has been one of the most highly-respected occupations in the black community. Had it not been for the diligent efforts of the first, second, and third generations of black teachers who taught in segregated schools, yet inspired their students, the present generation of black physicians, lawyers, engineers, and other professionals may not have chosen those careers. Indeed, the black community recognizes and values the significant contribution these teachers have made to progress.

The first black teachers had an enormous task before them; they attempted to educate a virtually illiterate population hungry for knowledge. In the racially segregated school system, few resources were available and financial inequities were pervasive. For example, most black teachers' salaries were only 60% of those offered white teachers.[1] The majority of secondary and post-secondary institutions established for blacks were also poorly funded, and their primary mission was to train new teachers for the masses of newly-emancipated slaves. Many of these institutions of higher education continue to train teachers, although they have expanded to train students for other careers as well.

Although segregated education has been prohibited for over twenty-five years and blacks are free to attend majority institutions, historically black institutions (HBI) continue to produce nearly as many black education graduates nationwide (48.3%) as do predominantly white institutions (51.6%). When viewed in a regional context, the contribution of black teacher-training institutions to the profession is even more significant. Of the 9,471 bachelor degrees awarded to blacks in 1980-81 in the education field, 6,518 were from southern institutions. The majority of the latter (62.9%) were issued by HBIs located in the south.[2]

Although laws requiring that black children be taught in black schools (and by black teachers) no longer exist, there is still a compelling need for minority teachers in the nation's classrooms. Yet minority teachers are quickly becoming a vanishing resource. Indeed, this tradition is threatened as fewer and fewer black students enter the teaching profession.

THE CRITICAL SHORTAGE OF BLACK TEACHERS

The complexion of the U.S. teaching force has paled in recent years. The percentage of black and other minority teachers has dropped dramatically in the past decade. Currently, approximately 6.9% of public school teachers are black, and 1.9% are Hispanic. Asians and Native Americans account for only 1.5% of the total teaching force.[3] Seven years ago, the teaching population was 8.6% black, 1.8% Hispanic, and .7% other.[4]

Data on education majors suggests that the non-white teaching force will continue to diminish in number. During the 1980-81 school year, 17% of education degrees went to blacks and Hispanics.[5] However, during the 1984-85 school year, only 10.4% of education degrees conferred went to blacks, Hispanics, Asians and Native Americans.

This decline in the numbers of minority teachers has been made worse by the fact that the black and Hispanic populations are growing more rapidly than is the white population, with many urban and suburban school systems becoming "minority/majority." Conservative projections indicate that non-white students already constitute at least one-third of the preschool age population.[6] The proportion of black, Hispanic, Asian, and Native American school-age children is nearly 30%. Yet, the total number of teachers from these groups may fall below 10% of the total teacher population.

This is not to suggest that non-white youngsters should be taught only by teachers of their own race, but that all students should and must be exposed to a wide variety of perspectives and role models that only a multicultural teaching force can provide. Moreover, consideration must be given to the multicultural training needs of majority teachers who are teaching minority youngsters. An education that fails to recognize and promote ethnicity in its teaching force is at best mundane, and at worst incomplete. Societal demands for an equitable and high-quality education will not be met until greater numbers of blacks and other minorities teach in the nation's classrooms.

Majority as well as minority students, have chosen professions other than teaching in recent years. Poor salaries and working conditions, coupled with the prospects of brighter futures in other careers have diminished the attractiveness of the profession. However, newly-imposed educational and assessment criteria in teacher education have had the greatest negative impact on blacks and other minorities entering teaching— greater than all other deterrents combined.

IMPROVED STANDARDS: A PUSH-PULL EFFECT ON QUALITY AND
QUANTITY

In recent years, the public has perceived a lowering of the overall quality of education.
The general consensus has been that teachers are to blame. While schools and schooling
suffer from a number of ills that also must be rectified, the focus of most educational
reform efforts has been placed on teachers and teaching methods.

In this regard, well-intended mandates for improvement have had unintended consequences. Most reform reports and subsequent legislation passed by individual states
deal with the broader issues related to teaching, e.g., quality assurance through assessment and testing, academic program content and design, and salary increases. Iron-
ically, many of these mandates have resulted in narrowly-focused, short-term, and
poorly-financed initiatives that exacerbate the current shortage of teachers. Moreover,
these mandates have had a differential impact on the participation of blacks and members of other racial and ethnic groups.

Individual states are primarily responsible for the quality of education and of educators provided in their locales. For the most part, the states have responded to problems in these areas by relying too heavily on scores. Nearly every state has imposed
testing requirements before, during, and/or after teachers are trained, with litle regard
for the reliability of such tests to assess quality teaching. Eighty-two percent of the states
use either a nationally standardized or state-customized test to assess teachers for
certification.[7] In addition, approximately 50% of schools, colleges, and departments of
education (SCDE) now require a program entrance examination, and nearly 20% have
instituted exit testing as a prerequisite to college graduation.

The impact of such tests on blacks is indisputable. When such tests were first administered in the mid 1980s, blacks and other minorities failed them at much higher rates
than did white students. Because states such as Georgia and Florida imposed sanctions
against colleges with particularly high failure rates on certification and other types of
examinations, many programs were discontinued.[8]

While state legislators have not singled out black teacher-training institutions for
reform, these schools bear the brunt of the testing phenomenon.[9] Most HBIs are located
in the South. These institutions have been at the forefront of the teacher-testing movement: States in this region were the first to use basic and professional skill competency
examinations as criteria for initial certification and recertification.

Black and Hispanic teacher education students have improved their performance on
certification examinations, but it has been a difficult process. In an attempt to retain
teacher education programs by meeting state-imposed passing rates, many schools,
colleges, and departments of education in majority and minority institutions have
significantly reduced their enrollments. Higher standards have been imposed for admission into SCDEs. More field work experience is being offered during training and fewer
method and more subject matter courses are required.

In some instances, it is no longer necessary to major in teacher education to become a
teacher. Because of shortages in certain discipline areas, e.g., math and science, states

such as New Jersey have instituted alternative certification programs to attract individuals from other occupations to teaching. Many new teachers must now participate in an induction program for one year beyond graduation, and practicing teachers are subject to more stringent evaluations and competency tests.

There are trends other than testing that are also counterproductive to producing more black teachers. Both the Carnegie Forum report[10] and *Tomorrow's Teachers: Report of the Holmes Group* suggest that teachers must have more subject matter knowledge and call for the elimination of undergraduate teacher education.[11] These groups suggest that aspiring teachers receive an undergraduate liberal arts degree and then learn educational methods and skills in graduate school. While there is no evidence that the 4 + 1 scheme (four years of liberal arts education and one year of teaching methods) will produce more effective teachers, a number of institutions are considering this approach.

Such a structural change in teacher education will likely have a negative impact on blacks and other minorities. The participation of blacks and Hispanics in four-year institutions has not kept pace with improved high school completion rates.[12] Hispanics and Native Americans attend two-year colleges at a higher rate than they attend four-year schools. Also, attendance at traditional four-year institutions is conditioned to a great extent by the availability of financial aid. Presently, financial aid in forms other than loans is scarce. Blacks and other minorities rely more heavily on such assistance than do white students. Clearly, the financial burden of five, rather than four years of schooling, to become a moderately paid teacher is not especially attractive, especially for minority students.

Further, many historically black institutions do not have or are not equipped to establish graduate education programs in short order. Because such institutions graduate nearly half of the black teachers in the U.S., and have a much higher program graduation rate for blacks than do majority institutions, the profession stands to lose an even greater number of much-needed teachers.

Although some of the measures taken to raise the quality of education may also help maintain an effective teaching force, precautions must be taken to ensure that the profession's multiethnicity is not lost in the process.

EASING THE PUSH-PULL EFFECTS

There is no single solution to establishing quality standards for teaching while also maintaining an appropriate supply of teachers, but it can be done. Legislators must consider the implications of their mandates and establish meaningful assessment criteria. Any changes to the program design and structure of teacher education must take into account the real need for minority teachers and add substantial support to those institutions that have a commitment to train minority teachers. Students must be informed early in their academic careers of the benefits of teaching and parents must recognize and encourage their youngsters to pursue careers in education. Community organizations and churches can also help by directing youngsters toward teaching careers and assisting new teachers in neighborhood schools to understand better the needs and temperament of the community.

A number of national, educational, and community organizations recognize the size and scope of this problem. Leaders from twenty-five such associations met recently to devise a plan of action to help alleviate many of these problems. Under the leadership of the American Association of Colleges for Teacher Education, the group identified a number of programs and activities that can help raise the issue of minority teacher shortages to national attention and refill the dwindling pool of candidates.

These recommendations include the establishment of:

- national and state scholarships for minority students;
- college and high school work-study programs that will allow students to work in school settings;
- incentive programs that will offer student loan forgiveness for college juniors and seniors willing to enter teaching;
- community assistance with teacher induction programs; and
- assessment demonstration grants.[13]

In conclusion, the critical shortage of black, Hispanic, and other minority teachers serves as a deterrent to progress in a competitive democratic society that makes great demands on education. Without a national imperative, existing state and organizational initiatives to recruit minorities for teaching will continue to flounder in isolation. Areas without established programs efforts will suffer most.

NOTES

1. Mary Dilworth, *Teachers Totter: A Report on Teacher Certification Issues* (Washington, D.C.: Howard University, 1984).

2. William Trent, "Equity Considerations in Higher Education: Race and Sex Differences in Degree Attainment and Major Field from 1976 through 1981" *American Journal of Education* (May 1984).

3. National Education Association, *Status of the American Public School Teacher, 1985-86*, July 1987.

4. Office of Educational Research and Improvement, 1983, *Condition of Education, 1983.*

5. Trent, "Equity Considerations."

6. Harold Hodgkinson, "Here They Come, Ready or Not," *Education Week*, May 1986.

7. Office of Educational Research and Improvement, *What's Happening in Teacher Testing: An Analysis of State Teacher Testing Practices* August 1987.

8. Dilworth, *Teachers Totter.*

9. Mary Dilworth, "Teacher Testing: Adjustment for Schools, Colleges and Departments of Education," *Journal of Negro Education*, Summer, (1986).

10. Carnegie Forum on Education and the Economy, *A Nation Prepared: Teachers for the 21st Century*, May 1986.

11. Holmes Group Inc. *Tomorrow's Teachers: A Report of the Holmes Group*, April 1986.

12. Office of Educational Research and Improvement, *Condition of Education, 1987.*

13. "Minority Recruitment and Retention: An AACTE Policy Statement", American Association for Colleges of Teacher Education, September 1987.

8
Improving Black Education: Perspectives on Parent Involvement

Diana T. Slaughter and Valerie Shahariw Kuehne

Lightfoot[1] reports that both teachers and parents have images and stereotypes of one another that stem from their own childhood experiences and guide their views of what schooling is, and ought to be, for the children for whom they are immediately responsible. She also states that Waller[2] expressed similar views nearly fifty years ago. Therefore, since the late nineteenth century, when public schools assumed significant educational functions in the lives of the majority of American children, the roles of teachers and parents have been debated.

Education professionals assume that both families and schools play significant roles in childhood learning and development because both primary institutions engage in child socialization.[3] Specifically, both are responsible for transmitting the culture and history of the broader community to children, and for insuring that these children, as adults, are capable of contributing positively and productively to society. The debates have centered around how best to describe the respective roles of parents and teachers, how to identify and document the consequences of differing perspectives about their respective roles in the education of children, and the educational policies to propose that are most consistent with optimal family-school relations. In summary, once public schools assumed significant, nationally-recognized educational functions, the debates of the newly-emerging education professionals stressed the authority and scope of parental involvement in the educational process.

Fein[4] argues that in American social and educational history, parents have been most likely to express particular concerns for informed childrearing practices whenever they have felt less confident about the ability of national and local community leadership to be responsible for the needs of their children. She points to the way in which the corruption of the Jacksonian presidency in the early nineteenth century may have helped to focus public interest upon the elements of quality childrearing:[5]

The authors wish to thank Dr. Rachel Lindsay of Chicago State University for her commentary on an earlier draft of this paper.

... the country discovered public corruption, greed, and immorality in high places ... It seemed that the nation had lost the virtues of an earlier time. In the self scrutiny that followed, there were many who suggested that America's fall from grace had occurred because children were no longer being reared as they ought to be ... Pamphlets, tracts, magazines, and sermons on child rearing innundated the public and were purchased by anxious parents ... the first publication for mothers, *Mother's Magazine* appeared in 1832 ... As memories of the Jacksonian exposes waned, interest in the informed parent waned. By 1850, *Mother's Magazine* had stopped publishing, and the first parenting crusade came to an end ...

Most black Americans have experienced continuing crises regarding their children's education. Lightfoot[6] points to a history in which the children of slaves were, by national and local policy, to be kept uneducated and illiterate. Further, in northern states, where slavery was abolished prior to the Civil War and Reconstruction, black children were generally legally forbidden to attend schools with white children, and public dollars were not, without repeated struggles by black parents and communities, allocated for the "separate but equal" education of black children. Even today, once allocated, the dollars are rarely allocated equitably. Desegregation efforts, initially pursued by black parents and communities to ensure that black children would have equal access to a high-quality education, have been systematically resisted and thwarted by white communities in all regions of the country.

In short, as Ogbu[7] and others[8] have suggested, the black community has long had a "crisis of confidence" relative to the benefits of public education for its children. There have been numerous efforts within the community for many years that have attempted to maximize parent involvement and participation in schools. Although the majority of black Americans still favor public education, they express continuing concern about the public schools influence on their children's learning and development.

There is yet another context in which the concept of parent involvement has particular salience for the black community. Many, indeed the majority, of black American families are middle to low-income households, and a disproportionately high number of these households that include children are in poverty. Chronic poverty is tied to an intergenerational history of lower-skilled, underpaid work, and to higher incidence of female-headed households; black families are disproportionately at risk of both of these sources of poverty. Even more important, according to Wilson,[9] in comparison to other American families, black families have been more vulnerable to changes in the labor market in the past fifteen to twenty years because black adults do not have access to prospering areas of the job market. This new source of deeply entrenched poverty affects even the hardiest of black families. Given this economic situation, we expect that black communities will continue to be involved in public schools; parents will have special responsibilities to ensure that their children are prepared for successfully living and working in the changed technology and labor markets anticipated in twenty-first century America.

CONTEMPORARY PARENT INVOLVEMENT:
ITS ROOTS IN PROJECT HEAD START

Valentine and Stark, as well as Fein,[10] report that Project Head Start, a program that achieved national prominence during the Johnson Administration's "War on Poverty" in the 1960s, shares several features with other poverty programs. Such programs were conceived as a response to the influx of blacks and Hispanics to urban metropolitan areas. Earlier migrants and immigrants, through intra-ethnic networking, had already garnered the traditional bases of political and economic power for their own communities. The overall poverty program, working through the various Community Action Programs (CAP) associated with Model Cities, promised a new "infrastructure" designed to facilitate maximum feasible participation. The newer residents, adults and children, could legitimately engage in significant decision-making, and therefore, eventually obtain the skills, contacts, and resources, both political and economic, with which to become upwardly-mobile.

Nearly all programs stressed the virtues of middle-class life styles, and the deficits or deficiencies of lower-class styles. Individuals were expected to use the service programs to transcend the limitations and barriers inherent to their communities, and to achieve upward social mobility. Shriver,[11] for example, sought scholarly legitimation for Head Start in the mental retardation research community, several of whose researchers had demonstrated the impact of environment and/or motivation on individual intellectual performance. Because lower-income youth, in comparison with other youth, scored significantly lower on typical intelligence tests, the prospect of good results in the mental retardation field appeared very promising. The basic intelligence of poor youth is modified under the right environmental conditions; specifically, the youth are educable. Early Head Start programs stressed parental involvement and participation so as to radically improve the child's home environment.

Eventually, many poverty program administrators came to perceive the participants as useful to program maintenance and continuity, particularly with the mandated citizen participation guidelines that emerged in the 1970s. For example, as the poverty child's home environment was believed to have resources, including community cultural traditions, education professionals facilitated the founding of the National Organization of Head Start Parents. The professionals aptly perceived that as a viable, organized infrastructure, parents could substantially support continuation of the program. Importantly, for many low-income parents, Head Start has served as a basis for excellent "grass-roots" training in political participation. According to Valentine and Stark, the best early example of this latter role was located in Mississippi. The Child Development Group of Mississippi (CDGM) at one time served more than 6,000 children in 84 centers throughout the state. Indigenous poor were responsible for all decision-making, including preschool curriculum and the hiring of staff at the centers. In such a climate, Head Start parent Fannie Lou Hammer emerged as an important political figure.

Valentine and Stark conclude that at least two quite distinct conceptual underpinnings of parent involvement in Head Start have existed from the beginning of the
program: the emphasis on social and political empowerment of parents, and the emphasis on parent education. Over time, greater emphasis has increasingly been given to
the latter perspective.[12] Without the emphasis on empowerment, however, they believe
that the essence of Head Start, as a program designed to help eradicate poverty, would
be significantly compromised because the parent and overall community's need for
control and self-determination are compromised. Regarding the fate of parent involvement in Head Start by the mid-1970s, the authors state:

> . . . the formal advancement of parent involvement paralleled the containment of
> those parent groups largely responsible for earlier changes in the overall program.
> With the vanguard of the institutional-change movement put in its place, the stage
> was set for parent education. The limits imposed on grassroots politics led rapidly
> to a widespread decline in participation, despite its formal legitimacy . . . Basic
> institutional change would seem to be a minimal prerequisite if individual
> changes made in childhood are to be sustained through the life cycle. [to date]
> only two studies . . . have considered institutional change as a potentially signifi-
> cant outcome of a good parent-involvement component . . . if the experience with
> parent involvement in Head Start has taught us anything, it is that self-determina-
> tion is not only an important component of quality education but the link be-
> tween education and the material and social progress of the poor.[13]

DEFINING PARENT INVOLVEMENT: MID-1970s TO MID-1980s

Examination of parent involvement studies reveals a recurring list of activities in
which parents may participate in schools, including preschools, parent meetings; workshops; parent-teacher conferences; classroom work as a volunteer, observer, or paid
employee; home tutoring; board membership; fundraising; community advocacy; and
general school program support.[14] Some of these activities are discussed in the context
of significant institutional changes that support development of individuals in the
programs.

A few authors have attempted to formulate a framework or identify more general
roles for parents or their involvement in their children's education under which specific
activities may be subsumed. Gordon's[15] conceptual paradigm of parent involvement
(Parent/Family Impact Model, School Impact Model; Community Impact Model) suggests typical activities for each of these models. For example, if parents tutor their
child(ren) at home in reading or attend parent-teacher conferences, these activities fall
under the Parent/Family Impact Model. The School Impact Model includes such parent involvement activities as classroom participation and advisory board membership,
all in an effort to change the school or agency. Some programs combine these two
models, in that parents hold the roles of both "learner" and "resource" to their children's development and education.

Gordon et al.[16] identify the simultaneous fulfillment of six parent roles as necessary to the Community Impact Model's success: volunteer, paid employee, adult learner, decision-maker, teacher at home, and audience (via items such as newsletters). Similar roles are documented in the work of Frierson and Hills,[17] where parents are described as teachers, learners, resources, decision-makers, and advocates. Specific activities in the Community Impact Model may be no different from the Parent/Family and School Impact models. However, with all six roles being filled simultaneously, a more comprehensive program for families, schools, and communities results. This is the perspective generally supported by Comer[18] and his colleagues in the successful intervention program pioneered in two New Haven public schools.

Warnat[19] has extended the Gordon Community Impact Model and its parent roles and activities, and suggests that parent involvement can be seen as strategies benefiting the child and parent, promoting social change. She proposes that parent involvement for the child involves a more passive role, in which parents might attend teacher-parent conferences regarding their child or open house activities at school to meet staff and other parents or respond to home visits by staff members. Alternatively, parent involvement for the parent would include volunteer or paid activities in the classroom or at an agency site. Parent involvement for social change encompasses such activities as board and committee memberships and other modes of community involvement (such as advocacy and fundraising) mentioned earlier.

Schickedanz[20] has classified various parent activities in schools into one of three levels of involvement. Once again, the activities included by this author are generally those identified by other authors. In this case, however, the author provides a framework for examining specific parent involvement activities as they affect the teacher's role as "expert," and on the decision-making role of school staff members. Schickedanz[21] states that Level One (also considered "low parent involvement") includes "parental activities that do not challenge the expertise of the teacher or the decision-making power of the school," Level Two includes "parental presence and participation in the educational setting," and Level Three includes "activities that involve parents in teaching their own children and in making decisions concerning educational policy."

Activities such as parent meetings and parent-teacher conferences would correspond to Level One involvement. At Level Two, parents would have active roles in the classroom, or on field trips, but control would still be maintained by the teacher and school. Parent involvement activities at Level Three include advisory committee membership and other decision-making activities described earlier.

Leler[22] states that at Level Three, the roles of teacher and school are both altered. While the teacher still remains an expert, his or her knowledge is now actively shared with interested parents. She further states that Levels One and Two of the Schickedanz[23] model are similar to Gordon's[24] Parent/Family Impact Model of parent involvement; conversely, Level Three relates more closely to the Community Impact Model.

In sum, while the list of possible parent involvement activities in the literature is rather "generic," conceptual perspectives with which to examine these activities are fairly different. Three such perspectives were presented: one views parent involvement as based on a triad of strategies, each having a different focus;[25] the second focuses on the direction of influence in home-school-community relations;[26] and the third concentrates on the degree to which "involved" parents alter the roles of teachers and school personnel.[27]

THE MAJOR ASSUMPTIONS OF PARENT INVOLVEMENT

Olmsted and Rubin[28] state that one of the most well-accepted and fundamental beliefs about parent involvement in education is that it positively affects children by encouraging their cognitive and affective development. Comprehensive reviews of literature on this subject are available but outside the scope of this study.[29]

Bronfenbrenner[30] has been specifically cited by at least two authors encountered and referenced by a host of others regarding an article that discusses parent involvement and children's achievement:

> The evidence indicates that the family is the most effective and economical system of fostering and sustaining the development of the child . . . Without such family involvement, any effects of intervention, at least in the cognitive sphere, appear to erode . . . once the program ends. In contrast, the involvement of parents as partners in the enterprise provides an on-going system which can reinforce the effects of the program while it is in operation and help to sustain them after the program ends.[31]

Two important assumptions of parent involvement, defined essentially as parent education, are that (a) it contributes to children's cognitive and affective development, and (b) intervention efforts with children are most effective when parents actively participate in those efforts. In addition to these two beliefs, these authors have identified at least five other key assumptions of the literature concerning parent involvement in general, several of which are implicit in Bronfenbrenner's comments.

(c) First, the parent is the major vehicle by which the society and community can reach the child and family;

(d) Second, linking the home and the school environments will be beneficial to parents, teachers, administrators, and especially children;

(e) Third, parents are resources and therefore a group worthy of investment. Indeed, the prescribed roles and activities of parents in the various parent involvement research and paradigms indicate that this group of adults is viewed as critically important to the developmental courses of children and potentially the community at large;

(f) Fourth, the family, not the school, provides the child with a primary source of values and behavioral reference points;[32]

(g) A fifth, related assumption regarding the uniqueness of the parent-child relationship as compared to teacher-child or peer-child relationships can also be identified.[33] Implicit in both the fourth and fifth assumptions is the view that the family and the parent-child dyad are of primary importance to a child's growth and development, while the school and school-based relationships play secondary roles. Involving parents in school-based programs inherently recognizes the family as having major childrearing responsibilities while further strengthening both the parental role and the family unit.[34]

Evaluation of Parent Education Programs

Clarke-Stewart[35] questions many of the major assumptions as applied to the parent education literature. First, she offers the reminder that statistical findings relating parental behavior to child achievement performance are typically correlational data, and do not necessarily represent a causal relationship. This author also challenges literature that describes the direction of influence in parent involvement programs as moving from program planner and program to parent(s) to child(ren). Her concern is that a "... chain of untested assumptions" extends "from the gleam in the program developer's eye to the last p-level in his final report."[36] Arguing that comparisons across such programs are not needed, she maintains that research into the differences between programs, while controlling for selected, confounding factors, would be of the greatest benefit.

Second, she questions the cross-racial applicability of many of these findings, an issue typically not considered in the literature. The issue of cross-cultural and subcultural generalizability is related to the questions of parental involvement. Because parent involvement is complex and multidimensional, it follows that families will differ both between and within cultures in the patterning of relationships formed on behalf of its children with other secondary institutions in which, for educative purposes, their children participate. To date, we have paid little attention to cultural differences in the natural variability of parent involvement. Further, we know little of how families in American society from different subcultural backgrounds will adapt to diverse planned programs of parent involvement.[37] This is no small matter, given the increasing proportions of culturally different child populations expected among our American children by the beginning of the twenty-first century.[38]

Why has such systematic investigation not yet taken place in the parent involvement arena? Tizard et al.[39] suggest that parent involvement is often part of a larger initiative or "educational package," and therefore its effects may not be easily disentangled from other program outcomes. Leler[40] notes that much of the evaluation research in the area of parent involvement is short-term, often in the form of doctoral dissertations with no follow-up.

Olmsted and Rubin[41] describe the evaluation of the federally-funded Follow Through program as incongruous with the important role parent involvement plays in this program's regulations. They state that descriptive methods were used to initially obtain evaluation data from parents, a method that many view as a weakness of parent involvement evaluations. These authors[42] further attribute the lack of evaluation data for Follow Through to personnel changes in the national headquarters and problems with data analysis and dissemination of results. Perhaps a similar scenario could be painted in cases of other government-supported programs that mandate parent involvement.

A final reason for the lack of evaluation data on parent involvement programs is that many programs are simply not required to evaluate their effectiveness. Although federally-funded programs, often designed for disadvantaged families, may be obliged by contract to report their outcome, privately funded programs are not, and these are more likely to involve middle and upper-income parents. Therefore, many opportunities for data collection and scientific research are not being utilized.

Parent Involvement: Issues of the Mid-1980s

Since 1980, there has been increasing acknowledgement in the literature that the changing nature of American families significantly impacts the concept of parent involvement in schools.[43] Many of the changes in American families are familiar because of extensive media coverage of these subjects.[44] For example, there has been a dramatic increase in the number of working women in the past fifteen to twenty years. Currently more than 50% of mothers of younger children work 20 or more hours per week. Women of all socioeconomic strata and racial/ethnic backgrounds are working. There is correspondingly less family time for active parent participation in school activities on behalf of children and their teachers.

After reviewing their findings of a study of parent involvement within private elementary schools, for example, Schneider and Slaughter[45] recently argued that the school social organization is a crucial factor in how parents participate, and further, that participation in activities may be a necessary but not sufficient indicator of parent involvement in schools. Other important factors, particularly for black and other ethnic minority parents, include the parents' sense of belonging and inclusion in the school community. As increasing numbers of parents find it necessary to work at times when many school activities are held, these more subjective measures of parental involvement in schools could eventually assume greater significance, insofar as they may most accurately reflect how children experience their families' relationships with their schools.

The number of single-parent households has risen sharply, and with this rise a larger number of lower-income and ethnic minority children live in economically-impoverished households. Earlier, this study discussed how the greatly increased vulnerability to poverty has severely impacted black families.[46] We have witnessed striking increases in the rates of homeless families and children throughout the nation.[47] Research from the 1960s and 70s has shown that poverty can have devastating effects on parent involvement with their children.[48] Generally, under impoverished conditions, many families are considerably more survival-oriented than child-centered, although for many such adults their children are their most precious possessions.

The current informal observations of Head Start directors are that they are seeing an increased number of impoverished families, and that the mothers of children in these families are themselves younger than in previous years. These observations probably reflect the high rate of black teen pregnancy, and recently-increasing rates among white youth.[49] These parenting situations can also mitigate against a child-centered approach to childrearing that includes active parental involvement.

The increasing numbers of mothers employed in the workplace, and the role of fathers, are two areas that require further attention in studies evaluating parent involvement,[50] because strategies for implementing parent involvement programs need to consider all forms of family life. This includes teenage parents and Warnat[51] suggests that junior and high school students comprise an important target group of future parents. In fact, Becher states that "developing an awareness of the possible impact of the changing roles and relationships of fathers and mothers is essential if policies and practices are to be appropriately adapted to changing social and parental norms."[52] Critical areas for research include documenting how differing family structures mediate the effects of recent program strategies.

Effects of Parent Involvement on Parents

Becher[53] lists a number of effects of parent involvement on parents; some of these effects are more extensively supported by literature than others. In essence, however, these outcomes may be classified into two groups: "external" and "internal" effects. External effects include such visible behaviors as parents gathering community support for programs, becoming more involved in their child's activities, and increasing their contact with school personnel. Such effects are relatively easy to quantify. Internal effects are more subjective and personal in nature and refer to attitude changes parents experience toward school personnel, or improved self-confidence and self-esteem.

Other authors identify outcomes of parent involvement programs for parents that can also be called "external." Washington and Oyemade[54] discuss the economic self-sufficiency that can result when parent involvement activities in Head Start help adults prepare for work through skill development. These authors suggest that evaluations of Head Start have primarily emphasized children's skill development and related parenting behaviors. The program has not systematically identified and studied the self-perceptions of participating parents. Laosa[55] offers a similar opinion regarding Head Start, which mandates parent involvement. He is critical of the fact that much of the research evaluating Head Start is typically focused on the child's cognitive or socioemotional development. Where are the parents in such evaluations?

An important question for systematic evaluation relates to the nature of any intervening variables between parent involvement and external outcomes, such as economic self sufficiency. Do improved self-esteem and self-confidence comprise such intermediate (internal) effects of parent involvement for parents? No data directly addressing this question can be found. Honig[56] suggests that the absence of evidence in the literature partly results from inadequate and/or unacceptable (to respondents) adult measures of self-worth. Nevertheless, this area of intermediate parental effects seems worthy of further study.

AN ECOLOGICAL PERSPECTIVE OF PARENT INVOLVEMENT

Bronfenbrenner[57] also provides an ecological approach to human development within which the phenomenon of parent involvement may be examined. He states: "In ecological research, the properties of the person and of the environment, the structure of environmental settings, and the processes taking place within and between them must be viewed as interdependent and analyzed in systems terms."

In his work, Bronfenbrenner characterizes the microsystem, mesosystem, exosystem, and macrosystem as concentric structures nested inside one another. This researcher describes the microsystem as the actual setting in which the person's behavior and development occur in face-to-face interactions with others. The mesosytem can be briefly described as many microsystems in which the same person may participate and it includes the relations between them. The exosystem refers to those settings whose events indirectly affect or are affected by events in the person's micro or mesosystems. Meso and exosystems are nested inside the characteristics of any given society or culture, known as macrosystems. Of course, macrosystems also directly affect developing persons.

Apart from the parenting that occurs in the home or microsystem, parent involvement perhaps takes place most clearly in the mesosystems, where the microsystems of school and home interact. Garbarino[58] suggests that where positive experiences for children result, mutual support exists between these two settings, with parents both interested and involved in school affairs. Parent involvement may also take place in the exosystem—in the worlds of work or local government—as parents lobby for services that support their families both individually and collectively. In this way, the macrosystem may be eventually altered in some way, supporting the view that parent involvement can function as a strategy for social change.

Importantly, we believe an ecological perspective offers the possibility of integrating the two historically thematic issues characterizing discussions of parent involvement in schools: parental empowerment and parent education.

Tizard, Mortimore, and Burchell[59] suggest that where parent involvement is related to schools, advocates share the belief that parents should become more active participants in their children's education. The notion of activity, common to the two perspectives of parent involvement presented thus far, is also included in a paradigm of the family described by Swick and Taylor.[60] Swick[61] suggests that by viewing family functioning as a "network of dynamic and complex relationships," a study of the family's ecology can lead to better parent involvement strategies in children's education. It is in the four contexts of work, family, neighborhood, and school that family members function on a daily basis. An ecological approach includes collecting information on how these persons relate to one another in view of the impact of their extrafamilial environments.

Bronfenbrenner and Swick are among those who argue that the social systems are interrelated and believe that parent involvement can have great impact on the family ecology, the relationships within the family, and the community in which the family lives. For example, if parent involvement activities result in an unemployed mother obtaining new skills and/or increased confidence, she could better qualify for work. Her employment will have an impact on relationships within the family, and further, the family as a unit will have ties to a new social system. Policies at the workplace could indirectly affect the mother's child care responsibilities and require help from members of the extended family. Further, the mother may be unable to take as active a role in the children's school activities as she may have prior to regular employment. The various social systems that constitute the family members' ecological worlds thus affect parent involvement, but parent involvement itself may also affect adaptation to those social systems.

FUTURE RESEARCH IN PARENT INVOLVEMENT

An ecological perspective on areas for further research in parent involvement might well include research focused on the "exosystemic" level, specifically an evaluation of policy issues associated with the practice of parent involvement. Additionally, such research might focus on the effects of parent involvement on changing American families, as well as individual parents. Finally, of course, little attention is still paid to the ways in which particular program features affect different aspects of individual development, to say nothing of how the cultural ecology interacts with service delivery in parent involvement programs.

Warnat[62] states that a successful parent involvement program is difficult to achieve. She adds that the three major barriers to success are professionals, the bureaucracy, and parent power. Other authors agree on at least the first two obstacles,[63] yet these two are the least often-studied dimensions of parent involvement.

The Professionals

Professionals generally identified as the "problem" in parent involvement issues are the teachers. Warnat suggests that teachers harbor an "antiparent sentiment," and as a result view parents as "unwelcome invaders" of their turf.[64] Garbarino[65] warns that if the school-home mesosystem is to be enhanced, parents and teachers cannot view one another as adversaries. Williams, Stallworth, and Kronkosky[66] state that conflict between teachers and parents is not surprising, and that at the root of such conflicts are differing views of parent involvement. Teachers see the parental role as minimally supportive and traditional, if not somewhat passive, in relation to the school and children's learning in school. The role of parents is primarily home-based. Parents, however, express interest in being active co-learners with their children, functioning as their advocates and participating in decision-making.[67]

There are several research questions that warrant study here. First, under what conditions do teachers really view parent involvement as more appropriately passive than active? Becher[68] suggests that teachers are often uncertain of parent involvement strategies, are concerned about the amount of time required to plan parent involvement activities, are worried that parents will undermine their authority and disrupt their classrooms, and predict that parents will not keep commitments.

A second research question concerns the view that teachers are inadequately prepared to facilitate new and support ongoing parent involvement.[69] Almy[70] maintains that although an emphasis on parent involvement in education seems to exist, teacher training continues to focus on strategies for working with children. Hence, she supports training for educators in interviewing skills and in parent development, needs, defenses and adaptations. Swick and Duff[71] add that teachers need additional instruction in communication techniques and effective group or team management. In considering the School Impact Model, Gordon[72] also stated that new modes of teacher education are necessary. Williams et al.[73] found in their study of educators and parents in six states that both groups supported policy changes mandating parent involvement training for teachers during their undergraduate education. Recent research showing bidirectional ties between teacher efficacy and parent involvement[74] is also supportive of these trends. Further research should address potential education policy initiatives as well as those already successful in facilitating parent involvement in schools nationally and internationally.[75]

The Bureaucracy

Warnat's definition of bureaucracy includes those at local, state, and federal legislative levels.[76] She suggests that individuals at each level interfere with parent involvement efforts in various ways. How these public officials or the systems themselves contribute to or interfere with parent involvement efforts is an important area for further research. In a statement made before a Hearing of the House of Representative Select Committee on Children, Youth, and Families, Coleman indicated that governmental provision of "meaningful" funding in the area of parent involvement is an important factor in such a program's success.[77]

Olmsted and Rubin[78] emphasize the need for funding for evaluation, in both the formative and summation periods. Support for evaluative research seems paramount to uncovering the reasons for nationwide successes and failures in parent involvement programs. For example, Coleman[79] views trust between parents and teachers as crucial to the success of parent involvement programs. Even if this is true, we need to know what other factors are characteristic of successful programs and under what conditions.

An example of state legislation supporting parent involvement in schools exists in Florida. In 1976 and 1979, legislation was passed requiring that "Parent participation be an integral part of every school district's education program . . . additional statutes have dealt with citizen participation through school volunteer programs."[80] For example, free day care is provided to school volunteers with young children, and three policies implemented by Florida's Seminole County School Board require training for all school volunteers, an advisory committee in each school, and the formation of parent/teacher organizations in which school principals play an active role. This state, and Seminole County in particular, have experienced success with their parent involvement programs at all levels of education. What have other states accomplished in this domain, and how effective have their efforts been? A comprehensive study of present legislation in this area is critical to advancing knowledge of parent involvement.

SUMMARY AND CONCLUSION

This paper has examined the major assumptions on which the practice of parent involvement in schools is based, particularly the recently-emergent assumption of the importance of the ecological perspective. This study has used an historical perspective to examine the conceptual underpinnings and typical definitions of parent involvement, as well as to identify areas for further research. The policy arena has been identified as one domain in which much work is needed. Special attention has been given to how social policies constitute potential supports and barriers for parent involvement and therefore to the developing relations between parents, teachers, and children.

Williams et al. state: "In order for parent involvement to be mutually acceptable and a more viable aspect of education, its definition must be clearer among parents and educators."[81] Such a mutually acceptable definition must be based on assumptions about parents, families, and communities that are dynamic and positive. If healthy, functioning families are the goal of parent involvement policies, programs, and activities, a deficit paradigm is not a useful framework.[82] These authors argue that recent history demonstrates that an ecological perspective on parent involvement is necessary to place both policy and/or program goals and objectives in context, and to render them most applicable to the lives of families. Bronfenbrenner[83] and Garbarino[84] also advocate competency-based paradigms for research on parent involvement. This study also endorses these positions. Social scientists must be more aware of their assumptions and the potential effects of their research on the policymaking process.

Many of the assumptions of school-based parent involvement programs could benefit from the results of sound research. For example, how do parents of children of different ages and social situations view their role(s) in parent involvement? Do they see themselves as a potentially powerful lobby group? Do they prefer active or passive roles in parent involvement programs? What legislation would they propose to support their vision of parent involvement? In addition, there are clear obstacles to parent involvement at the professional and bureaucratic levels.[85] These authors believe that these obstacles must be better researched so they can be evaluted and addressed, at least in part, by policy initiatives at the local, state, and federal levels.

We also believe that policymakers, social scientists, and constituents must not view parents, teachers, or children as the sole target group of parent involvement policies, nor should policies specifically directed toward parent involvement be the sole source of legislative concern for these groups. Cohen and Garet state that "policy researchers have traditionally assumed that applied research produced authoritative and socially relevant knowledge and it affects policy by affecting discrete decisions." Instead, they propose: "Most policy-oriented research, at least in education, tends to influence the broad assumptions and beliefs underlying policies, not particular decisions."[86] Garbarino[87] states that a more adequate approach to policy analysis is to consider the effect of a policy on all the microsystems, important mesosystems, and related exosystems that can significantly affect the target group(s). These authors support the position of Bowman and Brady,[88] who recently reminded social scientists and educators that both individuals and groups contribute to change that can affect the lives of everyone.

A continuing debate in American education centers around the respective roles of families and schools in children's learning and development. Black families have historically been particularly vulnerable to shifting ideological trends and perspectives on the roles of parent involvement in schools because of racial oppression and because disproportionate numbers of black families are also impoverished. Initially benefiting from an emphasis on community empowerment in the 1960s, blacks quickly found themselves repeatedly responding to diverse parent education and training programs. By the mid-1980s, the impact of changing American families had become another context in which to define the role of parent involvement in schools.

Policy-oriented research has questioned the feasibility of mandated citizen participation in American school programs.[89] Parent involvement in schools, from this perspective, has serious limitations as a tool of social reform and change to benefit children's development. Other authors have stressed the rights of children[90] or of broader American communities,[91] somewhat in contrast to the rights of families.

The Coleman[92] article indicates that even conservative proponents of the importance of family in schooling have voiced growing impatience with the slow pace of school reform, given the recent rapid and dramatic social changes in the American family. In such a climate of dissatisfaction, black families are among the most vulnerable, threatened by the necessity of some form of institutionalized childcare. The ecological perspective, in contrast, continues to embrace the child, and its family, school, and broader community as mutually interdependent, dynamic social systems to be stressed in any prevention and/or intervention/remediation efforts. If it is used to affirm the social and cultural integrity of both primary socialization institutions (families and schools), the ecological perspective has the potential to unite black families and their children's schools in a historically unprecedented bond that can only benefit black children.

NOTES

1. S. Lightfoot, *Worlds Apart: Relationships Between Families and Schools* (New York: Basic Books, 1978).
2. W. Waller, *Sociology of Teaching* (New York: Wiley and Sons, 1932).
3. R.D. Hess and D. Croft, *Teachers of Young Children* (Boston: Houghton Mifflin Co., 1978).
4. G. Fein, "The Informed Parent," in S. Kilmer (ed.), *Advances in Early Education and Day Care* (Greenwich, CT: JAI Press, 1980), pp. 155-85.
5. Fein, "Informed Parent," pp. 159-60.
6. Lightfoot, *Worlds Apart.*

7. J. Ogbu, *The Next Generation: An Ethnography of Education in An Urban Neighborhood* (New York: Academic Press, 1974).

8. D. Slaughter and B. Schneider, *Newcomers: Blacks in Private Schools. Final Report to the National Institute of Education, NIE-82-0040 Project No. 2—0450* (Washington, DC: NIE, 1986). ERIC Document Reproduction No. ED 274 769.

9. W. Wilson *The Truly Disadvantaged: The Inner City, the Underclass, and Public Policy.* (Chicago: University of Chicago Press, 1987).

10. J. Valentine and E. Stark, "The Social Context of Parent Involvement in Head Start," in E. Zigler and J. Valentine (eds.), *Project Head Start: A Legacy of The War on Poverty* (New York: Free Press, 1979), pp. 291-314; Fein, "Informed Parent."

11. The Hon. Sargent Shriver, "Head Start, A Retrospective View: The Founders," in Zigler and Valentine (eds.), *Project Head Start*, pp. 49-67.

12. A Honig, *Parent Involvement in Early Childhood Education.* (Washington, DC: National Association for the Education of Young Children, 1975); A. Honig, "Working With Parents of Preschool Children," in R. Abidin (ed.), *Parent Education and Intervention Handbook* (Springfield, IL: Charles C. Thomas, 1980), pp. 385-431.

13. Valentine and Stark, "Social Context," pp. 307, 310-11.

14. F. Frierson and T. Hills, *Planning For Parental Involvement in Early Childhood Education: A Guide for Teachers, Administrators, Parents and Parent Coordinators.* (Trenton, NJ: New Jersey State Department of Education, 1981). ERIC Document Reproduction Service No. 242 388; I. Gordon, "Parent Education and Parent Involvement: Retrospect and Prospect," *Childhood Education,* 54, no. 1 (1977), pp. 71-79; I. Gordon, P. Olmsted, R. Rubin, and J. True, "How Has Follow Through Promoted Parent Involvement?," *Young Children,* 34, no. 5 (1979) pp. 49-53; A. Honig, "Working With Parents"; H. Leler, "Parent Education and Involvement in Relation to the Schools and to Parents of School-aged Children," in R. Haskins and D. Adams (eds.), *Parent Education and Public Policy* (Norwood, NJ: Ablex, 1983), pp. 141-80; J. McKinney, *Evaluation of Parent Involvement in Early Childhood Programs 1979-1980.* (Philadelphia, PA: Philadelphia School District, Office of Research and Evaluation, 1980). ERIC Document Reproduction Service No. ED 204 388; P. Olmsted and R. Rubin, "Parent Involvement: Perspectives from the Follow Through Experience," in R. Haskins and D. Adams (eds.), *Parent Education and Public Policy.* (Norwood, NJ: Ablex, 1983), pp. 112-40; J. Schickedanz, "Parents, Teachers, and Early Education," in B. Persky and L. Golubchick (eds.), *Early Childhood Education.* (Wayne, NJ: Avery Publishing Group, 1977), pp. 331-33; D. Williams, J. Stallworth, and P. Kronkosy "Prepared Statement and Testimony, in *Improving American Education: Roles for Parents* (Washington, DC: U.S. Government Printing Office, 1984), pp. 115-22.

15. Gordon, *Parent Education.*

16. Gordon et al., "Follow Through."

17. Frierson and Hills, *Planning for Parental Involvement.*

18. J. Comer, *School Power: Implications of An Intervention Project* (New York: Free Press, 1980).

19. W. Warnat, *Guide To Parent Involvement: Parents As Adult Learners. Overview of Parent Involvement Programs and Practices.* (Washington, DC: American Univ., Adult Learning Potential, 1980). ERIC Document Reproduction Service No. ED 198 370; Gordon, *Parent Education.*

20. Schickedanz, "Parents, Teachers."

21. Ibid., p. 332.

22. Leler, "Parent Education."

23. Schickedanz, "Parents, Teachers."

24. Gordon, "Parent Education."

25. Warnat, *Parent Involvement.*

26. Gordon, "Parent Education."

27. Schickedanze, "Parents, Teachers."

28. Olmsted and Rubin, "Parent Involvement."

29. R.M. Becher, *Parent Involvement: A review of Research and Principles of Successful Practice.* (Washington, DC: National Institute of Education, 1984). ERIC Document Reproduction Service No. ED 247 032; J. Epstein, "Home and School Connections in Schools of the Future: Implications of Research on Parent Involvement," *Peabody Journal of Education,* 62 no. 2, 1985, pp. 18-41; Gordon, *Parent Education*; R. Hess and S. Holloway, "Family and School as Educational Institutions," in R. Parke (ed.), Vol. 7 of *Review of Child Development Research* (Chicago: Univ. of Chicago Press, 1985), pp. 179-222; Leler, "Parent Education;" Olmsted and Rubin, "Parent Involvement;" D. Scott-Jones, "Family Influences on Cognitive Development and School Achievement," in E. Gordon (ed.), Vol. II of *Review of Research in Education.* (Itasca, IL: Peacock, 1984), pp. 259-304; R. Seginer, "Parents' Educational Expectations and Children's Academic Achievements: A Literature Review," *Merrill-Palmer Quarterly* 29 (1983) pp. 1-23; D. Slaughter and E. Epps, "Home Environment and the Academic Achievement of Black American Children and Youth," *Journal of Negro Education,* 56 no. 1 (1987), pp. 1-20.

30. U. Bronfenbrenner, "Is Early Intervention Effective? Facts and Principles of Early Intervention: A Summary," in A. Clarke and A.B.D. Clarke (eds.), *Early Experience: Myth and Evidence* (New York: The Free Press, 1976), pp. 247-56.

31. See, for e.g., Honig, "Working With Parents"; D. Peters and J. Belsky, "The Day Care Movement: Past, Present, and Future," in M. Kostelnik, A. Rabin, L. Phenice, and A. Soderman (eds.), *Child Nurturance: Patterns of Supplementary Parenting* (New York: Plenum, 1982), pp. 101-29; the quote is from Bronfenbrenner, "Early Intervention," pp. 251-52.

32. L. Laosa, *Indices of the Success of Head Start: A Critique.* Paper presented at The Second Annual Meeting of the Minority Scholars Involved with Head Start Programs, Howard Univ., Washington, DC, October, 1985.

33. Becher, *Parent Involvement.*

34. Peters and Belsky, "Day Care."

35. K.A. Clarke-Stewart, "Exploring the Assumptions of Parent Education," in R. Haskins and D. Adams (eds.), *Parent Education and Public Policy* (Norwood, NJ: Ablex, 1983), pp. 257-76.

36. Ibid., p. 267.

37. D. Slaughter, "Programs for Racially and Ethnically Diverse American Families: Some Critical Issues," in H. Weiss and F. Jacobs, (eds.), *Evaluating Family Programs* (New York: Aldine Press, in press).

38. A. Pifer, *Final Thoughts, 1982 Annual Report: Carnegie Corporation of New York* (New York: Carnegie Corporation, 1982).

39. B. Tizard, J. Mortimore, and B. Burchell, *Involving Parents in Nursery and Infant Schools: A Source Book for Teachers.* (London: Grant McIntyre, 1981).

40. Leler, "Parent Education."

41. Olmsted and Rubin, "Parent Involvement."

42. Ibid.

43. S. Brice-Heath and M. McLaughlin, "A Child Resource Policy: Moving Beyond Dependence on School and Family." *Phi Delta Kappan*, April 1987, pp. 576-80; J. Coleman, "Families and Schools," *Educational Researcher*, 16, no. 6 (Aug.-Sept. 1987), pp. 32-38.

44. Slaughter, "Programs for American Families."

45. B. Schneider and D. Slaughter, "Parents and School Life: Varieties of Parental Participation," in P. Bauch (ed.), *Private Schools and Public Concerns* (Westport, CT: Greenwood-Praeger, in press).

46. Wilson, *The Truly Disadvantaged.*

47. P. Weingarten, "Children of the Homeless: Untreated Illnesses Are Constant Companions," *Chicago Tribune*, November 1, 1987, pp. 1, 16.

48. Bronfenbrenner, "Early Intervention"; U. Bronfenbrenner, *The Ecology of Human Development* (Cambridge: MA: Harvard Univ. Press, 1979); B. Goodson and R.D. Hess, "The Effects of Parent Training Programs on Child Performance and Behavior," in B. Brown (ed.), *Found: Long-Term Gains From Early Intervention* (Boulder, CO: Westview Press, 1978), pp. 37-78.

49. Personal Communication, Third Annual Head Start Minority Scholars Conference, Howard Univ., Washington, DC, September 21-22, 1987.

50. C. Hayes, and S. Kamerman (eds.), *Children of Working Parents: Experiences and Outcomes* (Washington, DC: National Academy Press, 1983); J. Eccles and L. Hoffman, "Sex Roles, Socialization and Occupational Behavior," in H. Stevenson and A. Siegel (eds.), Vol. 1 of *Child Development Research and Social Policy* (Chicago: Univ. of Chicago Press, 1984), pp. 367-420.

51. Warnat, *Parent Involvement.*

52. Becher, *Parent Involvement*, p. 47.

53. Ibid.

54. V. Washington and U. Oyemade, "Changing Family Trends: Head Start Must Respond," *Young Childern*, September 1985, pp. 12-19.

55. Laosa, *Indices of Success.*

56. Honig, "Working With Parents."

57. Bronfenbrenner, *Human Development*, p. 41.

58. J. Garbarino, *Children and Families in the Social Environmment.* (New York: Aldine, 1982).

59. Tizard et. al., *Involing Parents.*

60. K. Swick and S. Taylor, "Parent-child Perceptions of Their Ecological Context as Related to Child Performance in School," *Journal of Instructional Psychology* 9 (1982), pp. 168-75.

61. K. Swick, "Family Functioning, Parenting, and Parent Involvement Practices," *Journal of Instructional Psychology* 11, no. 2 (1984), p. 79.

62. Warnat, *Parent Involvement.*

63. See, for e.g., Becher, *Parent Involvement*; Bronfenbrenner, *Human Development*; Garbarino, *Children and Families*; Gordon, "Parent Education"; Olmsted and Rubin, "Parent Involvement"; A. Smith and A. Robbins, "Structured Ethnography: The Study of Parental Involvement," *American Behavioral Scientist* 26, no. 1 (1982), pp. 45-61.

64. Warnat, *Parent Involvement*, p. 85.

65. Garbarino, *Children and Families.*

66. Williams et. al., *Improving Education.*

67. J. Epstein, "School Policy and Parent Involvement: Research Results," *Educational Horizons* 86 (1984), pp. 277-93; J. Epstein, "Parents' Reactions to Teacher Practices of Parent Involvement," *The Elementary School Journal* 86, no. 3 (1986), pp. 277-93.

68. Becher, *Parent Involvement.*

69. H. Almy, "Day Care and Early Childhood Education," in E. Zigler and E. Gordon (eds.), *Day Care: Scientific and Social Policy Issues* (Boston, MA: Auburn House, 1982), pp. 476-96; K. Swick and K. Duff, *Parenting* (Washington, DC: National Education Association, 1979).

70. Almy, "Day Care."

71. Swick and Duff, *Parenting.*

72. Gordon, "Parent Education."

73. Williams et. al., *Improving Education.*

74. K. Hoover-Dempsey, O. Bassler, and J. Brissie, "Parent Involvement: Contributions of Teacher Efficacy, School Socioeconomic Status, and Other School Characteristics," *American Educational Research Journal* 24, no. 3 (1987), pp. 417-36.

75. M. McLaughlin and B. Shields, "Involving Low-Income Parents in the Schools: A Role For Policy?," *Phi Delta Kappan* (October 1987), pp. 156-60.

76. Warnat, *Parent Involvement.*

77. K. Coleman, "Prepared Statement and Testimony," in *Improving American Education: Roles for Parents.* (Washington, DC: U.S. Government Printing Office, 1984), pp. 82-95, 112-13.

78. Olmsted and Rubin, "Parent Involvement."

79. Coleman, "Families and Schools."

80. Ibid., p. 112.

81. Williams, et. al., *Improving Education.*

82. Slaughter, "Programs."

83. Bronfenbrenner, *Human Development.*

84. Garbarino, *Children and Families.*

85. Warnat, *Parent Involvement.*

86. D. Cohen and M. Garet, "Reforming Educational Policy With Applied Social Research," *Harvard Educational Review* 45, no. 1 (1975), pp. 17, 39.

87. Garbarino, *Childen and Families.*

88. B. Bowman and E. Brady, "Today's Issues: Tomorrow's Possibilities," in S. Hill and B. Barnes (eds.), *Young Children and Their Families* (Lexington, MA: Lexington Books, 1982), pp. 207-17.

89. P. Shields and M. McLaughlin, *Parent Involvement in Compensatory Education Programs.* (Stanford, CA: Stanford Univ. Center for Educational Research at Stanford [CERAS], 1983); McLaughlin and Shields, "Low-Income Parents."

90. Brice-Heath and McLaughlin, "Child Resource."

91. Coleman, "Families and Schools."

92. Ibid.

9

Test Fairness and Bias: Measuring Academic Achievement Among Black Youth

Sylvia T. Johnson

Americans like numbers. We depend on them for help in decision making at levels ranging from national policy to personal choices, from the Gross National Product (GNP) to the median family income, from the daily changes in the Dow Jones Index to the 2.1 children the average American family rear. Numbers are an important part of our daily lives; we view them as quick, reliable informers to help us to cut through the verbiage and make sense of it.

Scores on standardized tests are numbers with inherent egalitarian appeal. It seems logical that a test operates as a mental yardstick, so test scores should accurately reflect the appropriate level of knowledge of the person being tested. Such an interpretation however, presupposes that the test score is an implicit substitution for the "real thing" that we want to measure. However, the relationship between the test score and the characteristic being measured may not be the same for all examinees, particularly for blacks and members of other racial minorities who have been systematically excluded from educational benefits. As a result, a test score alone frequently is not a sufficient measure of aptitude, achievement, or other psychological and educational constructs for minority groups.

Yet test scores are increasingly used in educational and employment decisions at all levels. These decisions involve not only the educational programming or vocational placement of the individual students or job applicants who take the tests, but also are increasingly used in the evaluation of schools, school systems, and training programs in terms of their efficacy in providing educational experiences. In fact, the U.S. Secretary of Education, William J. Bennett, has recently urged that the regional college and university accreditation agencies consider the measurement of student learning as a major parameter for determining and renewing the accreditation of higher education institutions.

This broader usage of tests has had several positive outcomes. Community groups have responded to reports of low test scores in local public schools by developing school- and community-based strategies to improve the curriculum. Because of these efforts, improvements in the average scores on standardized tests have been achieved by these school systems. The knowledge that test scores will be viewed as barometers of a school's progress probably sensitizes teachers and administrators to the "fit" between curriculum and test, and encourages them to systematically cover the curriculum. Such use of tests does not necessarily validate the quality of the tests as measurement devices, but rather speaks to their effectiveness as spurs to curriculum development and instructional improvement.

THE HISTORICAL DEVELOPMENT OF TEST USE

Findings from use of tests have documented that both black and white children living in the South have improved their academic performance relative to their Northern counterparts since school desegregation began in the 1950s. An examination of the norms tables for Southern youths at various grade levels during the mid-1950s and current comparable tables shows that this gap has narrowed to the benefit of all Southern children, and thus has also benefited Southern commerce, technology, and culture.[1]

For example, prior to the 1954 integration of the District of Columbia Schools, the then predominately white school system had a composite mean test score for black and white sixth graders that was 2.3 years below the national norm. By 1958, with an 84% black population in these schools, sixth graders were achieving at a level equal to or above the national norm.[2]

As the innovative federal education agenda emerged in the 1960s and evolved throughout the 1970s, evaluation became an increasingly important component of all programs. With the proliferation of creative ideas, a well-grounded evaluation plan was a requirement for programs submitted for funding.[3] Evaluations included a wide variety of techniques—observations, checklists, assessments, interviews—and the melding of these to provide answers on program effectiveness, and help in decisions to raise, lower, or eliminate funding. But more importantly, evaluation meant a dramatic increase in the testing of children at all levels, and the firm and extensive planting of standardized tests as hardy perennials in the crowded garden of school activity.

The seeds of test use and school desegregation were as often scattered by the same as by opposing hands. Black and white liberals wanted tests to demonstrate the effectiveness of model programs to increase achievement of poor, often black youngsters, while reactionaries saw test scores as providing a basis for recreating what they were no longer able to do by law; separation of the races in the classroom.

Thus, the fairness of tests for black students is a thorny issue, not just because of the tests themselves, but because of the historical and contemporary use and misuse of standardized tests. The examination of the current status and performance of black students on standardized tests as reported in this article is presented in the context of test fairness and bias. The meanings of these findings for the educational development of black youth are also discussed.

The National Testing Programs

Black junior and senior high school students are tested along with their peers in nearly all schools using the major national standardized tests. Black youth at three grade levels from elementary to high school are proportionally represented in the National Assessment of Educational Progress (NAEP), conducted annually across the country. Those entering or considering entering the military take the Armed Services Vocational Aptitude Battery (ASVAB). For college admission, many students take either the Scholastic Aptitude Test (SAT), constructed by the Educational Testing Service for the College Entrance Examination Board, or the American College Testing Program (ACT) tests. A smaller number of students take both tests. Although some of these tests are titled as aptitude measures, they are generally regarded as measures of knowledge and skill attainment, or achievement.

How then do black students fare on these standardized tests? Scores achieved by blacks are roughly equivalent to or somewhat lower than scores of non-blacks with similar educational and income levels. The spread of scores tends to be lowest among blacks from low income levels with weak educational backgrounds.

Substantial variability exists among the mean test scores for black students from different communities and age groups. In those communities where the distribution of income and education among blacks is comparable to that of the total American population and the school systems are highly rated and well-supported, black students at all grade levels generally score at or above the national norm for all students. In strong urban school systems, test scores of black students also show moderate, steady annual increases as greater resources and improved instructional strategies are employed.[4]

For example, Table 1 shows test scores in mathematics, reading, and language arts for the Montgomery County, Maryland Public Schools, a suburban district near Washington, D.C. with a 15% black enrollment.[5] Among the local black population, the median levels of income and education are about the same as the figures for whites nationally, and the test scores shown in Table 1 are at or slightly above the national norms. The median income and educational level for all county residents is near the top for the United States as a whole, and the county-wide scores, well above national norms, reflect the importance of these antecedents.

This relationship between socioeconomic class and achievement as measured by test scores confounds and complicates the examining of test performance along other dimensions such as race. The correlation between socioeconomic status and individual student achievement has been estimated to be .22, and with an aggregated dependent variable, such as the school, the correlation is .55.[6] With an aggregated independent variable, parental income category, using the Medical Schools Admissions Test, it has been estimated as .95.[7] When test scores of black and white students are compared without controlling for socioeconomic and schooling effects, the differences between the average scores of the two groups are about one half to one standard deviation. Some black and white students achieve test scores at all levels, from the highest to the lowest, but the average scores among black samples are lower than the average scores among white samples.[8,9,10]

TABLE 1
Summary Results for California Achievement Tests 1982-1985, Montgomery County Md.
Normal Curve Equivalent* (NCE) Means

Grade/ Group	Math 1982–83	Math 1983–84	Math 1984–85**	Reading 1982–83	Reading 1983–84	Reading 1984–85**	Language 1982–83	Language 1983–84	Language 1984–85**
Grade 3									
Asian	75	77	78	64	65	66	70	72	73
Black	53	56	57	51	52	53	55	58	59
Hispanic	58	61	64	52	54	57	57	60	63
White	69	71	72	66	66	68	70	71	74
County Total	67	69	70	63	64	65	68	69	71
Grade 5									
Asian	76	80	82	64	65	67	72	74	77
Black	52	56	57	52	54	54	55	58	59
Hispanic	59	62	63	54	56	57	58	62	65
White	69	71	73	67	68	69	72	74	76
County Total	67	69	72	64	66	66	69	71	74
Grade 8									
Asian	76	75	77	62	63	65	65	64	67
Black	53	55	56	51	52	54	51	53	54
Hispanic	59	61	61	55	57	56	56	57	59
White	69	70	71	68	69	69	68	68	69
County Total	67	68	69	65	66	66	65	65	66
Grade 11									
Asian	72	74	73	57	61	60	60	65	64
Black	48	50	51	47	49	50	47	50	50
Hispanic	55	54	55	53	52	54	52	51	52
White	65	67	67	65	68	68	65	67	67
County Total	63	65	65	63	64	65	63	64	64

Source: Montgomery County Public Schools Department of Educational Accountability, 1985.
Notes:
  *The metric used here is not equivalent to a percentile rank.
  **Scores are from the November 1984 administration. NCE means are based on national norms.

Test Score Decline Among Upper Grade Students

In the early elementary grades, means or average scores of black students tend to be at about the national norm across a broad range of communities. In the upper elementary and high school years, the means for black students generally show an apparent decrease. This finding of decreased academic performance in the upper grades among low-income black youth has been found repeatedly.[11,12] The findings may be artificial in some cases, such as in communities that have large numbers of private and parochial junior and senior high schools. In such cases, the majority of elementary-age youth may be enrolled in the public schools, but a sizable proportion of the high-achieving group may opt to transfer out of the public school system. Test scores for junior and senior public high school youth, then, include nearly all of the lower-performing youth, but have a lesser number of high achievers.

This finding can be misinterpreted to mean that the performance of youngsters is decreasing as they move through the school system. In fact, it may simply mean that the best students are being lost from the school system, resulting in a lower average performance among the remaining youngsters. Adequate longitudinal records make it possible to assess whether this condition holds for a given school system. Unfortunately, high transiency rates and limited resources for staffing record-keeping functions in local schools may make the maintenance of such records the most difficult in locations where they would be most valuable.

When the presence of this decline in scores across grade level has been verified as an actual longitudinal effect, some large districts with substantial black enrollments have been able to improve the scores of the upper elementary and high school students to a statistically significant and important degree.[13] For example, Dallas and Fort Worth, Texas have achieved annual gains of one to four normal curve equivalents (NCE) during the last few years for black high school students, with larger gains being made in mathematics and language skills and smaller gains in reading.

NATIONAL ASSESSMENT OF EDUCATIONAL PROGRESS

The status of reading achievement among all Americans, as well as among black, Hispanic, and white subpopulations has been a major focus of the National Assessment of Educational Progress (NAEP) since its inception. Five federally-funded national assessments have been conducted—during the 1970-71, 1974-75, 1979-80, 1983-84, and 1985-86 school years. The first three assessments were conducted by the Educational Commission of the States. The 1983-84 and 1985-86 assessments were conducted by Educational Testing Service (ETS). Some findings from the 1983–84 assessment are discussed below.

The Reading Report Card

In the *Reading Report Card*, national trends in average reading proficiency for 9, 13, and 17-year-olds are presented.[14] The scores for all five assessment periods were converted by ETS to a 500-point scale on which certain levels of proficiency had been pegged to classifications of reading complexity. That is, a given score can be assigned meaning in terms of the degree to which persons receiving that score demonstrate certain skills. These levels, with their corresponding scores, are: rudimentary (150), basic (200), intermediate (250), adept (300), and advanced (350). The *Reading Report Card* defines these levels. Additional materials from NAEP provide more extensive background on the development of the scale and types of items that indicate proficiency levels. Virtually all black 13 and 17-year-olds can read at the rudimentry level according to the NAEP report.

Among black 13-year-olds, the percentage of children achieving at the basic, intermediate, and the adept levels has risen substantially from 1979 to 1984. Among 17-year-olds, it has risen even more. For example, in 1971, about 45% of black 17-year-olds were reading at the intermediate level, while in 1984, the figure was up to 65%. Among black students, 13-year-olds reading at the adept level was negligible for each assessment period, and while the percent of adept 17-year-olds has risen from about 5 to 15%, the number of advanced 17-year-olds is negligible. Considering the level of reading comprehension skills necessary for college and graduate school and for high-level professional work, these figures show a need for increased reading performance among black teenagers. Allowing for measurement error, the fact that 70% to 85% of black youth at the age of the typical high school senior are reading below the level required to comfortably and adequately handle college-level work virtually automatically sets limits on attainment and frustrates aspirations.

Literary Results Among Young Adults

To examine the longer-term implications of these findings in reading and writing on adult literacy, NAEP surveyed young adults from the 48 contiguous states in the 21-25 age range.[15] Literacy was examined with prose, document, and quantitative questions, and was viewed not "as simply reading, or reading plus writing, but an ability to use print for personal and social ends. . . . A functional skill in that it requires the application of various skills in common, everyday situations."[16] The overwhelming majority of young adults performed adequately at the lower levels on all three scales. Yet many were unable to do well on tasks of moderate complexity. While the majority of the young adults with the most severe literacy deficiencies are white, the proportion of blacks and Hispanics in these categories are well above their representation in the general population. Mean scores by ethnicity and educational background are shown in Tables 2 and 3.

Even when considered by educational level, there are mean differences, but the differences are a third smaller after college than at high school level. It should again be noted that although there are black students scoring at all levels, but the proportion scoring at lower levels is disproportionally large. Further, home support variables, such as the level of the parents' education and access to literacy materials, are significantly related to the literacy practices, the type of education, and the amount of education reported by young adults.

These findings among school-aged and young adult national and local samples are mixed. On one hand, black students are making steady, modest progress on school-related measures, and some black students are among those scoring at the highest levels on all tests. On the other hand, the proportion of black youth completing high school with high-level literacy skills, the sort of skills that enable students to do their best in college programs without developmental work, is disproportionally low. Greater school and community efforts are needed at the junior and senior high school levels to increase academic preparation for college and employment.

Tests For Higher Education

Many states now require students to pass competency tests in reading, mathematics, and other areas in order to graduate from high school. Results from these programs

TABLE 2
Mean Scores of Respondents on the Four Literacy Scales
by Race/Ethnic Group*

Scale	White	Black	Hispanic	Other
NAEP Reading	313.8	263.3	286.6	299.0
Prose	314.4	258.3	285.5	304.5
Document	315.7	255.7	278.7	298.2
Quantitative	314.6	259.1	280.3	306.4

TABLE 3
Mean Prose Scores of Young Adults by
Race/Ethnicity and Years of Formal Schooling Completed*

Years of Schooling Completed	White	Black	Hispanic
8 or Less	250.6	196.9	213.3
Some High School	274.9	230.3	247.4
High School Graduate, No College	300.6	253.0	285.8
College Degree, Two Years	332.3	289.6	—
College Degree, Four Years	345.4	308.7	340.9

Source: Venezky, R.L., C.F. Kaestle, and A.M. Sum, *The Subtle Danger-Reflections on the Literacy Abilities of America's Young Adults.* Report No. 16-CAEP-01, Center for the Assessment of Educational Progress, Educational Testing Service, Princeton, N.J., 1987).
Note:
*Scale of definitions of reading skills:
     150 = rudimentary
     200 = basic
     250 = intermediate
     300 = adept
     350 = advanced

have been widely reported in the press purportedly to show that schools fail to prepare students for adult life. In fact, the proportion of children of all racial groups who pass the tests have continued to increase, but in some states, the proportion of black children who fail is disproportionately high. High school seniors who do not pass the tests are typically given a "certificate of attendance" in place of a high school diploma.

The SAT and ACT tests are taken by high school students for college admission, but the results are often considered by the public as barometers of performance on school-related tasks. While these tests provide useful information when used in conjunction with high school grades and other data, they do not determine college admission, nor are they good indices to use to compare school performance. In admissions decisions, most colleges give strong weight to grades, activities, and other data. To compare school performance, the fact that the SAT is not designed to comprehensively cover the high school curriculum must not be forgotten. Even though the ACT, with subtests in natural science, social science, math, and English may be more closely tied to college pre-paratory high school curricula, the taking of either test is voluntary. In a particular high school, most students may take such tests, while at another school, only the best students take them. Moreover, because the ACT is more widely used by Midwestern schools, and the SAT is more prevalent in the East, the sample groups taking the two tests in any given area of the country will vary greatly.

The mean scores of black students on both tests are below the mean scores of whites. Within both groups, however, the same correlation between test scores and educational and socioeconomic variables is found. The scores of black youth have risen steadily since 1978, and done so at a rate much greater than the scores of non-blacks. This is a promising finding, especially because the number of students taking the test has also risen greatly.

Bias and College Admission Tests

Are blacks' low test scores due to academic background or to problems with the tests themselves? Recent research shows that this is not an either/or situation, but is instead "all of the above." According to student self-report information, black students taking the SAT have, on the average, taken fewer mathematics courses in high school than their white counterparts.[17] However, there is increasing evidence that special test preparation and coaching can increase SAT scores.

In 1984, the NAACP conducted a test preparation program in New York City, Atlanta, and San Francisco among black youth from low-income backgrounds.[18] Average math and verbal scores improved 70–85 points, with some students gaining as much as 200 points on one of the two subtests. The curriculum included test-taking strategies, review of fundamentals in algebra and geometry, and vocabulary and reading activities. The effectiveness of the program, which provided 36 hours of classroom instruction, was probably due to the improvement of academic skills, the lowering of test anxiety, and increased levels of motivation.

The importance of motivation in test taking is often not realized. If there are characteristics of the test materials that are not appealing, or even alienating, then although the person tested desires on one level to do well, performance may be decreased. The work of Banks has documented the effects of interest features on the performance of black students.[19]

The generally higher SAT score performance among students at independent preparatory schools and at high-income public schools may be due in part to the regular programs of test preparation and test-related curricular experiences these schools routinely provide. For example, one Washington, D.C. independent school offers a popular course in "analogous reasoning." Analogies are an important component of the SAT and many other standardized tests.

TESTING AND THE MILITARY

The Department of Defense (DOD) is the nation's largest test user. Through its construction and administration of the Armed Services Vocational Aptitude Battery (ASVAB), it has a profound impact on the broad range of American youth who desire to enter military service.

The dissemination and score reporting procedures of this program have not served black youth well. This is especially regrettable because of the tremendous financial investment in the program, its comprehensiveness, and the measurement skills of those involved.

In 1980, the DOD released a study, *Profile of American Youth*, that was conducted by the National Opinion Research Center and the University of Chicago.[20] This study reported that in the largest test validation and bias analysis done until that time, national norms had been established for the Armed Services Vocational Aptitude Battery test. Its ten subtests included traditional academic areas such as word knowledge, paragraph comprehension, numerical operations, and knowledge of mathematics, as well as familiarity with specialized areas such as automobiles, general shop, and electronics.

The report included findings about age, regional, and racial differences; these racial differences were badly distorted in press reports. In the overall DOD findings, race differences were confounded with academic achievement and attainment, yet such findings were reported in terms of "mental categories." All subjects took the same tests, but some twenty-five-year-old test takers had been out of school for eight years and had not taken a test since that time, while others of the same age were in graduate school. The greater proportion of white subjects in the latter category produced the confounding results. In addition, some sixteen-year-old test takers were enrolled in half-day distributive education programs, while others were taking chemistry and German, yet proportionally more black youngsters were enrolled in the non-academic, work-based programs. All of these differences were aggregated under the label of race, and reported in five score ranges called mental categories.

The detailed tables in the back of the DOD report show more meaningful comparisons. For example, the average score of whites whose mothers finished grades nine through eleven, Hispanics whose mothers finished high school, and blacks whose mothers just began college are about the same. The 1981 Census figures also indicate that these three groups of women have similar income levels, thereby suporting the link between test score, income, and parental background.[21] Further, within the white sample, the differences in test scores between young people whose mothers had low levels of education and those whose mothers were college-trained is far greater than any of the differences between ethnic groups.[22] Clearly, the experiences of these young people are major determinants of their performance.

If all of the ASVAB scores are ranked from highest to lowest, about 19% of blacks and 61% of whites fall above the middle point. Some students of each race were among the highest and lowest scorers on the test. However, the proportion of each group scoring above the middle point varied greatly by educational level, parents' level of education, parental income, and geographic area. There are sizable differences within each racial group. All of these factors make "average" scores misleading as accurate indices of group performance.

The *Profile* reports that the ASVAB has been found to have good predictive validity, so that enlistees who have high scores do better in a military training program than do enlistees with low test scores. It does not mean, however, that low scorers would not do well if given the necessary educational experiences to help prepare them for such training programs. Actually, the miliary should give attention to reducing the validity of its test for low-scoring youngsters by providing the technical assistance in skill-building that it is uniquely qualified to give. To do less might make the test look good, but will have long-range consequences for the future life patterns of young men and women. The tremendous measurement data base provided by the *ASVAB* could be used to structure instructional experiences to raise the job ceiling predicted for low-scoring enrollees. Such action would increase the employment potential of armed forces veterans, and would add substantially to our current knowledge base of instructional psychology.

BIAS AND FAIRNESS IN TESTING

As we examine the performance of blacks on various tests, the issues of fairness, bias, and overall accuracy of measurement are repeatedly raised. Are these tests fair to black students?

The issues of test fairness and test bias have been debated since the introduction of mental tests to the U.S. following the pioneering work of Alfred Binet in France.[23] Because the early construction and validation of these tests was based on socioeconomic distinctions, and many early test makers were part of the euthenics movement with political views that believed WASP groups to be intellectually superior, there is reason to question the fairness of the tests that were constructed and used. One of the earliest investigations of the relationship between test score and socioeconomic status was done by Allison Davis.[24] Davis was a black educational anthropologist at the University of Chicago with deep roots in the local black community, although his study was based on white students of varying socioeconomic backgrounds in a mid-sized Illinois city. In that landmark study, based on a large and diverse slice of Middle America, a strong relationship between socioeconomic status and standardized test scores was found.

As a result of these findings, Davis later developed a test designed to be free of the cultural effects he identified in the earlier study.[25] The measure had mixed results in subsequent research, but it was the first attempt to build a measure of general ability without a strong component based on common cultural experiences. Anastasi put forth an approach to measuring constructs across different cultural groups.[26,27] This researcher asserted that test makers needed to identify commonalities across cultures and base tests on these factors, or to develop instruments within cultures based on behaviors that represented intelligent, adaptive behavior within specific contexts. The Davis-Eells Games represented the first approach; this effort was followed by other attempts in succeeding years. The within-culture approach has been used in recent years among black groups by Robert Williams.[28]

The extent to which widely-used standardized measures may have strong cultural biases was demonstrated by Medley and Quirk.[29] Using a sample comprised of black and white college students, these researchers administered items from the National Teachers Examination (NTE), with a set of parallel items constructed to be of equal difficulty in terms of the reasoning and judgment required, but including information of interest to black subjects. As predicted, the black subjects did significantly better than white subjects in the experimental items.

The Academic Search for Test Bias

A series of articles published in the *Journal of Educational Measurement* and other professional periodicals during the 1970s debated the applicability of several models for use in identifying bias against any group on standardized tests used in the selection process. These models involved the predictive validity of the instruments in fairly identifying the persons likely to be successful, or the utility of the instruments in such a selection process.[30,31,32,33,34,35,36,37]

This work was followed by the development of various techniques for the identification of bias; numerous studies then employed these techniques. Much of this work involved item bias, that is the extent to which the individual test questions were equally fair to different groups. However, there are inherent problems in the study of item bias. Most techniques require either that items be compared with the entire test as a criterion or standard, or that groups of equal ability be compared on each item. With the first approach, the overall fairness of the entire test must be assumed. Otherwise, the aberrant items may be the fairest, rather than the most unfair, because the procedures simply identify them as behaving differently from the complete set of items.

The second approach assumes that there is a valid basis for determining that two groups are of equal ability. If a biased test is used to determine the equivalence of ability, then the group against which the test is biased actually has higher ability than the designated equivalent group, and items on which there is no difference between the supposedly equal-ability groups actually favor the advantaged group. More recent bias studies have tried to deal with these logical problems by constructing or locating the bias items, or by setting up artificial item statistics and comparing the performance of other items to these known biased items.[38] Moreover, the Differential Item Functioning (DIF) technique developed at the Educational Testing Service uses an iterative procedure for selecting the matched groups, so that items identified as having different score patterns are used to iteratively correct the selection of comparison groups.[39,40,41]

Jensen and Test Bias

The work of Arthur Jensen during the past twenty years has been arguably directed toward proving that the ability and intelligence of black Americans is inferior to that of whites. In a widely-quoted 1969 study, Jensen concluded that the compensatory education programs begun in the early 1960s had tried and failed.[42] Jensen's inadequate methodology coupled with the short time that these programs had operated suggested a more personal rather than scientific base for this finding.

Jensen's subsequent work was similarly directed. In *Bias in Mental Testing*, he prefaces the work by stating that individual and group differences would not disappear by abolishing tests—"One cannot treat a fever by throwing away the thermometer."[43] After reading the book, there is no doubt about the thoroughness with which its author has approached the fever of test score differences. But instead of using a thermometer, he has used calipers. That is, his mathematical tools are highly accurate, but often are not appropriate or applicable.

Jensen presents a thorough, extensive, and fair treatment of the literature on test bias, and concludes that there are systematic racial differences reflected on I.Q. tests. However, his conclusion regarding racial differences fails to emphasize the following points: 1) this test-measured difference is about the same size as the difference within families, and just slightly greater than the difference between families, all within the same racial group; and 2) within any racial group there are people with scores from the very highest to the very lowest, and thus the variance in test scores attributable to race is very small. In fairness, both of these points are mentioned by the author; however, they are not emphasized and highlighted to the same extent as is the racial difference in scores.

The author's problems in interpreting his findings reflect his deep concern with trying to derive causation from correlational data. He does not seem to understand the nature of the highly-confounded variables and the strong limitations this situation places on causal inference. Jensen's logic is akin to saying that because increases in the water temperature at Atlantic Ocean beaches are accompanied by increased drownings, higher water temperature causes drowning to occur.

Jensen's work gives insufficient attention to the number of measurement and methodological factors that must be considered in evaluating studies done with black subjects. These factors must be considered regardless of subject, but become even more essential when children of a different cultural background are studied. These factors were examined by Johnson, who proposed a model of test fairness and discussed major sources of bias (see Figure 1).[44,45]

The Nature of Measurement

The essential fact to recognize whenever psychological measurement is employed is that such measurement is never done directly. We do not measure minds the way we measure the length of a room.[46] Although physical measurement can also produce errors, errors in psychological measurement may be particularly difficult to detect and interpret. All psychological measurement is done on behavior, and from the behavior, an inference is made to a level of achievement, aptitude, personality, interest, or some other human characteristic that cannot be measured directly.

A low score on a psychological measure simply does not have much meaning. It may mean that the person tested has a low value on the construct or trait being measured, or it may mean that the construct or trait is present, but is not being tapped by the specific behavior measure being used. This axiom of psychological measurement is well known

FIGURE 1
Factors Affecting Test Score

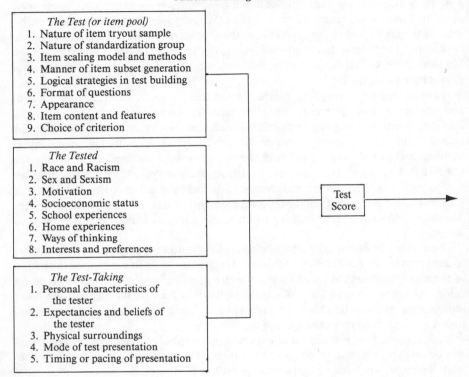

The Test (or item pool)
1. Nature of item tryout sample
2. Nature of standardization group
3. Item scaling model and methods
4. Manner of item subset generation
5. Logical strategies in test building
6. Format of questions
7. Appearance
8. Item content and features
9. Choice of criterion

The Tested
1. Race and Racism
2. Sex and Sexism
3. Motivation
4. Socioeconomic status
5. School experiences
6. Home experiences
7. Ways of thinking
8. Interests and preferences

The Test-Taking
1. Personal characteristics of
   the tester
2. Expectancies and beliefs of
   the tester
3. Physical surroundings
4. Mode of test presentation
5. Timing or pacing of presentation

Test Score

Source: Johnson, S.T., The Test, the Tested, and the Test Taking: A Model to Better Understand Test Performance. Paper presented at the Annual Meeting of the American Educ. Research Assn., New Orleans, LA, April, 1984.

to test makers, many of whom agonize over the lack of information provided by low scores. Yet, the less people know about measurement, the more they believe in the infallibility of the test score.

Modern measurement theory has made giant steps along the line of measuring achievement dimensions through the application of Item Response Theory (IRT), but increased precision in scaling techniques does not change the axiomatic relationship between behavior and inference, nor does such precision make the measure any more direct. IRT scaling procedures improve measurement by making it possible to identify sets of items with similar measurement features, to determine scale score values that do not depend on the specific set of test items administered, and to locate items with apparent bias or with other nondesirable features. Maintaining the integrity of a measurement scale over time is also facilitated by IRT procedures. However, modern scaling also tends to discourage more innovative uses of measurement that could examine the more unreliable creative and adaptive behaviors that do not "scale" well.

MEASUREMENT AND BLACKS

Issues in the testing of minorities have literally fueled much of the development of modern measurement methodology and practice, because much of the funding for measurement research has come from programs intended to broaden educational opportunities and increase access for these groups. Therefore, the measurement community has a responsibility to use these tools to improve the quality of instructional experiences available to black children. Because access to the rewards of our society is increasingly based on test scores, this becomes a special imperative.

Test scores must be used to facilitate academic achievement among low-income blacks, not to further depress their expectations. Instructional activities must be developed to capture the soul of learners, to truly motivate. Belief in the importance, value, and excitement of intellectual activity and knowledge of subject matter must be developed. Further, children need to believe that making the effort to learn something thoroughly will result in something positive happening to the learner.

The special stresses under which all poor families operate decrease the ability of many of them to facilitate academic achievement, and among black families, there are the additional stresses of racism and discrimination, and resultant job ceilings. Schools can and should provide information, assistance, and encouragement to families to help them increase the motivation of children toward academic achievement. Studies of achieving black youth illustrate many family and personal strengths. Clark's work with achieving and non-achieving low-income families is a landmark study, as is the earlier work of Billingsley in identifying the "screens of opportunity" that have operated among successful black families.[47,48] The personal characteristics that affect and are affected by school achievement among black teens are found to be quite similar to those affecting achievement among their peers of other racial or ethnic groups, and include self-concept, locus of control, and self-perception of ability.[49] The variable of task interest is applicable as well, and its usefulness highlights the fact that traditional measures have involved tasks of interest to whites but not necessarily to blacks.[50]

Thus, when considering achievement in school, it is necessary to carefully review the ways in which such achievement is measured. Models with strong scientific bases, built with a recognition of the reality of the black experience, have involved the skills of psychologists, sociologists, economists, and political scientists; such tests should also employ the expertise of those skilled in educational and psychological measurement.

CONCLUSION AND RECOMMENDATIONS

In this review of test fairness and the measurement of achievement, the findings are mixed. Although testing could be eliminated altogether, other information-gathering and decision-making systems have equal or greater problems of quality control and objectivity. The best solution seems to be to use test information where appropriate, change tests dramatically where needed, and discontinue use where warranted. The ultimate goal is to increase the achievement of youth and not limit the scope of their educational experiences.

Some information from tests has highlighted the need for greater community and school efforts, especially at the junior and senior high school levels to increase academic preparation for college and employment. When low test scores are earned by students who are not in school each day and are not receiving meaningful, substantive instruction, it makes no sense to blame the measure. A climate of expectation of achievement must be established and maintained within schools and communities so that time is spent on high-quality instruction, followed by well-planned home assignments that are completed and brought to school. If the length of time that students are exposed to meaningful academic work is limited, they can hardly be expected to show high performance. Regular, on-time school attendance supported by homework is a simple, mundane idea, totally devoid of the glamour one might expect from a solution to a pressing educational problem. However, these activities serve to orient students primarily toward schooling, and thus to allow the overall academic effort to have the best chance to make an impact.

We need to place tests in perspective—to remove the measurement mystique from the general public as well as the professional users. This can be done by improving the extent and quality of the training in measurement provided for teachers, counselors, and other professionals who use and interpret tests. More and better public information on testing is needed to make test results more accessible.

Related to the need to place testing in perspective is the need to recognize that tests are only part of the picture when examining and appraising abilities and achievements, so caution should be taken when making inferences from low test scores. Scores should be a part of the information examined, along with other indices of achievement and motivation. Although some of these data are rather "soft," they may have substantial validity in a reasoned appraisal of performance. Tests may be quite inappropriate for some measures of performance, and if so, they should not be used.

We should also demand better tests, using new technology where appropriate, but also including better measurement techniques. Cost must be considered; it makes little sense to make massive investments in testing without developing a superior academic program. A solid academic program should receive more resources as a result of the testing program, not less. Testing should be more selective to make measurement investments go further.

Finally, measurement scholarship must broaden its base to include various approaches to measuring important constructs, if such measures are to continue to play an important role in the determination of the rewards and positions within our society. Many talented, forward-thinking, and sensitive scholars have been drawn to the measurement field in recent years. The measurement of black children has drawn the interest of many researchers, but only a small percentage of such researchers are black themselves. If measurement research is to be carried out on black children, it should involve black professionals at the theoretical and conceptual levels, as well as in the other research activities because such researchers bring a broader perspective to the field. Graduate programs in measurement and research should recruit black students, and test publishers and others carrying out measurement research should seek to involve black scholars. Such scholars should have a broader role in investigating and documenting the measured achievements of black youth.

Such a mandate is no small task because potential measurement scholars may have had negative test experiences themselves. Further, such students may perceive researchers as less interested in doing the best measurement job and more interested in maximizing reliability and validity indices, regardless of whether the measure is appropriate for the construct. But, with the current challenges in measurement, the field must try to attract talented young blacks, thereby making the field a viable option for blacks considering graduate study and professional careers.

NOTES

The research for this chapter was supported by a grant from the National Research Council, The Commission on the Status of Black Americans.

1. Young, W.M. Jr., *To Be Equal* (New York, N.Y.: McGraw-Hill, 1964).

2. Young, *Equal.*

3. Echternacht, G, "Title I Evaluation and Reporting System: Development of Evaluation Models," *New Directions for Testing and Measurement* 8 (1980), pp. 1–16.

4. Montgomery (Md.) County Public Schools (MCPS) Department of Educational Accountability, "Progress Being Made by Minority Students," Internal memorandum from Wilmer S. Cody to the members of the Board of Education, July 30, 1985 (Rockville, Md.: Montgomery County Public Schools, 1983).

5. MCPS, "Progress."

6. White, K. "The Relations Between Socioeconomic Status and Academic Achievement," *Psychological Bulletin* 91: (1982), pp. 461–81.

7. Johnson, S.T. "The Measurement Mystique: Issues in Selection for Professional Schools and Employment," *Occasional Paper No. 2* (Washington, D.C.: Institute of the Study of Educational Policy, Howard Univ., 1979).

8. Ramist, L., and Arbeiter, S., *Profiles, College Bound Seniors* (N.Y.:N.Y. College Entrance Examination Board, (EEB), 1985).

9. MCPS, "Progress."

10. National Assessment of Educational Progress, *NAEP—Technical Report* (Princeton, N.J.: National Assessment of Eduational Progress, 1986).

11. MCPS, "Progress."

12. District of Columbia Public Schools, Student Assessment Office, *A Summary of Student Achievement on the Comprehensive Test of Basic Skills,* (Washington, D.C.: Student Assessment Office, Division of Quality Assurrance, District of Columbia Public Schools).

13. MCPS, "Progress."

14. National Assessment of Educational Progress, *The Reading Report Card: Progress Toward Excellence in Our Schools, Report No. 15-R-01* (Princeton, N.J.: Educational Testing Service, 1985).

15. Kirsch, I. and Jungeblutt, A., *Literacy: Profiles of America's Young Adults—Final Report.* Report No. 16-PL-01. (Princeton, N.J., National Assessment of Educational Progress, 1986).

16. Venezky, R.L., C.F. Kaestle, and A.M. Sum. *The Subtle Danger—Reflections on the Literacy Abilities of America's Young Adults,* Report No. 16-CAEP-01 (Center for the Assessment of Educational Progress, Educational Testing Service, Princeton, N.J. 1987).

17. College Entrance Examination Board (CEEB) *Equality and Excellence: The Educational Status of Black Americans* (N.Y.: CEEB, 1985).

18. Johnson, S.T., "The Test, The Tested, and the Test-Taking: A Model to Better Understand Test Performance," a paper presented at the Annual Meeting of the American Educational Research Assn., New Orleans, LA., April, 1984.

19. Banks, W.C., E.V. McQuater, and J.L. Hubbard, "Towards a Reconceptualization of the Social Cognitive Bases of Achievement Orientations in Blacks," *Review of Educational Research,* 48: (1978), pp. 381-98.

20. Bock, D., and R. Mislevy. *Profiles of American Youth* (Washington: D.C., U.S. Department of Defense, 1980).

21. U.S. Department of Commerce, Bureau of the Census, Vol. 2 of *Population Census Reports, PC80-2, Subject Report, Social and Economic Characteristics by Gender.* (Washington, D.C.: U.S. Government Printing Office, 1981).

22. Bock and Mislevy, *Profiles.*

23. Anastasi, A., *Psychological Testing* (2nd ed.) (New York: MacMillan, 1954).

24. Davis, A. *Social Class Influences Upon Learning,* (Cambridge: Harvard Univ. Press, 1948).

25. Davis, A. and Eels, K., *The Davis-Eells Games,* (Chicago: Univ. of Chicago Press, 1951).

26. Anastasi, A., "Some Implications of Cultural Factors for Test Construction," *Proceedings of the 1949 Invitational Conference on Testing Problems.* (Princeton, NJ: Educational Testing Service, 1950).

27. Anastasi, A. 1954, *Psychological Testing.*

28. Williams, R.L. "On Black Intelligence," *Journal of Black Studies,* (1973), pp. 29–39.

29. Medley, D.M. and T.J. Quirk. "The Application of a Factorial Design to the Study of Cultural Bias in General Culture Items on the National Teachers Examinations," *Journal of Educational Measurement* 11 (1974), pp. 235–45.

30. Cleary, T.A., "Test Bias: Prediction of Grades of Negro and White Students in Intergrated Colleges," *Journal of Educational Measurement* 5 (1968), pp. 115–124.

31. Thorndike, R.L., "Concepts of Culture Fairness," *Journal of Educational Measurement,* 8 (1971), pp. 63–70.

32. Einhorn, H.J., and A.R. Bass. "Methodological Considerations Relevant to Discrimination in Employment Testing," *Psychological Bulletin,* 15 (1971), pp. 15–19.

33. Sawyer, R.L., N.S. Cole and J.W.L. Cole. "Utilities and the Issue of Fairness in a Decision Theoretic Model for Selection," *Journal of Educational Measurement,* 13 (1973), pp. 59-76.

34. Linn,R.L., "Fair Testing Use in Selection," *Review of Educational Research,* 43 (1973), pp. 139-61.

35. Novick, M.R. and N.S. Petersen. Toward Equalizing Educational and Employment Opportunity, *Journal of Educational Measurement* 13 (1983), pp. 77–88.

36. Petersen, N.S. and M.R. Novick. "An Evaluation of Some Models for Culture-Fair Selection," *Journal of Educational Measurement* 8 (1976), pp. 253–61.

37. Gross, A.L. and W. Su. "Defining a "Fair" or "Unbiased" Selection Model: A Question of Utilities, *Journal of Applied Psychology* 60 (1975), pp. 345–51.

38. Shepard, L.A., G. Camilli, and D.M. Wiliams. Accounting for Statistical Artifacts in Item Bias research, *Journal of Educational Statistics,* 9 (1984), pp. 93–128.

39. Mantel, N. and W. Haenszel. "Statistical Aspects of the Analysis of Data from Retrospective Studies of Diseases," *Journal of the National Cancer Institute,* 22 (1959), pp. 719–48.

40. Holland, P.W. and D.T. Thayer. "Differential Item Functioning and the Mantel-Haenszel Procedure," *Program Statistics Research, Technical Report No. 86-69.* (Princeton, N.J., Educational Testing Service, 1986).

41. Schmitt, A.P., C.A. Bleistein and J.D. Schevneman. "Determinants of Differential Item functioning for Black Examinees on Scholastic Aptitude Test Analogy Items," paper presented at the Annual Meeting of the National Council on Measurement in Education, Washington, D.C., April, 1987.

42. Jensen, A.R., "How much can we Boost I.Q. and Scholastic Achievement?" *Harvard Educational Review* 39: (1969), pp. 1–129.

43. Jensen, A.R., *Bias in Mental Testing.* (New York: Free Press, 1980).

44. Johnson, S.T., "Measurement Mystique."

45. Johnson, S.T., *et. al.* "A Program to Increase Scholatic Aptitude Test Scores Among Low-Income Black Youth in Three Cities," Paper presented at the Annual Meeting of the American Educational Research Association, Chicago, Il., 1985.

46. Johnson, S.T., "Measurement Mystique."

47. Clark,R., *Family Life and School Achievement: Why Poor Black Children Succeed or Fail.* (Chicago: Univ. of Chicago Press, 1983).

48. Billingsley, A. *Black Families in White America.* (Englewood Cliffs, N.J.: Prentice-Hall, Inc, 1968).

49. Johnson, S.T. "Extra-School Factors in Achievement, Attainment and Aspiration among Black Adolescents," Paper prepared for the Commission on the Status of Black Americans, National Research Council, National Academy of Sciences, 1987.

50. Banks, W.C., *et. al.,* "Reconceptualization."

10
Sorting Black Students for Success and Failure: The Inequity of Ability Grouping and Tracking

Eva Wells Chunn

The public school system has long sorted and divided students into academic categories based on ability grouping and tracking. Substantial evidence abounds that non-minority students are often placed into higher academic ability groups, while blacks, particularly black males, are tracked into lower academic ability groups. Indeed, black, poor, and other minority students are less likely to be enrolled in programs for the gifted and talented, for they are disproportionately enrolled in special education programs. Moreover, such students are underrepresented in academic programs and overrepresented in vocational programs. Within those programs, Blacks receive less educational preparation in areas such as English, mathematics, and science.

It appears that administrative policies and practices, as well as teacher expectations about certain students' academic abilities and potential performances, affect curriculum placement as much as students' characteristics such as race, sex, and socioeconomic status (SES). Some commentators contend that these sorting practices are causing black students to lose ground in preparing for the technological society and employment opportunities of the 1990s and twenty-first century.

This article discusses academic sorting practices and their selective determinants such as teacher expectations, race, and socioeconomic status in influencing black students' scholastic success or failure. The contention is that these sorting mechanisms play a pivotal role in perpetuating and widening the achievement gap between black students and their white counterparts. Mindful of this inequity, this article provides some practical recommendations and strategies for minimizing and remedying the negative effects that ability grouping and tracking have on the academic achievement of black students.

ABILITY GROUPING AND TRACKING

Its Definition, Justification, and Use

Ability grouping entails the sorting of students into instructional groups or classes due to alleged differences in ability.[1] Homogeneous grouping, tracking, and/or skill grouping are labels that have been interchanged with ability grouping. Stated differently, students are usually sorted within classrooms into ability groups. On the other hand, tracking systems stratify classrooms by curriculum on the alleged basis of ability.

Four assumptions undergird ability grouping and tracking practices:

- that students learn better when they are grouped with other students who are similar to them academically;
- that slower students develop more positive attitudes in relation to themselves and their school if they are not sorted into groups with students who are more capable;
- that the placement process used to sort students into groups is accurate and fair and, in addition, reflects past achievements and innate abilities;
- that it is easier for teachers to accommodate individual differences in homogeneous groups; that similar students are easier to teach and manage.[2]

Ability grouping in elementary school classrooms sorts students into small ability-based groups for instruction in basic skill areas. Twenty-five percent of American school districts use cross classroom ability groups.[3] However, cross classroom ability grouping is more common in high school, manifesting itself in the form of tracking. High schools typically have two tracks or three tracks.[4] At the two-track high school, the tracks are known as "college-bound" and "non college-bound." Three-track high schools often label the tracks "gifted," "average," and "remedial" or "low ability." The top group or track is usually given a demanding curriculum with demanding standards of performance.[5]

Although various methods are used to sort students into tracks, such as standardized tests, grades, mental age, and administrative/counselor recommendations, a key determinant is personal perception: teacher expectations vis-a-vis selected student characteristics and perceived ability. Some observers contend that a teacher's expectations can become a self-fulfilling prophecy in determining the success and/or failure of students.[6] Thus, it is important that we learn more about the effects that teachers' values, beliefs, and attitudes have on students.

TEACHER EXPECTATIONS

Teacher expectations are inferences made by the teacher about present and future academic achievement and general classroom behavior of students. Teacher expectations can be significantly affected by information about test performance, performance on assignments, track or group placement, information obtained from other teachers, classroom conduct, physical appearances, race, socioeconomic status, sex, speech characteristics, and various diagnostic labels.[7] Expectations may be for the entire class or specific individuals such as black or minority students. Some general expectations held by teachers are:

- beliefs about the changeability versus the rigidity of students' abilities;
- beliefs about the students' potential for benefiting from instruction;
- beliefs about the difficulty level of the material for the students in general or for a particular subgroup;
- beliefs about whether the class should be taught as a group or individually.[8]

What teachers expect from students academically is critical because teachers interact with students over a long period of time. Throughout the life of a student, the teacher is a major force.[9] A student's scholastic performance can be influenced by a teacher in either a negative or positive direction. Teachers with positive influences encourage and challenge students to excel academically and to develop interest in and appreciation of particular subjects.[10] Moreover, influential teachers provide feedback and reinforcement that assist in the development of self-confidence, self-identification, and character. Indeed, teaching based on positive expectations contributes significantly to a student's performance.

One of the major functions of the school principal is to convey to teachers the critical influence of positive teacher expectation on a student's academic achievement. In many schools with black, other minority, and poor students, the principal may have written guidelines endorsing high teacher expectations, yet these guidelines may not be enforced. This may result in teachers' having lower expectations when interacting with their students, thus creating what is known as the self-fulfilling prophecy about academic performance.

Self-fulfilling Prophecy

The notion of a self-fulfilling prophecy has been most intensively studied as an expectancy effect.[11] The self-fulfilling prophecy begins as a false definition of the situation, which then causes a new behavior that makes the originally false conception come true. Thus with a particular expectancy, teachers are likely to behave in ways that bring about what they expect. Specifically, the self-fulfilling prophecy effect occurs when teachers consistently treat particular students as different from the way they actually are or can potentially become. This consistent pressure eventually causes the student to become more like what he or she is expected to be. In essence, the self-fulfilling prophecy describes situations in which teacher expectations influence student behavior.

Much public and scientific attention has been given to the influence of performance expectations on school achievement. Clark contended that many ghetto children might be the victims of low teacher expectations that then become self-fulfilling prophecies.[12] Ghetto teachers who believed that their students could not learn were seen as the cause of low achievement.[13]

Clark's contention that teacher expectations could become a self-fulfilling prophecy has been supported empirically by Rosenthal and Jacobson in their *Pygmalion in the Classroom* study.[14] Rosenthal and his associates reviewed fifteen years of research and found that teacher expectancy effects of some type occurred in two-thirds of the 345 studies reviewed.[15] Other scholarly evidence has identified a protocol of interactive behaviors of teachers who had low expectations of students. For example, such teachers:

- wait less time for low-expectation students (Lows) to answer questions;
- give "Lows" the answer or call someone else rather than trying to improve the Low's response through repeating the question, providing clues, or asking a new question;
- provide "Lows" with inappropriate reinforcement by rewarding inappropriate behaviors or incorrect answers;
- criticize "Lows" more often for failure;
- praise "Lows" less frequently than "Highs" for success;
- fail to give feedback to the public responses of "Lows";
- pay less attention to "Lows" and interact with them less frequently;
- call on "Lows" less often to respond to questions;
- seat "Lows" farther away from the teacher;
- demand less from "Lows" (it has been found that high-expectation, high-grouped, or high-tracked students are taught with more rapid pacing and less extended explanations or repetition of definitions and examples. Teachers may accept more low-quality or more incorrect responses from low-expectation students. Teachers are also more likely to attempt to improve a poor response from a high-expectation student than from a low-expectation student;
- interact with "Lows" more privately than publicly;
- differentially administer or grade tests or assignments in which "Highs," but not "Lows" are given the benefit of the doubt in borderline cases;
- give briefer and less information feedback to the questions of "Lows";
- exhibit less friendly interaction—less smiling, nonverbal warmth, eye contact, nonverbal communication of attention and responsiveness (forward leaning, positive head nodding) in interaction with "Lows";
- use less intrusive instruction with "Highs" so that there is more opportunity for them to practice independently;
- use less effective and more time-consuming instructional methods with "Lows" when time is limited.[16]

This protocol of interactive behavior of teachers with low expectations of students is particularly troubling because of its effect on the educational achievement of black, poor, and other minority children who are often in need of equitable treatment in education in order to achieve excellence.

Race and Class as Determinants of Teacher Expectations

Research abounds that race and socioeconomic status (SES) influence teacher expectations and thus contribute to the self-fulfilling prophecy effect. In 1970, Rist studied the influence of minority group status on teacher expectations on predominantly low and middle SES students enrolled in a school where most administrators, teachers, staff, and students were black.[17] Rist's findings revealed that black teachers, as well as white, have problems with teacher expectations. Rist longitudinally observed one class of black students during kindergarten, first, and second grades. The kindergarten teacher placed the children in reading groups that reflected the socioeconomic background of the students. These students remained in the same high or low reading groups throughout kindergarten and first and second grades.

This study pointed out some of the important problems of ability grouping, such as the lack of mobility between groups and the placement of low socioeconomic students in the lowest group. The teacher had certain expectations for the students. Indeed, the way the teacher behaved toward the different groups became an important influence on the students' achievement—a self-fulfilling prophecy. The nonflexibility in movement across groups further supports the view of ability grouping as a self-fulfilling prophecy.

Dusek and Joseph analyzed twenty-four studies in which teacher expectancies were assessed as a function of race of the child.[18] The twenty-four studies involved comparisons between black and white students who were included in the analysis. These studies were based on research performed during the period between 1968-1981. Based on their analysis, Dusek and Joseph concluded that race is a significant factor in the formation of teacher expectancies. Black students, so to speak, are expected to perform less well than white students.

Analysis was also performed on seventeen studies in which socioeconomic status was the basis for teacher expectancies.[19] Significant results were revealed. Teachers expect middle-class children to perform better than lower-class students. This, of course, has major implications for blacks, because most black students are from lower socioeconomic classes.

In discussing the education of black students and the influence of teacher expectations, it is noteworthy that characteristics peculiar to black students can help shape expectations. Research evidence clearly indicates that kindergarten teachers lowered their expectations of the academic abilities of black students who used dialect or spoke "black English." On the other hand, black students who spoke "standard English" were expected to have higher academic abilities.

Demeis and Turner investigated the nature of those characteristics that influence both the formation of teachers' expectations and their evaluation of students' performance.[20] White, female elementary teachers were requested to evaluate personality, academic abilities, and specific performance of fifth grade male students who varied by race (black and white), dialect, and physical attractiveness. Through this procedure, a direct examination of the relationship between teacher expectations of the students and their assessment of student performance was permitted. The results indicated that students who spoke "black English" were rated as having less academic ability than students who spoke standard English. Such results suggest that black children's race and dialect can result in a negative evaluation of their performance as well as their personalities and abilities.

In general, this research evidence underscores the fact that prejudice affects the judgments made by professionals who are trained to evaluate students' performances. Indeed, these judgments have important implications for black students in a society where academic achievement is a key to success.

FROM TEACHER EXPECTATION TO ABILITY GROUPING/TRACKING

In focusing on tracking and ability grouping, critics emphasize two themes: (1) socioeconomic status bias in educational policies and (2) the preference given to intellectually-advantaged students rather than to non-college track students. Alexander, Cook, and McDill reported that critics of tracking offer the following contentions:

- Tracking channels scarce resources to those who have the least need for them.
- Students in non-college tracks are denied access to students, teachers, counselors, and information that would broaden their interests, challenge their abilities, and improve their performance;
- Non-college tracked students are discouraged from competing with those students who are initially more advantaged, and thus are not required or even encouraged to strive for academic excellence.
- Students in non-college tracks are looked down upon as being unintelligent. As a result, they fail to develop attitudes and insights concerning education and institutional functioning that would allow them to compete successfully with their more advantaged classmates for post-schooling resources and rewards.
- Non-college track students are shunted into curricula that will impede their prospects for success in college. If they persevere in their college aspirations, they will be relegated to junior and community colleges which will further diminish their expectations.
- Being in a college track increases the probability of applying to college and enhances one's prospects for being admitted. Thus, sorting processes within high schools may substantially affect later SES attainment.[21]

Alexander, Cook, and McDill further contended that tracking serves the interests of higher status parents who exploit such mechanisms to ensure their children's success.[22] Higher status parents know how to manipulate the system to guarantee the placement of their children in gifted or honor tracks. These parents are aware that this is important to assist in obtaining admittance to the most prestigious colleges. In turn, graduates of prestigious colleges are most often the recipients of more prestigious jobs and the cycle repeats itself.

Differential Treatment of Ability Grouped/Tracked Students

Research has revealed that the learning context varies dramatically across ability groups.[23] For instance, students in low groups are instructed in an environment characterized by disruption from the teacher as well as from other group members. Conversely, high group members are instructed in a much less disruptive environment. Essentially, those students who are likely to have more difficulty learning are inadvertently assigned to groups whose social context is much less conducive to learning.

To be sure, homogeneous groupings compound initial problems by placing those children who have learning problems together in groups. An alternative would be to use some form of heterogeneous grouping. Although this might make learning more difficult for brighter children, it would benefit slower students by reducing the amount of inattention and management problems during their lessons. This change in grouping would help slower students who are most in need of positive learning environments.

Oakes, in a book and an article based on data from John Goodlad's project *A Study of Schooling*, contended that students in lower tracks of junior high and high school receive an education that is very different from students in the upper tracks.[24] The lower track education is qualitatively and quantitatively inferior to the upper track. For example, students of the upper tracks are taught differential equations, creative writing, and literature. Conversely, lower tracked students have basic arithmetic, grammar drills, and letter forms. Lower tracked students get less of whatever is distributed educationally. Oakes further argued that for low tracked students, schools are more of a burden than an asset. These students view knowledge as unrelated to their lives and instruction as an assault on their time. For them, school is a place to endure time rather than one to be used for self and social empowerment. School alienates and disrupts the lives of low track students. Therefore, if these students learn anything, it is in spite of the degradation they endure.

Overall, research indicates the following in relation to differential treatment of ability groups and/or tracks:

- that teachers are more demanding and give longer reading assignments to their high groups. Teachers interrupt low group students more quickly when they make a mistake in reading. Teachers are more likely to give the low group students the word or prompt them with graphic or phonetic cues rather than semantic or syntactic cues that are designed to help them intuit the word from its context;
- that with low groups, teachers were observed to have been less clear about their objectives, to make fewer attempts to relate the content of their courses to students' interests and background, to be less reasonable in their work standards, to be less consistent in their discipline, and to be less receptive to student input;
- that high track classes have teachers who plan and implement more independent projects and tend to introduce more higher-level and integrative concepts. Low track teachers stress more structured assignments dealing with basic facts and skills;
- that high track classes are seen more as an academic challenge, so teachers plan them more thoroughly. Low track teachers, in contrast, are less well prepared

and are much more likely to spend time correcting papers or allowing students to do activities of their own choosing rather than teaching academic content.[25]

TRACKING: DOES ANYONE BENEFIT?

Research on tracking and ability grouping suggests that it tends to have minor benefits for high track or high ability group students, but major disadvantages for students placed into low tracks or low ability groups.[26] Robert Slavin reviewed research on ability grouping and concluded that an entire class grouped by ability is the least flexible arrangement for pupils because they will experience changes in performance over the year.[27] Heterogeneous classes would offer beneficial peer pressure to perform better. Moreover, Slavin's study indicated that homogeneous low-ability classes attracted less-competent teachers who have low expectations for their students. Low ability class teachers' main goal is to be promoted to teaching "better" classes.

Other research on ability grouping in high schools and elementary schools has found that even when prior ability or achievement are controlled, students in high-ranking groups gain an achievement advantage over students in low-ranking groups by virtue of their group placement.[28] It appears that initial inequalities in achievement are actually increased over time by ability group systems.

A Case of Race and Class

The research reveals a positive correlation among race, socioeconomic status (SES) and the track or group into which students are sorted.[29] Indeed, it has been shown that students from upper SES levels are usually found in the highest ability group or track levels; students from minority groups (usually black males) and low SES levels are usually found in classes at the lower ability groups or track levels. Even high-achieving blacks tend to be placed in low ability groups or tracks, while low-achieving white, middle-class students tend to be placed in high tracks or ability groups.

A recent study by Epstein indicated that tracking and within-class ability grouping are used more often by teachers in southern schools who do not strongly support integrated education.[30] Black as well as white teachers most often used tracking when their class was predominantly black. Eighty percent of the teachers in the sample grouped children by ability within the classroom. Only one-fourth of the teachers reported track assignments flexible enough to permit twenty percent or more of the students to change tracks during their years in elementary schools. Epstein's study further indicated that flexible tracking, active learning, and equal status programs had a significant positive effect on the achievements of black students.

Thus, tracking or ability grouping as an organizational feature of school sorts students into groups that are reflective of social and economic divisions in society.

SORTING FOR SUCCESS AND FAILURE

Academic and Vocational Placement

We have thus far presented an amalgam of determinants for ability grouping and tracking. The end results of these determinants are clearly reflected when reviewed in the context of educable mentally retarded placements, academic vocational placements, and lack of gifted and talented placements. Within most high schools, blacks are underrepresented in academic programs and over represented and enrolled earlier in vocational educational programs where they receive less academic preparation in areas such as English, mathematics, and science.[31] Moreover, they are trained more for low-status occupations than are white students. It appears that these assignments are made by school personnel rather than by selection of students or their parents.[32]

Such assignments are related to educational achievement because students who are not in academic tracks are not placed in courses that will prepare them for college or allow them to obtain high scores on standardized tests (used as indicators that students are adequately prepared to begin college). Thus, black lose ground in terms of educational equity and achievement.

Recent research data from the first and second follow-up of *High School and Beyond* revealed that guidance counseling services are not equally available to all public high school students.[33] Low SES and minority students are less likely to have the guidance counseling necessary to make importance academic decisions. Students without access to guidance counseling are more likely to be placed in nonacademic curriculum tracks and to take fewer math courses. Counselors have a key role in high school curriculum track placement. Teachers have a key role in elementary school in ability group placement and in student placement in educable mentally retarded classes.

Educable Mentally Retarded (EMR) Placement

The high percentage of blacks placed in EMR classes is a glaring example of low expectations for blacks and sorting for failure. An examination of EMR placements of black students (see Table 1) for the periods 1976-1984 indicates the following:

- In 1976 and 1978, black students constituted 38% of the EMR enrollment, but were only 15% and 16% respectively, of the national enrollment in school generally;
- In 1980, when blacks constituted 16.1% of the national student population, the black EMR enrollment nationally rose to 38.7%;
- The 1984 data indicate a slight decrease of blacks enrolled in EMR classes to 37.3%. In 1984, blacks were 16.2% of the total national enrollment;
- The data for whites reveal that for the years 1976, 1978, 1980, and 1984, they constituted 76%, 75%, 73%, and 71%, respectively, of the national enrollment.

TABLE 1
EMR and Gifted/Talented Placements by Race

1976	Black	Minority[1]	White	Total[2]
Enrollment	6,773,600	10,483,760	33,229,249	43,713,009
Percent of Total	15	23	76	100
EMR[3]	249,707	289,843	371,326	661,169
Percent of Total	38	44	56	100
Gifted/Talented	31,713	56,660	348,400	405,060
Percent of Total	8	14	86	100
1978				
Enrollment	6,578,074	10,326,330	31,509,927	41,836,257
Percent of Total	16	25	75	100
EMR[3]	226,856	262,210	334,663	596,873
Percent of Total	38	44	56	100
Gifted/Talented	33,556	154,981	655,955	810,836
Percent of Total	10	18	81	100
1980				
Enrollment	6,418,194	10,652,272	29,180,415	39,832,687
Percent of Total	16.1	26.7	73.3	100
EMR[3]	214,912	247,276	308,731	555,943
Percent of Total	38.7	44.5	55.5	100
Gifted/Talented	93,560	184,538	840,424	1,024,912
Percent of Total	8.1	18.0	82	100
1984				
Enrollment	6,388,670	11,345,602	28,106,295	39,451,897
Percent of Total	16.2	28.8	71.2	100
EMR[3]	197,471	246,919	282,466	529,385
Percent of Total	37.3	46.6	53.4	100
Gifted/Talented	138,167	303,853	1,333,849	1,637,702
Percent of Total	8.4	18.6	81.4	100

Sources: U.S. Department of Education, Office of Civil Rights, *1976, 1978, 1980, and 1984 Elementary and Secondary Schools Civil Rights Surveys.*
1. Minority includes American Indian, Asian, Hispanic, and Black totals.
2. Due to rounding, percent total may be under or over 100%.
3. EMR refers to educable mentally retarded.

The white EMR rates for 1976, 1978, 1980, and 1984 were 56%, 56%, 56%, and 53%, respectively. The white EMR percentages have never exceeded the white national enrollment percentages during period, *while the black EMR percentages have been more than double their enrollment percentages for the period 1976-1984. Blacks, therefore, were overrepresented in EMR placement during this period.*[34]

Gifted and Talented (G/T) Placements

Blacks students during the period between 1976-84 were underrepresented in gifted/talented (G/T) classes as the following information indicates (see Table 1):

- In 1987, black students constituted 8% of G/T classes while whites comprised 85%. Black national enrollment was 15% of the total enrollment and whites were 76%;

- There was an increase from 1976-78 from 8%-10% for black students enrolled in gifted classes. White G/T decreased during this period, from 86% to 81%. National school enrollment figures for blacks and whites were 16% and 75%, respectively;
- The black G/T enrollment went down from 1978-80 from 10%-9.1%, while the white enrollment during this period in G/T increased from 81% to 82%. National school enrollment figures for blacks and whites were 16.1% and 74% respectively;
- In 1984 the black enrollment in G/T classes had further decreased from 9.1% in 1980 to 8.4%. There was a slight decrease in the white G/T enrollment to 81.4%, but their percentages still remained quite large. National school enrollment figures for blacks and whites, were 16.2% and 71%, respectively. White G/T percentages exceeded their enrollment percentages throughout the period 1976-84. This was not true for blacks.[35]

Such statistics reveal graphically that low expectations prevail for blacks as well as the inequitable sorting practices discusses earlier. The percentage of blacks in EMR classes has remained about the same from 1976-84. In the G/T programs for the same period, however, black G/T placements had fallen closer to the 1976 percentage.

INSTRUCTING WITHOUT ABILITY GROUPING: SOME RECOMMENDED STRATEGIES FOR SORTING FOR SUCCESS

Instead of current sorting procedures, it is possible to sort for success through the practice of high expectations for student performance and also by using more school programs that do not use ability grouping.

The Effective School Movement has shown that low SES black students can learn when effective school philosophies are used.[36] Research in this area documents that the principal can establish a school climate (environment) that promotes student achievement success. This climate results from the principal's as well as the teachers' commitment to high expectations for student success, which is then communicated to teachers and students and permeates the school. Indeed, for black, poor, and other minority students to achieve at high levels, it is important that principals manifest a commitment to and take the responsibility for high expectations.

A key strategy for remedying the negative consequences of ability grouping and tracking would be to develop more school programs that do not utilize ability grouping. For example, the District of Columbia Public School system has a program called the *Success in Reading and Writing Program (Success).*[37] This program operates in pre-kindergarten through sixth grades in 71 elementary schools and 191 classrooms. All interested teachers in the D.C. public schools can use this program to teach reading, writing, and spelling (the program also partially encompasses math and social studies) during a 2-2½ hour time period.

The *Success in Reading and Writing* program evolved from the studies of Dr. Anne Adams of Duke University. She concluded that anything in print, within reason, should be part of the basal reading program. Possible Instruction materials included the following: newspapers, fiction and non-fiction library books; content area textbooks; and magazines. Reading vocabulary evolves out of the students' experiences, and reading and writing skills are closely linked. The classroom decor includes charts containing the students' own vocabulary of words, word clusters, and sentences.

As well as changes in materials of instruction, the program also provides for changes in classroom procedure. Whole class teaching is preferred over grouping practices. This approach resulted from Dr. Adams' belief that certain grouping practices damage the teacher's effectiveness and the students' self-concepts.

Within this program, individualized instruction is a key element. It is defined as time (minutes or seconds) between the teacher and an individual student to focus on what the student is doing, has done, or should be doing academically. According to the program, such contact should occur three or four times during the course of a lesson; it is considered important to the affective student development.

The three main objectives of the program are reading skills, and writing skills (both in the cognitive area) and the development of a positive self-concept in the affective area. The *Success* manuals for grades one through six delineate specific achievements in these areas.

Students in the *Success* program have had significantly higher reading achievement scores when compared with those of students in regular reading programs that employ ability groupings. Thus, this nonability grouping program has been shown to be an effective teaching tool.

SUMMARY AND CONCLUSION

In summary, it is apparent that:

- academic sorting practices and their selective determinants, teacher expectations, and race and socioeconomic status influence black students' scholastic success or failure;
- black and/or low socioeconomic status students are most often in the lowest tracks or ability groups;
- tracking and ability grouping has few benefits for high track or high ability grouped students, but major disadvantages for low tracked or low ability grouped students.

To ensure equity and excellence in the education of the black student, there must be a partnership between parents, teachers, administrators, and the black community. Unfortunately, this type of collaboration is often weak or nonexistent. The National Urban League affiliates, through their Education Initiatives, are forging these needed partnerships. Such alliances are particularly important because many black students reside in single parent households, (often with teenage mothers usually of low SES), or in two-parent households (usually of low SES) where parents must work both full- and part-time jobs in order for the family to survive.

Many black parents have themselves had negative experience with the school system. Some black parents are school dropouts. Therefore, there is a need for black community-based groups to monitor the school system and to assist black parents in assuming responsibility for the equity and excellence of their child's educational experience. Parents and community-based organizations, in partnership, must act as advocates for black students.

Several avenues exist for the partnership to reach these goals. For example, community-based committees can be set up to explore teacher expectations and ability grouping tracking practices and the role such practices play in student achievement within schools where black students are located. Committees can meet with school superintendents, principals, and teachers to assess teacher expectations and ability grouping/tracking policies of local school systems and individual schools. They must be cognizant of the fact that although policies are often in place, they may not be implemented by individual principals. A monitoring process should also be initiated to insure implementation of the recommendations.

The growing activism within the black community to deal with and confront educational problems is particularly timely and warranted. The National Urban League's Educational Initiative, the National Alliance of Black School Educators, the McKnight Centers of Excellence, the Children's Defense Fund, and other organizations are working to assist black students to overcome the many barriers toward excellence and equity in education. It will take a concerted effort of parents, community members, and groups such as the National Urban League and concerned educators working together to form a movement to change the system in order to ensure that our black children are sorted for success.

NOTES

1. Brookover, W.B., "Can We Make School Effective for Minority Students," *Journal of Negro Education* 54, no. 3 (1985) pp. 257-63; N. Raze, *Overview of Research on Ability Grouping* (ERIC Document Reproduction Service, No. ED.252-927, 1984).

2. Oakes, J., *Keeping Track How Schools Structure Inequality* (New Haven: Yale University Press, 1985).

3. Rowan, R. and Miracle, A.W., "System of Ability Grouping and the Stratification of Achievement in Elementary Schools," *Sociology of Education* 56 (1983), pp. 133-44.

4. Raze, *Overview*.

5. Resnick, D.P. and Resnick, L.B., "Standards Curriculum and Performance: A Historical and Comparative Perspective," *Educational Researcher* 14 (1985) pp. 5-21.

6. Brophy, J., "Research on the Self-fulfilling Prophecy and Teacher Expectations," *Journal of Educational Psychology* 75, no. 5 (1983), pp. 631-61; J. Dusek and G. Joseph, "The Basis of Teacher Expectancies: A Meta Analysis," *Journal of Educational Psychology* 75, no. 3 (1983), pp. 327-46.

7. Ibid.

8. Ibid.

9. McKenzie, F., "Education, Not Excuses," *Journal of Negro Education* 53, no. 2 (1984), pp. 97-105; J.L. White, *The Psychology of Blacks* (Englewood Cliffs, N.J.: Prentice-Hall, Inc., 1984).

10. Johnson, S.T. and Prom-Jackson, S., "The Memorable Teacher: Implications for Teacher Selection," *Journal of Negro Education* 55, no. 3 (1986), pp. 272-83.

11. Miller, D.T. and Turnbull, W., "Expectancies and Interpersonal Processes," *Annual Review Psychology* 237 (1986), pp. 233-56.

12. Clarke, K. "Education Stimulation of Racially Disadvantaged Children," in A.H. Passover (ed.), *Education in Depressed Areas* (New York: Teacher College, Columbia University, 1963).

13. Clarke, K. *Dark Ghetto: Dilemma of Social Power* (New York: Harper and Row, 1965); Harlem Youth Opportunities Unlimited, *Youth in the Ghetto.*

14. Rosenthal, R. and Jacobson, L., *Pygmalion in the Classroom: Teacher Expectations and Pupils Intellectual Development* (New York: Holt, Rinehart and Winston, Inc., 1968).

15. Rosenthal, R. and Rubin, D., "Interpersonal Expectancy Effect: The First 345 Studies," *Behavior Brain Science* 1, no. 3 (1978), pp. 377-415.

16. Brophy, "Research."

17. Rist, R., "Student Social Class and Teacher Expectations: The Self-fulfilling Prophecy in Ghetto Education," *Harvard Educational Review* 40, no. 3 (1970), pp. 411-51.

18. Dusek and Joseph, "Basis."

19. Ibid.

20. DeMeis, P. and Turner, R., "Effect of Student Race, Physical Attractiveness, and Dialect on Teacher Evaluation," *Contemporary Educational Psychology* 3 (1978) pp. 77-86.

21. Alexander, K., M. Cook, and McDill, E.L., "Curriculum Tracking and Educational Stratification: Some Further Evidence," *American Sociological Review* 43 (1978) pp. 47-66.

22. Ibid.

23. Eder, D., "Ability Grouping and Self-fulfilling Prophecy: A Macro Analysis of Teacher-Student Interaction," *Sociology of Education* 54 (1981), pp. 151-62.

24. Oakes, 1985, *Keeping Track*; J. Oakes, "Tracking in Mathematics and Science Education: A Structural Contribution to Unequal Schooling," in Lois Weiss (ed.), *Race, Class and Gender in U.S. Education* (Buffalo: State University of New York Press, 1987).

25. Brophy, "Research."

26. Resnick and Resnick, "Standards Curriculum."

27. Slavin, R.E., *Ability Grouping and Student Achievement in Elementary Schools: A Best-Evidence Synthesis* (Baltimore: Center for Research on Elementary and Middle Schools, 1986).

28. Rowan, R. and Miracle, A.W., "System of Grouping."

29. Alexander, Cook, and McDill, "Curriculum Tracking."; Bowles, S. and Gintes, H., *Schooling in Capitalist America* (New York: Basic Books, 1976); Dusek and Joseph, "Basis"; National Coalition of Advocates for Students, *Barriers to Excellence: Our Children at Risk* (Boston: author, 1985); Oakes, *Keeping Track* and "Tracking in Mathematics"; Raze, Overview; Resnick and Resnick, "Standards Curriculum"; Rist, Student Social Class.

30. Epstein, J.L., "After the Bus Arrives: Resegregation in Desegregated Schools," *Journal of Social Issues* 4, no. 3 (1985) pp. 23-43.

31. College Entrance Examination Board, *Equality and Excellence: The Educational State of Black Americans* (New York: College Board Publications, 1985).

32. Ibid.

33. Eckstrom, R.B. and Lee, V.E., *Student Access to Guidance Counseling in High School* (Princeton, N.J.: Educational Testing Service, 1986).

34. U.S. Department of Education, Office of Civil Rights, *1976 Elementary and Secondary School Survey* (1976); U.S. Department of Education, Office of Civil Rights, *1978 Elementary and Secondary School Survey* (1978); U.S. Department of Education, Office of Civil Rights, *1980 Elementary and Secondary School Survey* (1982); U.S. Department of Education, Office of Civil Rights, *1984 Elementary and Secondary School Survey* (1986).

35. Ibid.

36. Moody, Sr., C.D., "Equity and Excellence: An Educational Imperative, in Williams, J.D. (ed.), *The State of Black America, 1986* (New York: National Urban League Inc., 1986) pp. 23-42; F. Jones-Wilson, "The State of Urban Education," in Williams, J.D. (ed.), *The State of Black America, 1984* (New York, National Urban League Inc., 1984) pp. 95-118; National Education Association, *The Role of Principals in Effective Schools, Number 4* (Washington, D.C.: author, 1986).

37. Chunn, E., *Success in Reading and Writing Pilot Project Final Evaluation Report* (Washington, D.C.: District of Columbia Public Schools, Division of Research and Evaluation, 1982, 1983, 1984).

11

The Eroding Status of Blacks in Higher Education: An Issue of Financial Aid

Mary Carter-Williams

Educational equity remains the most important unfinished business of American higher education. Although blacks made impressive progress in higher education during the 1960s and 70s, they have sustained major losses throughout the 1980s at all levels, exclusive of such professional programs as medicine, dentistry, and law (primarily because of the accelerated enrollment of black women). The historically black colleges (HBCs), whose students rely disproportionately on financial aid, have been particularly vulnerable.

The growing depression in black higher education does not augur well for the nation's future. Demographic trends suggest that larger numbers of blacks and other minorities will be needed in future years to meet the national demand for new skilled workers, talent in the sciences and information technology, and military officers. Moreover, the nation is just beginning to reap the benefits of the billions of federal dollars that were invested in elementary and secondary school minorities during the 1960s. In 1982, the eighteen-year decline in Scholastic Aptitude Test (SAT) scores came to a halt, primarily because of an improvement in the test performance of blacks.[1] Between 1970 and 1980, the most impressive gains in reading on the National Assessment of Educational Progress (NAEP) test were made by nine, thirteen, and seventeen-year-old blacks in the Southeast.[2]

This article will discuss the dilemmas of educational access and choice faced by blacks and the HBCs from the early 1970s to the present time from the perspective of student financial aid. This article is targeted toward black parents and students, higher education leaders and practitioners; public policymakers at local, state, and federal levels, and all citizens interested in preserving a hard-won, open system of higher education.

EARLY 1970s TO 80s SUCCESSES: A DREAM BEING REALIZED

In a quantifiable sense, between the early 1970s and the early 1980s, blacks advanced toward the center of American life. The number of employed black engineers and

TABLE 1
Persons 25 Years Old and Over Completing Four or More Years of College
(Percent)

Year/Sex	All Races	Black	White
1983			
Male	23.0	10.0	24.0
Female	15.1	9.2	15.4
1976			
Male	18.6	6.3	19.6
Female	11.3	6.8	11.6
1972			
Male	15.1	5.5	16.2
Female	9.1	4.8	9.4
1970			
Male	14.1	4.6	15.0
Female	8.2	4.4	8.6
1973			
Male	16.0	5.9	16.8
Female	9.6	6.0	9.9

Sources: U.S. Department of Commerce, Bureau of the Census, "Population Profile of the U.S.: 1976," Series p. 20, No. 307, pp. 20-21; Series p. 20, No. 243, pp. 18-30; "Educational Attainment," Series p. 20, No. 356, p. 60, and unpublished data.

school administrators increased by more than 100%, while the number of employed black bank officers/financial managers and lawyers/judges spiraled upward by more than 200%.[3] In current dollars, the median family income of blacks almost doubled,[4] while median weekly earnings more than doubled. By 1982, the proportion of black households with incomes under $10,000 had declined from roughly two-fifths of total black households to a little more than a third. The proportion of black households with incomes of $35,000 and above passed the 10% mark.[5] By the end of the decade, there were 5,500 black elected officials, about 282 of these people were mayors and congresspersons.

The accelerated increase in the number of college-educated blacks was a major contributor to the improvement in living conditions. Between 1973 and 1983, the proportion of blacks with 4 or more years of college education increased from nearly 12% to 19.2% (see Table 1). In 1983, the labor force participation rate of blacks with 4 or more years of college was 92%, compared to about 85% for those with 1 to 3 years of college, and less than 60% for those with less than 4 years of high school. Blacks with college training were significantly more likely to hold executive or professional positions than were those who did not attend institutions of higher education. The unemployment rate of college-educated blacks was only about 41% of that for those who had less than 4 years of high school.

The federal student financial aid system was pivotal to making professional advancement possible for blacks. In 1983, about 1.1 million (8.9%) of students enrolled in higher education were black. Half of all students (6.7 million) were recipients of aid especially targeted toward minority and low-income students. Such forms of aid included Pell grants, supplementary educational opportunity grants, college-work study, national

TABLE 2
Recipients Of Major Federal Student Assistance Programs, FY 1973–83

| Fiscal Year | Pell | TYPE OF LOAN | | | | | Total Recipients |
		Supplementary Educational Opportunity	State Student Incentive	College Work-Study	National Direct Student	Guaranteed Student Loan	
1973	176	331	—	556	655	1,030	2,748
1974	567	395	813	570	680	938	3,963
1975	1,217	390	902	570	670	991	4,760
1976	1,944	449	1,104	697	765	1,298	6,257
1977	2,011	499	1,161	845	715	973	6,367
1978	1,893	510	1,218	852	809	1,085	6,367
1979	2,538	595	1,278	923	953	1,510	7,797
1980	2,538	717	1,242	819	812	2,314	8,442
1981	2,709	659	1,210	739	803	2,746	8,866
1982	2,601	636	1,253	721	810	2,939	8,960
1983	2,781	648	1,524	885	860	3,285	9,983

Source: U.S. Department of Education, Office of Planning, Budget and Evaluation, and Office of Student Financial Assistance Fiscal Years 1982, 1983, and 1984, Unpublished data: U.S. Department of Education, Office of Planning, Budget and Evaluation, *Annual Evaluation Report*, Fiscal Year 1983, pp. 501–06.

direct student loans, and state student incentive grants[6] (see Table 2). In 1973, about 417,000 fewer blacks were enrolled in U.S. colleges and universities than in 1983, but their proportional representation in the total student population remained nearly the same (8.4%). Only 2 of 10 of all higher education students received aid other than guaranteed student loans, and 1 of 10 was a guaranteed student loan recipient.

With regard to college entry rates, in 1973, when Pell grants were extended to all eligible freshmen, about a third of all black high school graduates went to college. In comparison, nearly half of all students and half of all white students attended college.[7] In 1977, when Pell grants were made available to all eligible undergraduates, about the same proportion of black high school graduates entered college as the proportion of both the total student population and white students.

Blacks gained impressively at all levels of higher education during this period. Between 1972 and 1982 black undergraduate enrollment expanded by 458,000 and total minority enrollment was up by 1.2 million (see Table 3). Black graduate enrollment increased the most, expanding by 257%, (compared to a 99% increase at the undergraduate level), with a 44.4% increase in medicine, law, and other professional programs. Total minority participation in professional programs grew by 164.2%, compared to increases of 52.7% for whites and 105% for students of all races. Black participation in medical education increased by 27.6%, compared to 32.7% for all students.

Shifts in the degree programs chosen by blacks reflected national trends. Education continued to attract large numbers of blacks, but business and management took over first place, and public affairs and services became the second most popular major. Black enrollment in MBA, doctoral education, and law programs shot upward, reflecting the

TABLE 3
Enrollment in Institutions of Higher Education, by Race, 1972 and 1982

Ethnic/ Racial Group	1972								1982								Percentage Change 1972-1982			
	All Students		Under-graduate		Graduate		First Professional		All Students		Under-graduate		Graduate		First Professional		All Students	Under-graduate	Graduate	First Professional
	No.	%	No.	%	No.	%	No.	%	No.	%	No.	%	No.	%	No.	%				
Native American	34	0.6	32	0.6	2	0.5	.4	0.2	88	0.7	72	0.7	4	0.4	.9	0.3	158.8	125.0	100.0	125.0
Asian	68	1.1	56	1.0	8	2.0	2	1.1	351	2.8	272	2.8	26	2.4	8	2.9	416.2	386.0	250.0	300.0
Black	495	8.1	465	8.4	21	5.2	9	5.0	1,101	8.9	923	9.5	55	5.0	13	4.6	122.4	98.5	257.0	44.4
Hispanic	139	2.3	131	2.4	6	1.5	3	1.7	519	4.2	570	5.6	30	2.7	9	3.2	273.4	335.0	400.0	200.0
Total Minority	736	12.0	685	12.4	37	9.1	14	7.8	2,059	16.6	1,837	18.9	115	10.5	31	11.1	179.8	168.1	275.6	164.2
Percent Black of Total Minority	—	67.3	—	67.8	—	56.8	—	64.3	—	53.5	—	50.3	—	47.8	—	41.9	—	—	—	—
Nonresident Alien	NA	NA	NA	NA	NA	NA	NA	NA	331	2.7	202	2.1	99	9.0	3	1.1	NA	NA	NA	NA
White	5,392	88.0	4,858	87.7	369	90.8	165	92.2	9,997	80.7	7,694	79.1	881	80.5	246	87.9	85.4	58.4	138.7	52.7
Total	6,129	100	5,542	100	406	100	179	100	12,388	100	9,733	100	1,095	100	280	100	102.1	75.6	169.7	105.0

Source: U.S. Department of Education, National Center For Education Statistics, *Condition of Education: 1982* (Washington, D.C.: GPO, 1982), p. 134; NCES Racial Ethnic Enrollment Data From Institutions of Higher Education: Fall 1972 (Washington, D.C.: GPO, 1972), p. 76; NCES, Unpublished data, 1984.

growth in the number of blacks employed as banking/financial officials, lawyers, and school administrators.

The Role of the Historically Black Colleges

During most of the decade 1973-1983, the historically black college sector, composed primarily of degree-granting four-year institutions, strengthened its role as the nation's major producer of black professionals. As a product of the segregationalist policies and practices of the Old South, this small but diverse[8] group of colleges had been plagued by grave financial uncertainties since its inception. Hence, the expansion of the federal role in financing higher education during the 1970s was fundamentally important in expanding HBC enrollments: because of disproportionately low family income, 90% of the students attending this group of institutions relied on student financial assistance. In the early 1970s, more than 43.8% of all federal aid dollars received by the historically black colleges was in the form of student aid, compared to 25.6% nationally.[9] Toward the end of the decade, federal student aid dollars comprised 53.5% of such aid received by these institutions, in contrast to 36% for all institutions.

In 1983, the total enrollment of HBCs stood at 221,962, representing a 17.9% growth, yet still lagging behind the increase in total higher education enrollment at 25.8%.[10] The enrollments of the public black colleges, especially their 4-year enrollments, climbed steadily, growing more than twice as fast as private black college enrollments. Between 1973 and 1982, the first-time freshmen enrollments of the HBCs increased by 23.5%, or more than twice as rapidly as the number of entering students nationally (11.4%). Over the decade, the graduate and professional enrollments of these institutions grew phenomenally.

Between 1973 and 1976, the growth in the number and diversity of the degrees conferred by the historically black colleges mirrored the improvements that had occurred in their enrollments and programming.[11] These institutions produced increasingly more graduates at the baccalaureate and master's degree levels, and had significantly larger numbers of students majoring in business and management, public affairs, and engineering.[12] At the baccalaureate level, education remained an important, but significantly less popular discipline compared to its standing during most of the years of the existence of these colleges.

Losses: A Dream Deferred

When the higher education gains made by blacks are weighed against selected population parameters and the higher education gains of whites, an erosion in progress of blacks is clearly visible. Between 1973 and 1983, the number of blacks ages 18 to 24 (the typical age range for undergraduate students) increased by 32%, compared to an increase of 11% for whites (see Figure 1). The number of blacks ages 25 to 34, the typical age range for graduate and professional students, grew by 63%, compared to 36% for

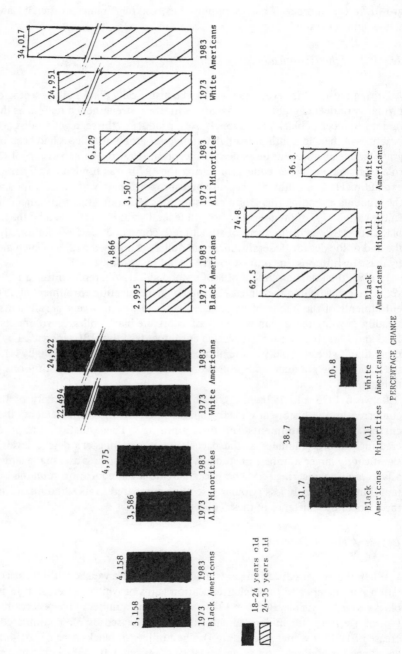

FIGURE 1

Distribution of Selected College-Age Chohorts by Race, 1973 and 1983

Source: U.S. Department of Commerce, Bureau of the Census, Current Population Report, Series P-25.

TABLE 4
Change in Higher Education Enrollment and Degrees Conferred to White Females

Subject/Level Enrollment	1976 Number	1976 % Change 1974-80	1976 Number	1976 % Change 1976-80	1978 Number	1978 % Change 1978-80	1980 Number	1980 % Change 1980-82	1982 Number
Total	3,652	18.9	3,715	16.9	4,580	− 5.2	4,344	3.2	4,483
Total Graduate	420	6.1	411	8.5	423	5.4	446	− 2.0	437
Total First Professional	42	61.9	48	41.7	56	21.4	68	10.3	75
Law	16	125.0	27	33.3	32	12.5	36	− 11.1	32
Medicine	8	87.5	11	36.4	13	15.4	15	6.6	16

Degrees Conferred	1975-76	1980-81	Percentage Change
Total	505,276	552,114	9.3
Total Graduate	129,846	134,251	3.4
Total First Professional	8,513	16,910	98.6
Law	5,521	10.545	91.0
Medicine	1,830	3,251	77.7

Source: NCES Unpublished HEGIS 1982 data and OCR, Racial/Ethnic and Sex Enrollment, and Earned Degrees Conferred in Institutions of Higher Education.

whites. The number of recent black high school graduates continued to rise rapidly, as that of whites began to taper off sharply.

Nonetheless, the college-going rate of recent black high school graduates reached a high of 51% in 1974 and, after a decline, rose to 50% in 1977. By 1983, blacks' rate of entry was down to 39%, compared to 55% for whites and 53% for students of all ages. The gap between the proportion of college-educated blacks and whites ages 25 and older widened by 5.4 percentage points (from 14.8% to 20.2%).

The erosion in the college-going and college-enrollment rates of blacks affected their participation at all levels of higher education. Black undergraduate education peaked at 10.2% in 1976, and by the end of the decade had fallen to 9.5%—or significantly below their 12% representation in the 18 to 24 age cohort. Black representation in graduate education and first-professional education decreased to 5% (from 5.2%) and 4.6% (from 5.0%) respectively—although blacks represented 10.5% of the 25 to 34 age cohort. The representation of blacks in medical education dropped to 5.8%, after peaking at 6.3% in 1974. Total minority participation in professional and graduate education improved because of the continued growth in Hispanic and Asian enrollments. The overall growth in professional enrollments was due to the rapidly-rising participation of white women (see Table 4).

Between 1976 and 1983—a period of accelerated emphasis on the role of expert knowledge in revitalizing and expanding the national economy—the overall production of black doctorates fell by 15.4%, compared to 10.6% for whites and 10.7% for all races.[13] This decline was primarily due to a sharp drop in the number of blacks majoring in education at the master's and baccalaureate levels. Between 1976 and 1981 alone, the number of blacks majoring in education at the bachelor's and master's levels fell by 33.2% and 30.5% respectively, compared to losses of 24.5% and 22.1% nationally.[14] In

1982-83, nearly 25% of all black undergraduate degrees were in business and management and almost 20% were in public affairs.[15] Only 10.2% were in education, which until 1976 was still the most popular undergraduate major among blacks. At the master's level, education still remained the most popular major among blacks, although the number of blacks opting for it had dropped sharply.

Over the decade, the rapid decline in the participation of black males in higher education was one of the most ominous signs of retrenchment for blacks.[16] Traditionally, black women have outnumbered black men in higher education, particularly at the post-baccalaureate level. However, the number of black males in higher education in 1983 was about the same as it was in 1973, despite a 41% increase in the number of black males ages 18 to 24.[17] Black male enrollment peaked in 1977 and tended to decline thereafter.[18] By the end of the decade, the number of black women in higher education had doubled, compared to a 35% increase in the number of black women ages 18 to 24.

The distribution of degrees granted to blacks by sex differed significantly from national trends and selected ethnic/racial trends in most instances. In 1982-83, when 60.7% of black recipients of baccalaureate degrees were women, only about half of all such degree recipients nationally were women.[19] At the master's level, the predominance of women was greater: 63.8% of the black degree recipients were women, compared to a little more than half, nationally. In professional programs such as medicine and law, men predominated in all cases. However, women comprised 39.5% of black earned degrees, compared to 26.9% nationally. Whereas a little more than half of the black doctorates were granted to women, the reverse was true for all students and all other minority groups exclusive of Native Americans.

Similar to black higher education in general, most of the enrollment growth of the historically black college sector occurred in the early years of the decade. The steady growth in the numbers of students entering HBCs ended by the middle of the decade. For example, between 1973 and 1975, these institutions experienced a 38.4% growth rate for entering students, compared to a 13.2% increase of entering students nationally. Throughout the remainder of the decade, the first-time freshmen enrollments of HBCs were very volatile, reflecting year-to-year changes in federal student financial aid policies and declining economic conditions. Between 1980 and 1982, first-time freshmen enrollments declined by 12%. By the fall of 1985, the total enrollment of these institutions was down to 213,776 (see Table 5).

After accelerating from the middle 1960s to the early 1970s, graduate enrollments peaked in 1975 at the public black colleges, and in 1978 at private black colleges.[20] Between 1976 and 1980, total graduate enrollment at these institutions decreased by 14.3% (compared to a 2.3% increase nationally) due to substantial losses sustained by the public black colleges. By 1982, the graduate enrollment of both public and private black colleges was alarmingly lower than previous years.

By the early 1980s, the extraordinary degree production capability of the historically black colleges had been sorely tested. With the exception of professional degrees, the number of degrees conferred by these institutions reached a high in the mid- to late 70s.

TABLE 5
Selected Statistics, Traditionally Black Institutions of Higher Education[1]

		Traditionally Black Institutions			
	Total	Public		Private	
		4-year	2-year	4-year	2-year
Number of institutions, fall 1985	99	38	5	49	7
Enrollment, fall 1985					
Total enrollment	213,776	146,111	6,050	60,292	1,323
Men	94,998	65,617	2,370	26,387	624
Women	118,778	80,494	3,680	33,905	699
Full-time enrollment	165,670	105,485	4,662	54,270	1,253
Men	75,429	49,440	1,714	23,676	599
Women	90,241	56,045	2,948	30,594	654
Part-time enrollment	48,106	40,626	1,388	6,022	70
Men	19,569	16,177	656	2,711	25
Women	28,537	24,449	732	3,311	45
Earned degrees conferred, 1983-84[2]					
Associate	1,849	1,101	399	120	229
Men	630	410	100	29	91
Women	1,219	691	299	91	138
Bachelor's	21,229	13,789	—	7,433	7
Men	9,344	6,283	—	3,054	7
Women	11,885	7,506	—	4,379	0
Master's	4,090	3,194	—	896	—
Men	1,780	1,400	—	380	—
Women	2,310	1,794	—	516	—
Doctor's	118	22	—	96	—
Men	74	11	—	63	—
Women	44	11	—	33	—
First professional	913	239	—	674	—
Men	565	166	—	399	—
Women	348	73	—	275	—
Financial statistics, fiscal year 1984					
(in $000)[2]					
Current-fund revenues	$1,757,100	$937,526	$25,305	$781,676	$12,594
Tuition and fees	317,856	124,218	3,216	187,641	2,780
Federal government[3]	398,736	133,759	5,144	256,299	3,534
State governments[3]	477,976	453,830	12,597	11,467	83
Local governments[3]	64,146	62,495	1,381	271	0
Private gifts, grants, and contracts ...	90,764	8,081	664	78,794	3,225
Endowment income	20,648	1,259	0	19,201	187
Sales and services	343,838	135,287	1,914	204,125	2,512
Other sources	43,136	18,596	390	23,878	272
Current-fund expenditures	1,723,305	915,461	27,082	769,218	11,544
Educational and general expenditures	1,382,512	793,021	25,558	554,524	9,410
Auxiliary enterprises	206,056	122,440	1,524	79,957	2,135
Hospitals	134,736	0	0	134,736	0
Endowment (market value)	278,507	14,886	—	263,387	235
Buildings (replacement value)	4,183,929	2,748,302	66,197	1,343,500	25,931

Sources: U.S. Department of Education, Center for Education Statistics, "Fall Enrollment in Higher Education, 1985," "Earned Degrees Conferred, 1983-84," and "Financial Statistics of Institutions of Higher Education, Fiscal Year 1984" Surveys (Sept. 1986).

Notes: [1]Includes institutions established prior to 1954 for the education of black students (mainly in southern and border states.
  [2]Includes degree and finance data for Lomax-Hannon Junior College but excludes enrollment data.
  [3]Includes appropriations, grants, and contracts.
  —Data not reported or not applicable.
  —Because of rounding, details may not add to totals.

By 1982, the HBCs produced fewer baccalaureate and master's degrees than during the peak year for each level, due to a decline in the number of degrees granted in education.

CONTRIBUTING FACTORS: WHY THE EROSION?

The declining status of blacks in higher education after 1976 was part and parcel of the developing retrenchment in equal opportunity as a national objective. This retrenchment was accelerated during the early 1980s by the policies of the Reagan administration. The administration drastically reduced the funding level of some Title IV and special-purpose programs, while threatening to eliminate others. By the 1983–84 school year, loans accounted for nearly half of all aid awarded to stuents, resulting in an alarming increase in student indebtedness. Support for the original beneficiaries of the system dissipated as major battles were publicly fought about the rising cost of student financial aid, the role of loans versus grants, and other related issues.

Organization and Administration of Student Aid

Between the fiscal years of 1973 and 1983, federal student financial aid policies evolved into a massive delivery system. This system was primarily designed to meet the special circumstances of underserviced populations, while also addressing the difficulties experienced by middle-income students in paying for college costs. Despite the success of the system in reaching its intended beneficiaries during most years, serious flaws were evident.

One problem was the categorical status of the Pell grants that form the centerpiece of equal opportunity in higher education. Although federal support of these grants went up greatly between 1973 and 1983, the funding level was governed by appropriations rather than by entitlement, as intended by the 1972 Education Amendments. Proportionately, the number of recipients averaged about 20% less than the number of eligible recipients. However, before 1980, less than half a million applicants were turned away annually; after 1980, the number of eligible applicants denied Pell grants averaged 637,000 annually (see Table 6).

These statistics do not take into account the thousands of college aspirants who were discouraged from applying for Pell grants because of the appropriations process. At times, highly-charged federal debates on funding levels and rules and regulations had bottlenecked the Pell grant delivery system. Neither parents and students nor the participating institutions knew what to expect.

The complexity of the federal student aid system posed another major challenge. Generally, any U.S. citizen or eligible non-citizen qualified for student financial assistance if he or she was enrolled in school at least half-time, demonstrated financial need, made satisfactory academic progess, and complied with the requirements of the draft (males) loan repayment. However, unique rules existed for each of the six major programs. For example, students' eligibility for Pell grants was affected by the type of institution or program in which they were enrolled, their dependent status, and educa-

TABLE 6
Trends In Selected Characteristics, Pell Grant Program 1973-83

Fiscal Year	Number of Applications	Number of Valid Applications	Percent Valid Application	Number of Eligible Applicants	Number of Recipients	Percent of Recipients' Valid Applications
1973	513	482	93.9	268	176	65.7
1974	1,305	1,114	85.3	682	567	83.1
1975	2,339	2,179	93.1	1,455	1,217	83.6
1976	3,590	3,409	94.9	2,258	1,994	86.1
1977	3,844	3,622	94.2	2,390	2,011	84.1
1978	3,885	3,401	87.5	2,229	1,893	84.9
1979	4,188	3,868	92.3	3,030	2,538	83.8
1980	4,813	4,512	93.7	3,367	2,538	75.4
1981	4,883	4,615	94.5	3,337	2,709	81.2
1982	5,119	4,686	91.5	3,327	2,601	78.2
1983	5,454	4,920	81.0	3,337*	2,781*	83.3*

*Estimated
Source: U.S. Department of Education, Office of Planning and Budget and Evaluation, Unpublished Fiscal Year 1982 Report; U.S. Department of Education, Office of Student Financial Assistance; Unpublished Fiscal Year 1982 Report; U.S. Department of Education, Office of Planning, Budget and Evaluation, *Annual Evaluation Report, Fiscal Year 1983* (Washington, D.C.:, 1984).

tion costs. Moreover, students could use any of five different forms to apply for grants, awards could be made either directly to institutions or to students, and students were required to reapply every year.

Information dissemination was also a problem. Using a scale of 0 to 10, one study found that minority student awareness of the purposes and rules govering the major student financial aid programs ranged from 0 to 4. In the 1978 academic year, 70% of approximately 373,000 black students reported that they received no high school counseling on student financial aid. For Hispanic and Native American students, 70% and 78% respectively, reported that they did not receive student aid counseling in high school, compared to 74% of all undergraduates.

Although these data are incomplete, undergraduates in the lowest income group (less than $6,000) tended to report the least likelihood of receiving high school counseling. Students having family incomes in the $12,000–$17,999 and $18,000–$24,000 ranges reported the highest probability of access to aid information. Similarly, the 1980 study High School and Beyond[21] found that the higher the students' income levels, the more likely they were to be informed about student financial assistance.

Several factors affected the accessibility to information of black and other minority students. These factors included limited governmental support for information dissemination, the concentration of minority students and understaffing of high schools in the central cities, and the first-generation status of the overwhelming majority of black college aspirants.

Rising Cost of Student Financial Aid

Prior to the passage of the Middle Income Student Assistance Act, increases in total federal appropriations reflected the rapid extension of Pell grants to all eligible and

TABLE 7
Growth in Total Student Aid Compared to Growth in Loan Programs, 1973–83

Fiscal Year	Total Student Aid		Guaranteed Student Loans		National Direct Student Loans	
	Current	Constant*	Current	Constant*	Current	Constant*
1973	1,186	2,608	291	640	293	644
1974	1,676	3,384	398	804	298	602
1975	2,443	4,437	594	1,079	329	598
1976	3,137	5,323	807	1,369	331	562
1977	3,283	5,264	357	572	323	581
1978	3,734	5,610	479	720	326	490
1979	4,672	6,419	945	1,298	329	452
1980	5,310	6,435	1,609	1,950	286	347
1981	6,383	6,936	2,581	2,805	201	218
1982	6,642	—	3,073	—	193	—
1983	6,707	6,422	3,090	2,959	193	185

Note: *measured in 1982 dollars.
Source: Table 15, ISEP Staff Calculations.

potentially-qualified undergraduates who desired higher education or training of some kind after school. Between fiscal years 1978 and 1981, the accelerated rise in aid dollars reflected the extension of Pell grants to middle-income students with incomes above $15,000, the loosening of eligibility requirements for independent students, and the uncapping of guaranteed student loans. During this period, the total federal appropriations of the U.S. Department of Education for student aid programs grew by $3 billion (see Table 7). The total aid awarded to students by the U.S. Department of Education escalated from approximately $6 billion to $12.1 billion. In fiscal year 1981, the total aid available to students, including nondirect federal outlays, peaked at $16 billion.[22]

The distribution of participation in the Pell grant and campus-based programs was immediately affected. Between academic years 1978 and 1979, although the total number of Pell grant participants escalated sharply, the number of dependent recipients with family income under $6,000–$12,000 decreased by 5%, and those in the above-$12,000 category increased by 154%.[23, 24] Between fiscal years 1979 and 1981, the state student incentive grant, college work-study, and national direct student loan programs sustained a collective loss of 402,000 students (see Table 2). During this two-year period, the number of participants in the guaranteed student loan program grew by 1.4 million. In fact, 54.8% of the gain in recipients in this program during the 1973-1983 decade occurred between fiscal years 1979 and 1981.

The Omnibus Budget Reconciliation Act of August 1981 radically altered federal spending patterns for student aid as well. In addition to recapping guaranteed student loans to control costs, the bill cut back student aid programs targeted for underserviced populations (e.g., veterans education benefits and social security education benefits).

Inflationary pressures and unemployment exacerbated the effects of redirections in federal spending on the ability of black and poor families to finance schooling. In real terms, between 1973 and 1983, federal support of need-based aid, exclusive of guaran-

TABLE 8
Total Appropriations, Need-Based Student Financial Aid Programs, 1973-83
(In millions)

Year	Current Dollars	Constant Dollars*	Percentage Change
1973	685	1,506	—
1974	1,273	2,570	70.0
1975	1,849	3,359	30.7
1976	2,330	3,953	17.7
1977	2,926	4,692	18.7
1978	3,255	4,890	4.3
1979	3,727	5,120	4.7
1980	3,016	3,655	− 28.6
1981	3,802	4,131	13.0
1982	3,569	3,569	13.6
1983	3,617	3,463	3.0

Note: *measured in 1982 dollars. Guaranteed students loans are excluded.

Source: Table 4. Inflation-adjusted dollars based on Consumer Price Indices in D. Kent Halstead, *Inflation Measures for Schools and College* (Washington, D.C.: U.S. GPO, Sept. 1983), p. 15.

teed student loans, increased only by 130% (see Table 8). At the same time, real increases in student charges at four-year private colleges stymied the ability of black students to enroll in the more prestigious colleges and universities.

Nonetheless, poor and middle-income families and students had historically borne the major responsibility for financing college costs. In academic year 1983, at both public and private schools, dependent federal aid recipients and their parents contributed more than two-fifths of college costs. In fall 1982, full-time financial aid recipients from families with incomes under $15,000 and enrolled by institutions with freshman expenses of under $3,000 financed more than a fifth of college costs. Those enrolled by institutions with expenses ranging from $3,000 to $4,499 provided nearly 25% of college costs.

In summary, between fiscal years 1973 and 1977, the large increases in student aid significantly outpaced inflation and compensated for the disproportionately low black family incomes. Because of losses in purchasing power and actual dollars, for most of the years after 1978 the income provided by need-based student assistance programs was insufficient to counteract rapidly-rising student charges and a paralysis of black family incomes.

Grants

The Middle Income Student Assistance Act accelerated the dismantlement of grants as the linchpin of undergraduate access. In academic year 1979, grant aid as a proportion of total appropriations dropped to 61% from 66.8% in academic year 1978 and 67.4% the previous year (see Table 9). Four-year public and private colleges registered dramatic decreases in the proportion of entering freshmen reporting supplementary educational opportunity grants and state grants as sources of funds. At the predomi-

TABLE 9
Grant and Loan/Work Study Appropriations as a Percent of Total Student Aid Appropriations

Year	Total Student Aid		Grants		Loan/Work Study	
	Number	Percent	Number	Percent	Number	Percent
1973	1,186	100	332	28.0	854	72.0
1974	1,676	100	705	42.3	966	57.8
1975	2,443	100	1,100	45.0	1,343	55.0
1976	3,132	100	1,609	51.3	1,528	48.7
1977	3,283	100	2,213	67.4	1,070	32.6
1978	3,734	100	2,494	66.8	1,240	33.2
1979	4,672	100	2,848	61.0	1,824	39.0
1980	4,625	100	2,165	46.8	2,460	53.2
1981	6,383	100	3,051	47.8	3,332	52.2
1982	6,642	100	2,848	42.9	3,794	57.1
1983	6,707	100	2,834	42.3	3,873	57.7
1984	6,242	100	3,251	52.1	2,991	47.9
1985	7,926	100	4,064	51.3	3,862	48.7

Source: U.S. Department of Education, Office of Planning, Budget, and Evaluation, vol. II of *Annual Evaluation Report: FY 1981*, (Washington, D.C.: U.S. GPO, 1981), pp. 357, 366, 374, 384, 391, and 396.

nantly black colleges, the decline in grant support was disproportionately worse, especially in the case of Pell and supplementary educational opportunity grants. In 1977, when the Pell grant program was fully implemented, grants peaked at 70% of total federal appropriations for student aid.

Throughout the decade, grants played a small role in financing postbaccalaureate education. The Graduate and Professional Opportunity Fellowships and the Council on Legal Education Opportunity were the only nonrepayable efforts of the U.S. Department of Education targeted to blacks, other minorities, women, and the economically disadvantaged. However, federal appropriations for these programs never exceeded $11 million, regardless of the authorization levels (see Table 10). Additionally, the $4,500 and $1,100 stipends offered by each program (plus $3,900 for the participating institutions) remained the same. Meanwhile, the family income of black graduate students, which averaged about $10,000, eroded disproportionately. Before 1980, graduate tuition charges increased about 10% annually; thereafter, such charges rose about 11% to 13% annually.

Loans

The 1972 Education Amendment established loans as the financing option of last resort for blacks, other needy students, and middle-income students otherwise unable to obtain the benefits of an undergraduate education. The Middle Income Student Assistance Act reversed this principle. In fiscal year 1983, guaranteed student loans made up nearly half of total appropriations, as opposed to about 25% in fiscal year 1973 (see Table 11). In the fall of 1981, loans contributed 17% of the educational costs incurred by entering full-time freshmen, compared to 9.1% in the fall of 1978; such loans increased by 138.9% in dollars (see Table 12). During this period, the loan share for

TABLE 10
Appropriations, Selected Financial Aid Programs, 1973-85
(in millions)

Programs	1973	1974	1975	1976	1977	1978	1979	1980	1981	1982	1983	1984	1985
TRIO	70.3	70.3	70.3	70.3	85.0	—	140.0	145.5	156.5	150.1	154.7	164.7	174.9
Talent Search	6.0	6.0	6.0	6.0	8.9	—	—	15.3	17.1	16.4	17.5	[1]	[1]
Upward Bound	38.3	38.3	38.3	38.3	41.5	—	—	62.5	66.5	63.8	68.3	71.0	[1]
Equal Opportunity Centers	—	3.0	3.0	3.0	4.0	5.0	—	7.7	8.0	7.6	7.7	[1]	[1]
Special Services for the Disadvantaged	23.0	23.0	23.0	23.0	30.6	—	—	60.0	63.9	61.3	69.0	[1]	[1]
Title IX	—	—	—	—	—	—	19.5	22.3	16.0	12.3	13.5	15.5	17.2
GPOP	—	—	—	—	—	—	8.0	8.8	10.0	8.6	10.0	11.0	11.7
Public Service Grants and Fellowships	—	—	4.0	4.0	4.0	4.0	4.0	4.0	2.0	1.9	1.9	2.5	2.5
Mining Fellowship	—	—	1.5	3.0	4.5	4.5	4.5	4.5	[2]	—	—	—	—
CLEO	0	.75	.75	.75	.75	1.0	1.0	1.0	1.0	.96	1.0	1.0	1.5
LSCE	—	—	—	—	—	—	2.0	4.0	3.0	.96	.60	1.0	1.5

Notes: [1]Included in total TRIO figure.
[2]Program unfunded after 1981.

Source: *Higher Education Daily*, July 24, 1979, Aug. 27, 1980, Oct. 25, 1982, Feb. 3, 1983, and Oct. 22, 1984; U.S. Department of Health, Education and Welfare, Office of Planning, Budgeting, and Evaluation, *Annual Evaluation Report on Programs Administered by the U.S. Office of Education: FY 1977* (Washington, GPO, 1977).

freshmen with family incomes of less than $9,999 and $10,000–$14,999 increased by 82% and 95%, respectively.

This principle of last resort did not negate the substantial flexibility offered by low-cost national direct student loans for financing black and needy students at all levels of the higher education system. However, over the decade the federal capital contributions for direct loans plummeted. Between fiscal years 1973 and 1983, in inflation-adjusted dollars, direct loans decreased by 71.3%. At the postbaccalaureate level, losses in direct loan income were compounded by major cutbacks in college work-study and programs administered by the U.S. Department of Health and Human Services (e.g., National Health Services Corps Scholarships and Exceptional Financial Need Scholarships). At the undergraduate level, this erosion in direct loans was discernible in the shifting distribution of the source of support for full-time freshmen. Between 1978 and 1981, direct loans as a proportion of all aid for full-time, first-time freshmen with family incomes of less than $9,999 decreased from 13.2% to 10.3%. This rate continued downward until the fall of 1983, when direct loans as a proportion of all aid went up for all income groups.

THE EARLY 1980s AND BEYOND

From the early to mid-1980s, the eroding presence of blacks in higher education reached crisis proportions. In 1982, blacks represented 8.9% of total enrollment (1.1

TABLE 11
Loans As a Percentage of Total Student Financial Aid, 1973–83

Fiscal Year	Total Student Aid Amount	Total Student Aid Percent	Total Loans Amount	Total Loans Percent	Guaranteed Student Loans Amount	Guaranteed Student Loans Percent	National Direct Student Loans Amount	National Direct Student Loans Percent
1973	1,186	100	584	49.2	291	24.5	293	24.7
1974	1,676	100	696	41.5	398	23.7	298	17.8
1975	2,443	100	923	37.8	594	24.3	329	13.5
1976	3,137	100	1,138	36.3	807	25.7	331	10.6
1977	3,283	100	680	20.7	357	10.9	323	9.8
1978	3,734	100	805	21.6	479	12.8	326	8.7
1979	4,672	100	1,274	27.3	945	20.2	329	7.0
1980	5,310	100	1,895	35.7	1,609	30.2	286	5.4
1981	6,303	100	2,782	43.6	2,581	40.4	201	3.1
1982	6,642	100	3,266	49.2	3,073	46.3	193	2.9
1983	6,709	100	3,283	48.9	3,090	46.1	193	2.9

Source: Table 7; ISEP Staff Calculations.

TABLE 12
Loans As A Proportion Of Total Aid And Educational Costs

Selected Income Group	Guaranteed Student Loans 1978 Total Aid	Guaranteed Student Loans 1978 Cost	Guaranteed Student Loans 1981 Total Aid	Guaranteed Student Loans 1981 Cost	National Direct Student Loans 1978 Total Aid	National Direct Student Loans 1978 Cost	National Direct Student Loans 1981 Total Aid	National Direct Student Loans 1981 Cost
Less than $9,999	10.7	33.0	19.1	38.3	13.2	22.9	10.3	24.1
$10,999 to $14,999	12.5	36.2	25.3	39.3	13.6	24.8	11.4	24.8
All Groups	10.9	40.3	27.3	42.5	8.5	25.0	8.1	25.7

Notes: Data is for entering freshmen enrolled full-time in U.S. colleges and universities, fall semester.
Source: Adopted from an unpublished Fiscal Year 1982 report of the U.S. Department of Education, Office of Planning, Budget, and Evaluation.

million) and 9.7% of total undergraduate enrollment. In 1984, their participation had dwindled to 8.8% (1.0 million). In 4-year institutions, black enrollment had stabilized at 8.0%, while their representation in 2-year institutions had declined from 10.2% to 10.1%. Total minority enrollment in higher education had increased nearly 6% because of the across-the-board growth in Hispanic and Asian participation. In 1985, according to Blake, total black enrollment fell below the 1 million mark, a landmark level that had been reached by blacks back in 1976.[25]

At the postbaccalaureate level, both erosion and progress had occurred. Black participation in graduate education eroded precipitously, declining from 5.0% in 1982 to 4.8% in 1984. Consistent with national trends, the participation of blacks in professional education again inched upward from 4.6% to 4.8%, because of the accelerated entry of black women to this sector of higher education. The participation of blacks in medical school peaked at 6.3% in 1974. However, between 1984 and 1985, black enrollment in medical school declined by 4.9%, compared to a small decrease for whites and a small increase for Hispanics;[26,27] enrollments of Native Americans suffered most, declining by 7.5%. Between 1983 and 1985, blacks sustained a small gain in medical graduates, increasing to 5.1% of all graduates.[28] However in 1982, blacks had represented 5.6% of all medical graduates. Total minority representation peaked at 7.8% in 1982.

The picture was as bleak at the historically black colleges. Total enrollment in the HBCs had peaked at 222,218 in 1982. Nationally, total enrollment had peaked at 12.5 million in 1983. Between 1983 and 1985, enrollments at these institutions continued to fluctuate, decreasing from 221,962 to 213,776[29,30] (by 3.7%), compared to 1.7% nationally (from 12.5 million to 12.2 million). With the exception of the private 2-year sector, these institutions experienced across-the-board losses.

The continued ascent of loans in the federal student financial aid system as the income of first resort for students contributed to the crisis in black higher education. Although between 1983 and 1985 the average amount of pell grants went up by 30%, the number of recipients increased by a mere 2.1%. The reverse was true for guaranteed student loans: the number of guaranteed loan recipients increased by 26.8%; while the average size of guaranteed student loans only increased by 2.1%. The number of students receiving campus-based dollars grew slightly: in 1985, loans represented 51.7% of total federal aid, in contrast to 49.2% in 1983.

A recent study of the private black colleges graphically demonstrates the powerful implications that the evolving transformation of the federal student aid system has for the survival of black students and black institutions. Between 1983 and 1984 at the private HBCs, the percentage of students receiving loans rose to 46% from 37%.[31] Forty-eight percent of the students whose incomes were under $10,000 used loans to finance their schooling. In 1980, only 10% of the students in these schools had received loans, yet 42% of the full-time students had family incomes below the poverty line, and 30% were from families with incomes of $6,000.

The private black colleges have had little or no ability to reverse this situation because they have been historically plagued by low endowments and inequitable federal support. Yet they have set tuition levels significantly lower than private institutions nationally in order to preserve the right of blacks to educational choice.

The unwillingness of black students compared to white students to take out loans, the inequitable access of blacks to loans, and the effect of loans—compared to grants and college work-study—on the persistence of black students have been well-documented elsewhere. The exacerbation of these predispositions by an increasingly unresponsive student aid system—in addition to the jolts of a recovering economy, the reemergence of hostile conditions on many predominantly white campuses, a new focus on test scores as entry and exit criteria, and the ongoing challenges to affirmative action—has wrought an environmental milieu very hostile to the production of educated blacks.

CONCLUSIONS AND RECOMMENDATIONS

The creation of a broadly-educated black citizenry in the U.S. is vital to the national interest. Progress toward this goal would have been minimal without the powerful federal incentives embodied in the Higher Education Act of 1965, as amended through the mid-1970s (and the groundwork laid by black student activism and the Civil Rights movement of the 1960s). Likewise, national redress of the current crisis in black higher education will be impossible without the reemergence of a federal student aid system more responsive to the special needs of blacks.

The stepped-up commitment of the states to educational equity in recent years has been impressive. However, this commitment varies according to the individual states' wealth, their educational and economic agendas, and their willingness to promote social justice. Further, the recent upsurge in state budgets is far below the real dollar improvement required to compensate for the massive losses in revenue and expenditures sustained between fiscal years 1981 and 1983 because of inflationary pressures and changing federal policies.[32,33]

During the early 1970s—when the economy was still expanding, a Civil Rights consensus was still intact though frayed, and the American public was feeling generally optimistic about the potential of the American dream—opening the doors of higher education to blacks and the poor was viewed as both necessary and morally right. A pro-black student aid system flowed out of this realization. Our challenge today is to reestablish the higher education of blacks as a moral issue of national proportion, an issue that has enormous economic implications for the future well-being of the nation. Such a plan will require (1) broad use of the media in clarifying public misperceptions of the conditions of black America and black higher education; (2) careful, objective, and timely assessment and dissemination of the effectiveness of public/private programs designed to promote educational equity and diversity; and (3) broad cooperation among black and nonblack institutions of all kinds in order to forge a power elite fully supportive of an egalitarian system of higher education.

Once a context for change begins to form, fundamental renewal of the federal student financial aid system will become possible. Such renewal should address:

- reestablishment of a grant-centered student aid system;
- expansion of grants at the postbaccalaureate level;
- expansion of low-cost direct loans as a financing option of last resort at the undergraduate level;
- greater articulation between the student financial aid system and the high schools and social organizations serving large numbers of black and poor students; and
- incentives for promoting the college education of black males, for attracting more blacks into the teaching profession, and for developing cadres of black doctorates skilled in science and technology.

The fact that this article has focused on the federal government's role in financing postsecondary education for blacks and the poor in no way negates the principle of shared responsibility in financing the cost of education. Neither does it suggest a nostalgic return to the 1960s and early 1970s. The emphasis on the federal role speaks to the validity of the spirit of the 1960s and to the larger purpose of government in promoting the welfare of all the nation's people. The crisis in black higher education is a national problem. National problems require national solutions in addition to the substantial commitment of students and parents.

NOTES

1. Carter-Williams, Mary with Doris James-Wilson. The Fifth Status Report of Black Americans in Higher Education 1970 to 1982 (unpublished book): Washington, D.C.: Howard University Institute for the Study of Educational Policy, 1985), p. 67.

2. Ibid.

3. U.S. Bureau of the Census, Table No. 696, "Employed Persons, By Sex, Race and Occupations: 1972 and 1982." In Statistical Abstract 1984: National Data Book and Guide to Sources, 104th Edition, p. 419.

4. U.S. Bureau of the Census, Table 2, "Money Income and Poverty Status of Families and Persons in the United States: 1983." In Current Population Report. Series P-60, No. 145. Washington, D.C.: GPO, 1984, p. 8.

5. U.S. Bureau of the Census, Table 2, "Households, by Total Money Income in 1967 to 1982 (In Current Dollars), Race, and Spanish Origin of Householders." Current Population Reports, Consumer Income, Series P-60, No. 142, Money Income of Households, Families, and Persons in the United States: 1982, p. 6.

6. Over the years, state agencies have had considerable flexibility in selecting the recipients of state student incentive grants. The 1980 Amendments charged that such recipients should be selected on the basis of financial need. However, while some states use family income as the major criterion in selecting students, others define need based on the difference between students' expense budgets and their resources.

7. U.S. Department of Labor.

8. The historically black colleges are not monolithic in nature. Although most are small church-related liberal arts institutions, some are land-grant, and others are affected by the desegregation mandate.

9. Carter-Williams, and James-Wilson, Fifth Status Report, pp. 219-22.

10. American Council on Education Office of Minority Concerns, Fifth Annual Status Report 1986: Minorities In Higher Education. (Washington, D.C.: American Council on Education, 1986), p. 45.

11. Carter-Williams and James-Wilson, Fifth Status Report, p. 219.

12. The role of the historically black college sector in producing black engineers is significant because six HBCs have Colleges of Engineering: Howard Univ., North Carolina A&T. Univ, Prairie View A&M Univ., Southern Univ., Tennessee State Univ., and Tuskegee Institute.

13. American Council on Education, Fifth Annual Status Report (1986), p. 24.

14. Carter-Williams and James-Wilson, Fifth Status Report, pp. 154-55.

15. Ottinger, Cecilia A., 1986-87. Fact Book on Higher Education (Washington, D.C.: American Council on Education Division of Policy Analysis and Research, 1987), pp. 161-64.

16. Carter-Williams and James-Wilson, Fifth Status Report, pp. 172-79.

17. Extrapolation derived from Ottinger, Cecilia A., 1984-85 Fact Book on Higher Education (Washington, D.C.: American Council on Education Division of Policy Analysis and Research, 1987), p. 4.

18. Carter-Williams and James-Wilson, Fifth Status Report Table 104, p. 378.

19. Ottinger, Cecilia A., 1986-87 Fact Book on Higher Education. (Washington, D.C.: American Council on Education Division of Policy Analysis and Research, 1987), pp. 161-64.

20. Hill, Susan T, The Traditionally Black Institutions of Higher Education 1860 to 1982. (Washington, D.C.: National Center for Education Statistics, 1984), pp. 19-20.

21. U.S. Department of Education National Center for Education Statistics, High School and Beyond: A National Longitudinal Study for the 1980's. (Washington, D.C.: GPO, 1980).

22. Gladieux, Lawrence E, "The Future of Student Financial Aid," The College Board Review 126 (Winter 1982-83), p. 5.

23. U.S. Department of Education Office of Evaluation and Center for Education Statistics, "Program Management," 1984, pp. 19-20, Vol. II of Fiscal Year 1980, Annual Evaluation Report, pp. 141-42.

24. U.S. Department of Education Office of Planning, Budget, and Evaluation, Vol. II of Annual Evaluation Report Fiscal Year 1981, pp. 360-65.

25. Reported by Dr. Elias Blake, Jr. at the 1987 Black Caucus brain trust session on black higher education.

26. American Council on Education, Fifth Annual Status Report, p. 29.

27. American Council on Education, Fourth Annual Status Report, 1985, p. 15.

28. American Council on Education, Fifth Annual Status Report, p. 34.

29. Ibid., p. 45.

30. See Table 5.

31. United Negro College Fund, Inc. and National Institute of Independent Black Colleges and Universities, Access to College: The Impact of Federal Financial Aid Policies At Private Historically Black Colleges (Washington, D.C., 1987).

32. National Governors' Association Office of Reserch and Development and National Association of State Budget Officers, Fiscal Survey Of The States 1981-1982 (Washington, D.C.), pp. 1-11.

33. National Governors' Association Office of Research and Development and National Association of State Budget Officers, Fiscal Survey Of The States 1983 (Washington, D.C., June 1983), pp. 1-7.

12
The Intended and Unintended Benefits of School Desegregation

Charles V. Willie

SCHOOL DESEGREGATION: UNRAVELING ITS INTENT

Over the years, the purpose of school desegregation has become so obfuscated that many have forgotten this simple fact: Litigation for desegregation was undertaken because blacks wanted better educational opportunities for their children.

The beginning of the obfuscation of *Brown v. Board of Education* (1954), which determined that "separate educational facilities are inherently unequal," may be found in James B. Conant's book *Slums and Suburbs* (1961). He counseled "those who are agitating for the deliberate mixing of children to accept *de facto* segregated schools as a consequence of a present housing situation and to work for the improvement of slum schools whether Negro or white."[1] Apparently, Conant did not realize that one reason for separating population groups is precisely for the purpose of according them differential treatment. And differential treatment that is discriminatory is likely to be unfavorable to the population group that is subdominant in the community's power structure.[2] For this reason, the separate-but-equal doctrine prescribed by the U.S. Supreme Court in the 1896 *Plessy v. Ferguson* decision was doomed to fail.

Probably the best example of the inappropriateness of advocating segregated facilities is the educational experience of handicapped students. Rostetter, Kowalski, and Hunter observed that "if handicapped children [are] to be successful participants in society, including having the opportunity to become economically independent, then the opportunity for education [has to] include integration with nonhandicapped peers in educational and community activities."[3] These authors state that this principle is central in Public Law 94-142; this law was necessary for the purpose of making available "a free appropriate public education . . . to all handicapped children in the least restrictive environment."[4] Rostetter et al. assert that "systematic direct instruction with nonhandicapped peers is the only remedy to the interaction deficits that result from segregated education."[5] This is another way of stating the finding of the Supreme Court in *Brown* that separate educational facilities are inherently unequal and deprive the children of minority groups of equal educational opportunities, opportunities which are essential to their success in life.

According to Donder and York, in most instances, services provided for handicapped children and racial minority children in segregated institutions have been "woefully inadequate."[6] Kluger describes such services as a "disgrace."[7] Blacks sought a way to reverse the deficit experiences of a segregated education in *Brown*; in response, the Supreme Court mandated desegregation as soon as practicable. Advocates for the handicapped sought to overcome the deficit experiences of a segregated education in PL 94-142. These efforts resulted in a congressional mandate for integration in the least restrictive environment. It is fair to conclude that "the foundation for the development of a right to education for handicapped children is based on the *Brown* decision . . ."[8]

PLANS, STRATEGIES, AND STRUGGLES TO IMPLEMENT SCHOOL DESEGREGATION

The processes of achieving both desegregation and integration have been most difficult. The implementation of some desegregation plans has compromised the rights of blacks. John Finger, a desegregation planner for several communities, admitted that some plans may be "inequitable."[9] The outcome of this process for some blacks has been disillusionment with desegregation and bitterness about unfulfilled promises. Martin Luther King, Jr. observed that "the reality of equality will require extensive adjustments in the way of life of some of the white majority,"[10] an adjustment many are unwilling to make. An analysis of several desegregation plans sustains Finger's conclusion. The plans have been designed not so much to achieve the greatest practicable amount of desegregation for blacks and other racial minorities, but to be least offensive to whites.

Despite the success of nonviolent demonstrations in Montgomery and elsewhere, King encountered resistance to this approach in the Freedom March through Mississippi, initiated by James Meredith in 1966.[11] Meredith was shot but not fatally wounded on the first day of his solo march. To signify that blacks "would never again be intimidated by the terror of extremist white violence," King and other civil rights groups continued the march.[12] Immediately there was bickering among the leadership as to whether the march should be all black and whether the participants should embrace the principle of nonviolence.

Although King's philosophy won on both issues, there was residual bitterness.[13] King said that he was not attuned to such bitterness, but felt he should have known that "in an atmosphere where false promises are daily realities, . . . where acts of unpunished violence toward Negroes are a way of life, nonviolence would eventually be seriously questioned." "I should have been reminded," he said, "that disappointment produces despair and despair produces bitterness."[14]

The right to a desegregated education, which the Supreme Court affirmed in *Brown v. Board of Education*, has been experienced more frequently during the past decades by whites than by blacks. The *Brown* plaintiffs were black, and although the Court sustained their allegations of segregation and discrimination in public education, it actually gave more desegregative relief to whites than to blacks. Cities such as Atlanta, Milwaukee, and St. Louis have adopted desegregation plans that prohibit any all-white schools, but accommodate several all-black schools.[15]

Boston was one setting in which disillusionment and bitterness were manifest over the failure of school desegregation to fully redress the grievances of the black plaintiffs. Boston Latin School and Boston Latin Academy are among the most prestigious secondary schools in the city. The school desegregtion plan required that blacks and other racial minorities be offered up to 35% of the seats in the entering classes in these schools. In general, the court-ordered plan required the racial enrollment in city magnet schools to be proportional to the size of each group in the public school population. Blacks, who constitute 47% of all students, have a similar proportion of magnet school seats, and whites, who comprise 28%, receive a like proportion of places. But in the most prestigious Latin schools, whites occupy 57% of the seats. Because whites are overrepresented and blacks are under-represented at these prestigious magnet schools, some blacks call this arrangement unfair.[16]

Moreover, the desegregation that the Boston Plan initially promised appears to be eroding over time. Unless attendance zones are adjusted, Court-appointed experts have said that "each year, the number of segregated schools . . . will increase . . ."[17]

Blacks who initiated the court case in Boston proposed a modification of the plan so that the promise of school desegregation might be more fully realized. The Boston School Committee decided to experiment with a more flexible plan in 1985, ten years after the initial Court-ordered plan. Boston communities selected for the experiment were those in which the black population was a minority, ranging from 13 to 25%. Communities in which blacks constitute a majority (78 to 81% of the school-going population) were left out of the experiment, despite the fact that these were the kinds of communities that could become more segregated if efforts were not made to reverse the trends.

The disillusionment of some northern blacks in the 1980s, was not unlike that experienced by some southern blacks in the 1960s. In Boston, this disillusionment led some parents of the plantiffs and one of their attorneys to advocate scrapping the entire Court-ordered student assignment desegregation plan and institute a freedom-of-choice plan in its place. Despite the past failures of such plans to achieve desegregation, however, some blacks supported the proposal because nothing else, including the existing Court-ordered plan, offered the promise of fulfilling the desegregation goal for which litigation had been undertaken.[18]

Moreover, even the modest school desegregation that blacks had experienced throughout the nation placed an unequal burden on members of their racial group during implementation. Milwaukee, for example, transported nine times as many blacks as whites in its school desegregation plan. This situation prompted Mary Haywood Metz to comment that no one should present a plan that requires such an imbalanced use of transportation by race as a model of equity.[19] Blacks have also expressed resentment about desegregation plans in which whites are always the majority in their schools. Such plans are particularly onerous in communities where blacks are a majority.

In 1987, the public school-going population in St. Louis was approximately 80% black. Yet the magnet schools in that city were supposed to be 50% black and 50% white according to the plan in effect that year. The white students enrolled in magnets included both city and county students, but black students were recruited only from among city dwellers. Clearly, the black students of St. Louis did not have their fair share of magnet school seats. Yet, some attorneys associated with the case resisted a plan to modify the racial ratio for magnet school students by raising the black proportion to 60% and lowering the white proportion to 40%. These attorneys asserted that this modification would make it difficult to market the magnet schools to whites, especially county dwellers who dominate suburban school systems.

In 1979, Milwaukee broke with the practice of attempting to guarantee a majority presence for whites in all magnet schools. The city adopted a new racial ratio to define desegregation in magnet schools because it "comports with the change in the relative black percentage in the school system." Further, school administrators frankly acknowledged that "a school can be majority black (60%) and still be considered racially balanced."[20] By 1984, thirty-five of Milwaukee's magnet schools were dominated by minorities.

DO DESEGREGATED SCHOOLS PROMOTE HIGHER ACADEMIC ACHIEVEMENT?

The reluctance of communities to encourage whites to enroll in black-dominated schools is anchored, in part, in the 1960s research of James Coleman.[21] He discovered that black children in classrooms where more than half of the students are white score higher on achievement tests than do other black children; black children in classrooms with fewer whites reveal a wider spread in test performance.[22] Pettigrew questioned whether the achievement benefits reported by Coleman were due to the racial composition, the social class composition, or some other compositional characteristic of the classroom learning environment. Pettigrew states that Coleman is equivocal on these points.[23]

A review of the literature reveals that many social scientists are unclear about the plurality of factors and their interrelationships that contribute to producing effective education. Unable to comprehend the complexity of these relationships, they often limit explanations to obvious factors such as race, gender, and social class. Comer attributes this tendency to "the traditional American flair for ignoring behavioral complexities." He states that "intellectual and academic achievement is only one part of the school mission. . . . The school has an important role in promoting socialization and psychological development. Tests and measurement of academic achievement should not be the only indicators of the child's school success."[24]

Since 1968, Comer and his collaborators have been examining "the complex forces at play in a school."[25] In a 98% black New Haven school, located in an attendance zone where 50% of the households receive public welfare, Comer and his associates demonstrated that it is possible to generate a positive social climate with minimal student conflict, high motivation, and desirable interpersonal relationships among parents, staff, and students. Moreover, it is possible in a learning environment such as this to encourage above-average levels of achievement and a high attendance rate.[26] These outstanding results were achieved by making the kinds of administrative changes that are necessary to establish order, bringing together parents and staff in a way that permitted them to know each other as reasonable people with common goals, and helping parents and staff think and plan from a shared perspective.[27]

Whereas Coleman reported results of black children in predominantly white desegregated schools, Comer reported similar achievements in a predominantly black school. Comer's findings cast doubt on Coleman's hypothesis that the level of achievement of black students is a function of the proportion of white students in their classrooms, and that blacks in majority white schools always perform better than blacks in majority black schools. It is quite possible that the alleged association between the proportion of whites in a school and the achievement level of blacks is a spurious correlation and results are due largely to the fact that only the racial attributes and achievement scores of individuals were studied. These are input and outcome variables. When information on the process of education is ignored, predictions about educational outcomes are likely to be inaccurate. Coleman had little, if any, information on the educational process the students experienced.

Based on this analysis, it is easy to understand the resentment that has developed among some blacks on school desegregation when it is suggested that high levels of black achievement are dependent upon schooling in predominantly white learning environments. This was the conventional wisdom of the nation until evidence from studies on black achievement in predominantly black settings began to emerge in the 1980s. Barbara Sizemore claims that minorities had been excluded from the desegregation research, planning, and policy-making processes and that these exclusions resulted in plans that have been deleterious for black children.[28] Obviously, more comprehensive data contribute to better educational planning.

THE UNINTENDED BENEFITS OF SCHOOL DESEGREGATION

The prevailing research during the 1960s and 1970s about school desegregation seldom indicated any benefits for whites who were schooled in predominantly black learning environments. Only recently have data been reported that indicate beneficial effects may accrue to whites who participate in predominantly black institutions. Pascarella and his colleagues have studied the influence of 1971 college students' academic and social self-concepts. A follow-up study on these individuals was conducted in 1980. They concluded that academic and social experiences during college have significant and direct effects on the development of self-concept.[29]

These authors found that "for white men, attending a black institution had a positive direct effect on social self-concept."[30] Indeed, Pascarella discovered that "attending a primarily black institution had a significantly stronger effect on social self-concept for white men than it did for black men."[31]

The findings about the beneficial effects of an education for some whites in a predominantly black setting is similar to a finding tucked away in Coleman's report about the self-concept effects of an education in a predominantly white setting for some blacks. Coleman found that "blacks in schools with a higher proportion of whites have a greater sense of control" and that "when minority students have a belief that they can affect their own environments and future, . . . their achievement is higher than that of whites who lack that conviction."[32] This researcher explained the stronger self-concept among blacks in predominantly white settings this way: "they see they can do some things better than whites . . . knowledge which they never had so long as they were isolated in all-black schools."[33]

Coleman's explanation suggests that some blacks in an integrated setting overcame a false sense of inferiority. This author sees a similar explanation for the stronger self-concept of some whites who must function in an integrated setting, which whites do not control: such white students probably gain an understanding that blacks can perform as well as or better than whites, knowledge they could never obtain in a segregated, all-white setting. Thus, an integrated education helps white males, in particular, to overcome a false sense of superiority.

Standley's 1978 study of 1,189 whites enrolled in twenty predominantly black colleges and universities in the South is instructive. An overwhelming majority of the students told her that "black schools provide a good education, that teachers in these schools help all students and are not partial because of the race of a student, and that the courses that the schools offer can contribute to future job plans."[34] The white students in predominantly black schools also reported that they learned a great deal about race relations through their contacts with blacks on campus. More than 80% said they now feel comfortable communicating with a person of a different race and 75-80% were more concerned about achieving equal opportunity for all and had a heightened appreciation of cultural diversity. Moreover, these white students on predominantly black campuses felt that their multiracial, multicultural experiences would help them to be more effective in their careers.[35]

CONCLUSION

With new information about desegregation and a definition of educational outcome that goes beyond academic achievement, racial minorities can now assess the benefits of school desegregation for whites as well as themselves in both predominantly black and predominantly white settings. If they realize that a high-quality education can occur in a setting in which any population is the majority, blacks will be more inclined to support school desegregation, as long as faulty assumptions and defective strategies of implementation of the past are changed.

The past resentment of blacks is actually resentment about unfairness in the school desegregation process rather than against the concept of desegregation itself. In Boston, for example, a majority of blacks (71%) said that if they had the option, they would choose an integrated over a segregated school; however, the black population was split over whether busing was good. Busing, of course, is an implementation strategy, the burden of which has fallen disproportionately on the black population. In general, busing has been unfair to blacks and therefore they resent it. Distinctions should be made between resentment against the goal of an integrated society and resentment against unfair methods of achieving it.

This author believes that most blacks still favor desegregation because they remember the harm that they experienced under conditions of segregation. They also recognize the educational reforms that have come about under conditions of partial if not full integration.

The Boston experience is not unlike that of blacks in other cities. Under a court order to desegregate, the Boston administrative and teaching staffs were diversified; unsafe and unfit schools were closed; system-wide curriculum objectives were developed; promotional standards were created and school-based management was established; community and parental involvement was increased; and partnerships between businesses and schools and colleges and schools were formed. These quality-enhancing experiences were direct outcomes of school desegregation.[36]

For reasons such as these, Boston blacks, like blacks throughout the U.S., have continued to support school desegregation. A poll conducted in the early 1980s revealed how Boston blacks felt about school desegregation: 73% thought that an end to court-ordered school desegregation would be a setback for them.[37] School desegregation no longer is an issue for most blacks, but the methods by which it will be achieved are.

School desegregation is a social movement over which no group—the majority or the minority—has full control. Social movements seldom fulfill all of their intended goals, and there is no precise beginning or end to such a movement. In addition, because of the suffering and sacrifice usually associated with social change before, during, and after social movements, success is hard to assess.

Social scientists have had difficulty assessing school desegregation because they have not recognized it as a social movement. Moreover, they have erred by attempting to ignore behavioral complexities. White citizens tend to measure the success of school desegregation in terms of the achievements of racial minority children in communicating and calculating skills and measure their success by majority group standards. Black citizens, on the other hand, tend to measure the success of school desegregation in terms of the empowerment of minorities to control their own destinies. In the end, school desegregtion may achieve some, but not all, of these goals fully.

This analysis has revealed the unintended consequences of school desegregation that were goals of neither the majority nor the minority. Although school desegregation was demanded by blacks and resisted by whites, it has been experienced more frequently by the resisting group. This fact is abundantly clear when social scientists measure desegregation not in terms of the proportion of black students enrolled in predominantly white schools, but in terms of the decreasing proportion of all-white schools. In most cities of the U.S., few all-white schools remain, although several all-black schools may be found.

The interracial educational experience of whites is profoundly different from their segregated educational experience before the *Brown* decision.

That the desegregation movement has had a greater impact upon the white than black population is truly an unintended outcome. Desegregation has also enhanced the self-concepts of individuals in both racial populations by enabling blacks in predominantly white settings to overcome a false sense of inferiority, while whites in predominantly black settings have overcome a false sense of superiority. These outcomes of school desegregation help equip students in both racial populations acquire the kinds of attitudes they need for adult living. Although the outcomes have little if anything to do with empowerment and academic skills, they are fundamental in promoting socialization and psychological development which, according to Comer, is an important function of a formal education.[38]

In summary, school desegregation has achieved for the nation much more than blacks anticipated, but much less than they demanded. Indeed, school desegregation has accomplished more for the white population that resisted it than for the black population that requested it. It is a puzzlement not easily comprehended, but worthy of continued effort and study.

NOTES

1. Conant, James B., *Slums and Suburbs* (New York: McGraw-Hill Book Co., 1961).

2. Willie, Charles V., "Deprivation and Alienation: A Compounded Situation," in C.W. Hunnicutt (ed), *Urban Education and Cultural Deprivation* (Syracuse, N.Y.: Syracuse University School of Education 1964), pp. 83-92.

3. Rossetter, Dave, Ron Kowalski, and Dawn Hunter, "Implementing the Integration Principle of PL 94-142," in Nick Certo, Norris Haring, and Robert York (eds.), *Public School Integration of Severely Handicapped Students,* (Baltimore: Paul H. Brookes, 1984), pp. 293-320.

4. Ibid., p. 295.

5. Ibid.

6. Donde, Daniel J. and Robert York, "Integration of Students with Severe Handicaps," in Nick Certo, Norris Haring, and Robert York (eds.), *Public School Integration of Severely Handicapped Students* (Baltimore: Paul H. Brooks, 1984), pp. 1-14.

7. Kluger, Richard, *Simple Justice* (New York: Vintage Books, 1975).

8. Rostetten et al., "Implementing the Integration Principle."

9. Finger, John, "Why Busing Plans Work" in Florence Hamlish Levinsohn and Benjamin Drake Wright (eds.), *School Desegregation,* (Chicago: University of Chicago Press, 1976), pp. 58-66.

10. King, Martin Luther, Jr., *Where Do We Go From Here* (Boston: Beacon Press, 1968).

11. King, Martin Luther, Jr., *Stride Toward Freedom* (New York: Harper and Row, 1958).

12. King, *Where Do We Go.*

13. Ibid, pp. 23-66.

14. Ibid, p. 26.

15. Willie, Charles V., "The Future of School Desegregation," in Janet Dewart (ed.), *The State of Black America 1987* (New York: National Urban League, 1987), pp. 37-47.

16. Willie, Charles V., "A Ten-Year Perspective on the Role of Blacks in Achieving Desegregation and Quality Education in Boston," in Phillip L. Clay (ed.), *The Emerging Black Community in Boston* (Boston: Trotter Institute of the University of Massachusetts at Boston, 1985), pp. 145-80.

17. Dentler, Robert and Marvin Scott, *Schools on Trial* (Cambridge: *Abt Books,* 1981).

18. Hughes, L.W., W.M. Gordon, and L.W. Hillman, *Desegregating America's Schools* (New York: Longman, 1980).

19. Metz, Mary Haywood, *Different by Design* (New York: Routledge and Kegan Paul, 1986).

20. Bennett, David A., "A Plan for Increasing Educational Opportunities and Improving Racial Balance in Milwaukee," in Charles V. Willie, *School Desegregation Plans That Work* (Westport, Ct: Greenwood Press, 1984), pp. 81-118.

21. Coleman, James S., et al. *Equality of Educational Opportunity* (Washington, DC: U.S. Government Printing Office, 1966).

22. Pettigrew, Thomas F., *Racially Separate or Together* (New York: McGraw-Hill, 1971).

23. Ibid., p. 63.

24. Comer, James P., *Beyond Black and White* (New York: Quandrangle Books, 1972).

25. Comer, James P., *School Power* (New York: Free Press, 1980).

26. Ibid. pp. 74-75.

27. Ibid. pp. 104-5.

28. Sizemore, Barbara, "Educational Research and Desegregation: Significance for the Black Community," *Journal of Negro Education* 47 (Winter 1978), pp. 58-68.

29. Pascarella, Ernest, John C. Smart, Corinna Ethington, and Michael T. Nettles, "The Influence of College on Self-Concept: A Consideration of Race and Gender Differences. "*American Educational Research Journal* 24 (Spring 1987), pp. 49-77.

30. Ibid., p. 72.

31. Ibid., p. 62.

32. Coleman, "Equality", p. 23.

33. Coleman, James S., "Equality of Educational Opportunity," Integrated Education 6 (Sept.-Oct., 1968).

34. Willie, Charles V., *The Ivory and Ebony Towers* (Lexington: Lexington Books, 1981).

35. Ibid, p. 82.

36. Willie, "A Ten-Year Perspective," p. 150.

37. Willie, "Future," p. 39.

38. Comer, "Beyond," p. 55.

13

The Case for a Separate Black School System

Derrick Bell

A group of black parents, educators, and legislators, led by long-time activist Dr. Howard Fuller, disturbed the lazy days of late summer 1987 in Milwaukee, Wisconsin, by announcing their intention to seek legislation creating an independent and largely black school system. Their proposal calls for the creation of either a new district or a special neighborhood district within the existing city public school system. It would encompass nine schools, serving more than 6,000 children (97% of whom are black) in the heart of the black community. The proposal shocked the city and was immediately opposed by Milwaukee school officials, the NAACP, and the media, who condemned the plan as both unconstitutional[1] and symbolizing a return to "separate but equal" schools.[2]

Proponents of the new district were unfazed by the storm of criticism. They deny that the new school system will violate constitutional standards. Rather, they view it as the last clear chance to rescue black children from schools that remain mainly black and educationally ineffective after two decades of school desegregation litigation. The black parents' concerns are supported by school department statistics that reveal serious disparities between the performance of black and white children attending the Milwaukee Public Schools. For example, for the 1985-86 school year, 33% of black children in the fifth grade are "low performing" students in reading, compared to only 15% of white children in this grade. In the seventh grade, the figures are 32% for blacks and 14% for whites, and by the tenth grade, 42% of black children are in the low performing category, compared to 14% for whites.[3]

Similarly, in math performance, the percentage of low performing white students remains fairly stable (about 12%) from grades five through ten, but for blacks, the figures are progressively worse: 23% in the fifth grade, 26% in the seventh grade, and 36% in tenth grade. School board officials would likely point out that the percentage of low performing blacks has decreased significantly over the last ten years.[4]

In their proposal, entitled *A Manifesto for New Directions in the Education of Black Children in the City of Milwaukee* (see the addendum to this article), advocates express disenchantment with proponents of integration from both races who continue to view "the body shuffling of black children" as a viable means of achieving academic excellence. Voluntary busing plans, such separatists argue, will not provide the parental involvement, teacher morale, and accountability to students and parents that are the hallmarks of good schools across the country.

The manifesto quotes a number of prominent blacks, including W.E.B. DuBois, former NAACP General Counsel, Judge Robert L. Carter, Dr. Sara Lawrence Lightfoot, and Dr. Ron Edmonds who support their view. These people agree with Dr. DuBois that black children need quality education rather than either segregated or mixed schools. These people deny that the "equal educational opportunity" promised by the U.S. Supreme Court requires an integrated setting, and reject the notion that it is not possible to achieve academic excellence in a predominantly black school environment.

In addition to mastery of basic skills, the manifesto writers set goals for the new system that include the development of analytical ability needed for effective functioning in today's world and the confidence to influence, control, and change the world that comes from knowledge of the value and strength of black history and culture.

WONDERING WHAT MIGHT HAVE BEEN

Reading the Milwaukee manifesto, this author felt empathetic toward those black leaders and parents in Milwaukee, sharing their sense of despair with the large percentage of black students who remain in all-black schools after almost three decades of hard-fought desegregation litigation. Writing out of this despair several years ago, this author probably shocked "civil rights" colleagues by suggesting such an extreme remedy. Acknowledging that it may have seemed cruel and unprecedented, the author wondered whether the educational interests of black children might have been better advanced had the Supreme Court, after declaring segregated schools unconstitutional in 1954,[5] ordered a deferral of pupil desegregation for several years.[6]

After all, this author reasoned, the Court's refusal in 1955[7] to grant the black petitioners' request for injunctive relief that would immediately desegregate the schools, resulted in a decade-long period of litigation with very little progress. If instead of a vague order to desegregate "with all deliberate speed," the Court had specifically ordered the ten-year delay of any requirement that school boards "mix the races," the Court could have ordered the immediate and total equalization of school facilities and resources.

One can further imagine that in addition to orders mandating the early equalization of all facilities and resources, the Court—exercising in 1955 as much insight into the racist motivations of school segregation as we have now gained through bitter experience—recognized that separation of students by race is basically a convenient means of perpetuating the real evil: white dominance over blacks in public education. Based on such an understanding, the Court could have required that blacks immediately be provided representation on school boards and other policymaking bodies in each school system in percentages equal to the percentage of black students in the particular system. This remedy would have given blacks meaningful access to school board decisionmaking, a prerequisite to effective schooling still not attained today in many mainly black systems in the South and in major urban school districts around the country. In addition, enforcement of such an "equal representation" rule would have provided early policy-level protection for the thousands of black teachers and principals who were dismissed by school systems in the 1960s and 70s when racial balance-oriented school desegregation plans were implemented.

As the Court, in fact, did in *Brown II,* it might have urged school districts to proceed voluntarily with the elimination of their dual school systems. But until the end of the equalization period, the major emphasis would have been placed, not on desegregating children, but on desegregating money and control. The approach this author suggested was, of course, not that actually followed by the Court. For with the exception of striking down instances of total recalcitrance, as in Little Rock in 1957,[8] the involvement of courts in the first ten years of school desegregation after *Brown* was generally non- and often counter-productive.

If civil rights groups and black parents had known in advance that the courts would not order schools desegregated for ten years, what might they have done? Surely, the possibility exists that they would have become discouraged by the delay in student desegregation and simply done nothing until the Court was willing to issue such orders. More likely, they would have done what was eventually needed in each community where a desegregation decision was issued: to organize both parents and the community to effectively implement the court-ordered equal money and control mandates within still all-black schools.

Impossible? Perhaps. But a "no desegregation" order by the Court might have caused civil rights lawyers to focus on the primary goal of black parents: the effective schooling of their children. Civil rights leaders might have recognized earlier the now-obvious fact that attainment of racially-integrated schools in a society still committed to white dominance would not ensure that black parents and their children gained the equal educational opportunities for which they have sacrificed so much and waited so long.

Black parents and leaders of their communities learned the hard way that there can be no effective schooling for black children—even in racially-balanced schools—without having both parental involvement in the educational process and meaningful participation in school policymaking. Often painful experience has taught them that neither objective is brought closer by enrolling their children in mainly white schools, particularly if those schools are located a long bus ride from their homes and neighborhoods.

Sadly, the number of black children attending schools that are "separate and unequal" in fact, although desegregated in law, provides a continuing opportunity to try the course neither ordered by the Supreme Court nor followed by civil rights lawyers. Black parents in Milwaukee now urge this alternative in its most dramatic form: the creation of a separate school district that will be mainly black.

THE ALTERNATIVE PLAN'S CONSTITUTIONALITY

Given the circumstances facing black parents in Milwaukee's still all-black and poorly-performing schools, a proposal to create a separate or semi-autonomous school district for the purpose of dramatically increasing academic achievement, parent and community involvement, and reducing drop-out rates should be upheld as constitutional by the courts. School board officials and civil rights spokespersons who condemned the plan as a return to "separate but equal" schools are misguided and wrong and reflect a too-rigid adherence to the original ideal that black children can obtain their constitutional entitlement to "an equal educational opportunity" in racially-balanced schools. In Milwaukee, where a large percentage of the district's black students attend schools that are both racially isolated and educationally inept, the racial balance goal is neither feasible nor required by law.

The *Brown* decision declared that separation of black children "solely because of their race generates a feeling of inferiority as to their status in the community that may affect their hearts and minds in a way unlikely ever to be undone." That language, however, must be read in light of the facts of those cases: blacks were required by law to attend inferior schools that were racially segregated and denied blacks any control over school officials or participation in educational policymaking.

In dozens of urban school systems across the nation, demographic realities and subsequent judicial rulings have rendered an end to racially separate schools all but impossible. But barriers to racial balance do not define the entitlement of blacks under the *Brown* decision. Recognizing the "educational components" in *Brown,* in a 1977 decision, the Supreme Court approved a plan supported by the black community in Detroit that (1) rejected an NAACP plea that racial balance be maximized in the already 70% black district; and (2) approved a series of proposals intended to improve the quality of schooling in all black schools.[9]

In reliance on the Detroit decision, a federal district judge in Dallas approved a community-supported, mainly black sub-district in that school system—again over NAACP objections.[10] The judge acknowledged that the plan departed from long-accepted legal principles of school desegregation relief, but the judge was influenced both by the plan's potential for improving minority student achievement and the widespread support for the "education over racial-balance" approach prevalent in the local black community.

In a later opinion in the same case, the Dallas court observed that the decades since the Supreme Court's decision in *Brown v. Board of Education* "have exacted a toll on the traditional goals of school desegregation litigation." The judge predicted with a prescience significant in the Milwaukee controversy that "the remedies designed for the 1980s may have to be dramatically different from those developed in the past."[11]

The Milwaukee manifesto is simply the next logical step in the continuing effort by black people to obtain effective schooling for their children. While there is little direct precedent for this form of school desegregation relief, the cases previously cited and others like them point in this direction. The manifesto, it should be noted, does not seek a court order requiring the establishment of a new school district. Moreover, if the legislature approves the plan, it will not be vulnerable to charges that it creates a segregated school system that already exists.

Critics fail to recognize that the new district's emphasis will be on control and not color. Black parents seeking to transfer from the new district will be able to do so.

Whites seeking to enroll their children will be welcomed. And, if the new district succeeds in implementing the programs that have been effective in improving the academic performance of inner-city black children in several schools around the country, experience indicates that whites will also desire to enroll their children in the new school system.

Let us be honest. Can we, whose children are not required to attend the inner-city schools honestly condemn the manifesto writers and their supporters? After all, when middle class parents—black and white—lose faith in the administration of a public school, they move to another school district or place children in private schools. Inner-city black parents who cannot afford such options seek a legislative remedy as a group that may, after a long struggle, enable them to do what can be achieved independently by those of a higher economic status.

The manifesto is a dramatic response to a critical situation. Those who support the plan deserve better than the hypocritical charge that they are seeking to perpetuate the poorly-functioning, segregated schools that years of civil rights efforts have been unable to change. The city attorney's finding that the manifesto's proposal is unconstitutional is ironic and sad. It is ironic because his conclusion relies on the dozens of school desegregation decisions that blacks have won over resistant school boards, including Milwaukee's; and it is sad because none of those decisions has brought real relief to those black parents who are supporting the plan for a new school district.

Finally, the Milwaukee manifesto does not threaten the long-held ideal of integrated schools. It simply seeks to attain it by first putting administrators and faculty in place who are both accountable to the community and dedicted to improving the quality of schools now serving black children, schools that by even the board's own admission are not serving these students well.

CONCLUSION

Constitutional validity does not guarantee political viability. Whatever its efforts to improve the schooling of black children, the Milwaukee School Board can be expected to spare neither energy nor resources in resisting the manifesto's proposal that if implemented could cost the board an estimated $55 million per year under state school funding formulas.

Whatever the outcome of the proposal, the debate it has engendered is healthy. As an editorial in the Milwaukee Times Weekly Newspaper put it: "At the very least, a proposal to create a separate, largely Black school district within the Milwaukee Public School System has put the question of quality education in the front of everyone's mind."[12]

Of course, the pressures of racism may well doom any plan to educate minority children to failure; this is especially true for the children of the poor. Surely all black parents should have the option of sending their children to predominantly white schools if they choose. However, given the uncertain educational outcome of exercising that option more than thirty years after *Brown*, black parents who prefer to do now what perhaps the Supreme Court should have done in 1955 ought to be encouraged, not assailed.

At least these parents are trying to learn from our losses. The barriers of continuing white resistance, a less than supportive Supreme Court, and the growing concentration of most poor blacks in large urban areas render continuing efforts to achieve compliance with *Brown* through reliance on racial balance plans preposterous. The chances for further progress lie with those who have decided that the better route to educational quality is in schools in which black children and their parents are not treated as strangers.

ADDENDUM
A MANIFESTO FOR NEW DIRECTIONS IN THE EDUCATION OF BLACK CHILDREN IN THE CITY OF MILWAUKEE

> ... theoretically, the Negro needs neither segregated schools nor mixed schools. What he needs is Education. What he must remember is that there is no magic, either in mixed schools or in segregated schools. A mixed school with poor and unsympathetic teachers, with hostile public opinion, and no teaching of truth concerning black folk, is bad. A segregated school with ignorant placeholders, inadequate equipment, poor salaries ... is equally bad. Other things being equal, the mixed school is the broader more natural basis for the education of all youth. It gives wider contacts: it inspires greater self-confidence; and suppresses the inferiority complex. But other things seldom are equal, and in that case, Sympathy, Knowledge, and the truth, outweigh all that the mixed school can offer.
>
> W.E. Burghardt Du Bois (1935)

For years many citizens have expressed concern, indeed outrage over the poor academic achievement level of the majority of students attending Milwaukee Public Schools (MPS). First, the administration denied that there was a serious problem, but within the last three years, independent and scholarly research has documented the gravity of the situation. For example, staff findings from the Governor's Study Commission show that the *majority* of high school freshmen in MPS either drop out or are graduated with less than a "C" average.

In response, MPS has turned to a new strategy of blaming the victims. Now, we are told the poor performance of poor and minority students, most of whom are Black, is the logical and *predictable* extension of their race or family income.

Needless to say, a great deal of frustration and anger has built up in the Black community as a result of this entire situation. Over the last several months this frustration has been increased by the events and the information coming out of the so-called "Metropolitan Desegregation Suit." Once again our children's educational needs and indeed our children themselves have become pawns in a larger power game; a game which offers no real hope for equal educational opportunity for the majority of students nor, for that matter, provides for the equitable racial desegregation of public education in Milwaukee.

We find ourselves listening to Black and white proponents of "integration no matter what the cost" expound on the various means of increasing the body shuffling of black children—a practice that is the bulwark of Milwaukee's "voluntary" deseregation plan. This body shuffling continues although the evidence, contrary to MPS pronouncements, shows that the integration program promoted by MPS has failed as a catalyst for excellence in the academic achievement of the vast majority of poor Black students.

In fact, the preponderance of independent research suggests that Milwaukee's "voluntary" busing program works directly at cross purposes with the factors which must be present for learning to occur—strong parental involvement and a three-way partnership between the parent, school, and child. Too often, the MPS program of dispersing Black children to schools miles from their home prevents this partnership from developing. If any lawsuit is justified, it would be a suit against MPS for implementing a pupil assignment program which prevents key elements of the learning process from flourishing.

We can remain silent no longer. We are compelled to raise our voices in protest- ENOUGH IS ENOUGH!! This MADNESS must stop!! We must make a break from the old solutions based on myths and come to grips with the present situation so that we might chart a clear path that will meet the current and future educational needs of our children.

Dr. DuBois was right when he said that what we need is EDUCATION. The most valid research shows a direct correlation between higher achievement levels of students and (1) parental involvement, (2) teacher morale, and (3) accountability to students and parents. The scientifically credible research is equally clear that there is little discernible correlation between effective education and mere shuffling of Black bodies to achieve the "right" mix with non-black bodies. If the last 34 years of desegregation have proven anything, it is that busing to achieve "racial balance" does not improve learning. Busing works when it reflects the conscious decision of individual parents—Black or non-black—to send their children to schools of their choice; schools in which the parents have confidence; schools which open their arms to parents and children and are accountable to them.

Therefore, the time has come for the citizens of Milwaukee to call a halt to body shuffling and get down to the business of spending our money and our energies on developing the framework that will promote and implement effective educational strategies for our children in the schools they choose to attend. Federal Judge Robert Carter, one of the leading attorneys in the *Brown* litigation spoke directly to this point when he stated,

> Integrated education must not be lost as the ultimate solution. That would be a disaster in my judgement. For the present, however, to focus on integration alone is a luxury that only the black middle class can afford. They have the means to desert the public schools if dissastisfied, they can obtain remediation if necessary,

and get their children into colleges or some income producing enterprise. The immediate and urgent need of the black urban poor is the attainment in real life terms and in settings of virtually total black-white school separation, at least some of the constitutional guarantees that *Brown* requires. The only way to ensure that thousands of black urban poor will have even a remote chance of obtaining the tools needed for them to compete in the market place for a decent job and its accompanying benefits is to concentrate on having quality eduation delivered to the schools these blacks are attending, and in all likelihood will be attending for at least another generation.

We reject metropolitan desegregation as a remedy to poor academic achievement. It is an idea rooted in the racist assumption that it is impossible to achieve academic excellence in a predominantly Black environment. It is an idea that accepts as an axiom the notion that the Black community is so pathological that only a dispersal methodology offers any possibility of hope for our children. It is an idea that misrepresents the history of Black educational achievement in this country. We believe that such a strategy can in no way address the massive undereducation and miseducation facing the vast majority of poor Black children in Milwaukee in 1987. Rather than pursue a strategy of dispersal, we believe a consolidating effort that utilizes the resources and strengths available within the Black community itself is what is needed at this time. Such an effort can work only if Black people are placed in a position to exercise power over the educational process for their children. As Sara Lawrence Lightfoot stated so eloquently,

> . . . a critically important educational success for black and white children lies in the power relationship between communities and schools, rather than in the nature of the student population. Mixing black and white bodies together in the same school and preserving the same relationships and perceptions between schools and the families they serve is unlikely to change the structures, roles, and relationships within schools that define the quality of the educational process. The nature and distribution of power among schools, families and communities is a crucial piece of the complex puzzle leading toward educational success for all children.

The "divide them up and disperse them" strategy of the metropolitan desegregationists is antithetical to the notion of Black people working together *and accepting responsibility* for creating the conditions needed to take on the task of effectively educating our children.

We believe we must turn to a strategy that is rooted in a different definition of equal educational opportunity. We believe equal educational opportunity in today's world means assuring that our children receive an education that not only grounds them in the basic skills of reading, writing, and arithmetic, but also helps them develop the thinking and analytical abilities necessary for them to influence, control, and, where necessary, change their world.

In addition to giving our children these fundamental skills, the educational process must also teach our children the value and strength of their own history and culture. As Janice Hale stated, our children "need an educational system that recognizes their strengths, their abilities, and their culture and that incorporates them into the learning process."

Therefore, we demand that legal options be developed to wrest from MPS political and policy control over the targeted area cited in the enclosed maps. This is an area which already exists by virtue of policies and practices developed and implemented by MPS over the last decade.

We ask that support be given to effect a pilot project which has as its objectives:

(1) a dramatic increase in the students' level of academic achievement
(2) a substantial reduction in the drop-out rate
(3) increased parent and community involvement in the schools
(4) increased excellence through increased parental choice.

We specifically propose the creation of either a new school district for this neighborhood, independent of MPS, or a special neighborhood district within MPS. Within this district, residents could choose to enroll their child in a school outside the district, for whatever reason, be it integration or the belief that another school offered a better education program. Parents from outside the district could apply to send their children to schools in the district if space were available. In other words, *no child would attend a school in this district if his or her parent did not make that choice.*

At first glance, it may be argued, this plan is not much different from the current situation in which schools are attended by black students who live in the neighborhoods in which the schools are located. In fact, the difference would be dramatic because in a new district, the power and responsibility would be focused on the parents, children, and educators within the district. For most of the parents, it would be either their first opportunity to have real power over the education of their children, and, therefore, the future of their children. The current climate in these schools too often is one of futility and resignation that change will never be approved by those in power at Central Administration. That excuse, too often valid, sometimes a cop-out would be gone.

There are some who contend that the inability of MPS to educate the vast majority of poor non-white children is the result of few resources, specifically money. These same forces will almost certainly contend that the proposed district will not have the financial resource to provide an adequate educational program. It is our contention that lack of money is not the reason children are not learning in MPS. Children are not learning because MPS is a system that does not foster local control, is not accountable, and only gives lip service to parental involvement. In any event, state school aid formulas operate in a way that will provide levels of per pupil spending comparable to current MPS spending; the biggest difference is that a new district might be able to channel more dollars into the classroom and less into a bloated central bureaucracy.

The time is now for a system of education based on accountability and results. We cannot afford the loss of another generation of our youth. Give us—the parents, the students, and determined educators—this chance to make a difference.

> . . . demographic desegregation must take a backseat to instructional reform or we will remain frustrated by a continuing and widening gap between black and white pupil performance in desegregated schools . . . we must abandon the legal perspective that treats desegregation litigation as a matter solely of racial balance and assumes quality education comes with that balance.
>
> Dr. Ron Edmonds (1980)

NOTES

1. The Milwaukee city attorney issued an opinion on September 17, 1987, condemning the manifesto plan as unconstitutional under both the federal and state constitutions.

2. The media's opposition to the plan has been clearly expressed. See, e.g., "Blacks, whites criticize school resegregation plan," Milwaukee Journal, Aug. 13, 1987, p. 1; "Idea for Inner City school district greeted with dismay." Milwaukee Sentinel, Aug. 12, 1987; "Plan for a black school district seen as condoning segregation," Milwaukee Sentinel, Aug. 18, 1987; "Black clergy group opposes independent school district," Milwaukee Journal, Sept. 9, 1987.

3. Dept. of Educational Research and Program Assessment, Milwaukee Public Schools, *Preliminary Report No. 2, City-Wide Test Results, School Year 1985-86, Displays of Disaggregated System Test Data:* 17 pp.

4. *Ibid.* Grade point averages for black students in the Milwaukee public schools are much lower than those for whites throughout the high school years. The system operates on a four-point scale, with A = 4.0, B = 3.0, C = 2.0, D = 1.0, and F = 0. In the 1986-87 school year black students averaged 1.32 in the ninth grade, compared to 2.05 for whites. The gap remained in the twelfth grade, where black grade points averaged 1.87, compared to 2.45 for whites. These figures are contained in a report compiled by the Milwaukee Public Schools Educational Research Department, *Milwaukee Today: A Racial Gap Study,* Aug. 4, 1987.

5. 347 U.S. 354 (1954).

6. Bell, *Learning from Our Losses: Is School Desegregation Still Feasible in the 1980s?* Phi Delta Kappan 64, no. 572 (1983).

7. 349 U.S. 294 (1955).

8. Cooper v. Aaron, 358 U.S. 1 (1958).

9. Milliken v. Bradley II 433 U.S. 267 (1977).

10. Tasby v. Wright, 520 F. Supp. 683 (N.D. Tex. 1981).

11. Tasby v. Wright, 542 F. Supp. 134 (N.D. Tex. 1982).

12. Times editorial: "By whatever method, Black youth must be educated," Milwaukee Times Weekly Newspaper, Sept. 16, 1987, p. 4.

14
Desegregating with Magnet and One-Race Elementary and Secondary Schools

Alvin Thornton and Eva Wells Chunn

This article explains the circumstances that led to the development of Prince George's County, Maryland's magnet-based desegregation plan. The article also describes the major provisions of the court order under which the plan is being implemented, describes the magnet programs, analyzes the continuing role of one-race schools, and offers some continuing concerns about the desegregation program.

Prince George's County is one of the largest suburban counties in the U.S. It is located adjacent to Washington, D.C. and has a population of approximately 676,000, 46% of whom are black. The relatively high percentage of blacks in its population is the result of thirty years of black suburbanization and some movement of whites out of the county. The major shift in the racial composition of its public school student population is a good indication of the general demographic changes the county has experienced. During the school year 1970-71, the public school system had 160,547 students. White students, constituted 76.1% of the total, while black students represented only 22.4%. The most recent student census (1987-88) shows that the system now has 103,325 students—31% white and 62.6% black.[1]

Since 1954, the county has maintained a non-unitary public school system. Much of its attention and resources from 1970-87 have been devoted to finding ways to desegregate the public schools while adjusting to major political, economic, and social changes occasioned by expanding business and industrial development and rapid increases in the black population.

The county's response to the demand that it desegregate its public schools may be separated into three stages. The initial response was massive resistance and involved various types of "freedom of choice" plans and bureaucratic non-responses. This was followed by a period of massive involuntary busing in response to direct orders from the federal courts. The third stage, which is still in progress, has been characterized by a combination of involuntary busing and magnet programs with an increased focus on equal educational opportunity and academic achievement for all students.

A 1985 report commissioned by the Board of Education of Prince George's County made several observations about public education in the county. It observed that the public schools had undergone significant stress in the past decade. For fifteen years, the report indicated, desegregation was contested in the courts at great expense. The Board further pointed out that following a drop in enrollment of approximately 60,000 students, 65 schools were closed in the late 1970s and early 1980s, and the number of instructional and support staff were dramatically reduced under the Tax Reform in Maryland (TRIM) initiative. The community, the report stated, had strong concerns about escalating costs, lack of discipline, and most important, a decline in educational achievement.

The Board of Education therefore decided to shift its focus from relying on involuntary busing to achieve a unitary school system to a "school system of choices" based on diversified magnet schools at all instructional levels.[2] The Board's decision to adopt the magnet-based desegregation plan came at the end of a period of extended legal controversy about school desegregation that was conditioned by changing attitudes about the best way to achieve equal-quality education and the rapidly-changing racial demographics of the county. However, the board's decision to develop a number of single-race schools as an important ingredient in the overall desegregation program was not mentioned in the report.

BACKGROUND OF THE MAGNET/MILLIKEN II DESEGREGATION PROGRAM

The formal desegregation effort in Prince George's County was initiated by a group of black adult residents on behalf of the area's school age children. Their claim for injunctive and declaratory relief was based on alleged violations of the law as enunciated by the U.S. Supreme Court in *Brown v. Board of Education*[3] and *Swann v. Charlotte-Mecklenburg Board of Education.*[4] The case was filed in the U.S. Federal District Court for the District of Maryland and captioned as *Sylvester J. Vaughns, Jr. et. al v. Board of Education of Prince George's County, Maryland, et. al.*[5] Judge Frank A. Kaufman, who presided in the original case in 1972, determined as a matter of law that until 1954 (the year of the first Brown decision), Prince George's County had maintained a legally segregated dual school system. After the 1972 decision, the district court retained jurisdiction over the case to supervise the implementation of the desegregation plan that was adopted.[6]

Between January 1973 and November 1974, all of the non-student attendance issues were tentatively resolved by agreement. However, from March 1975 until September 1981, there were no developments in the case that suggested that the Board of Education was moving to develop a unitary public school system. The plaintiffs therefore moved to reopen the case, alleging violations of outstanding orders of the Court by the board and seeking relief.[7] The court held, among other things, that although the board had not intentionally discriminated on racial grounds in connection with faculty assignments, special education, and talented and gifted programs, the plaintiffs were entitled to relief because the board had not acted to remove all vestiges of pre-1973 segregation, which the court's earlier orders were intended to eliminate. In September of 1983 the Court resumed jurisdiction of the case and rendered additional orders consistent with those issued previously.

The school board and the plaintiffs appealed to the U.S. Court of Appeals for the Fourth Circuit. The board argued that the district court had no jurisdiction in the case because the school system had achieved unitary status. The three-judge appellate panel rejected the board's argument and affirmed the findings of the lower court. The appeals court did reverse the district court on the narrow issue of burden of proof regarding the special education and talented and gifted programs.

Subsequent to the appellate court decision, the *Final Report on Desegregation of Prince George's County Public Schools* (The Green Report) was filed with Judge Kaufman (who had ordered it.) The report called for a major program of two-way busing involving some 30,000 students, pairing of schools, and school closings to achieve effective desegregation of the school system.[8]

The Green Report caused acrimony in the community. People on both sides of the debate generally agreed that another solution was necessary. There was a general objection to involuntary busing from both the black and white communities, as many blacks had grown tired of school closings in their communities and resented that their children bore the primary burden of busing. Moreover, many parents felt that there was inadequate evidence that the children were achieving academically as a result of being bused.[9] Whites joined blacks in expressing concern about the anticipated cost of implementing the Green recommendations. Some continued to argue for the neighborhood school concept. Still others took the position that involuntary busing would not work because the student population had become more than 60% black. In this atmosphere, in the summer of 1985, the Board of Education and the plaintiffs agreed to an interim magnet-based desegregation plan that featured one-race (Milliken II) schools, and was implemented in the 1985-86 school year. The essential elements of the desegregation plan were included in what has come to be called the "Memorandum of Understanding."[10] The key components of the memorandum are summarized in the next section of this case study.

GOVERNANCE: PROVISIONS OF THE MEMORANDUM OF UNDERSTANDING

The Memorandum of Understanding, which now serves as the governing document for the magnet-based desegregation of the Prince George's County public school system, contains five primary provisions: (1) selected magnet schools; (2) a limited number of one-race (Milliken II) schools; (3) a Community Advisory Council with a monitoring subcommittee; (4) a mandatory backup involuntary busing plan to the magnet-based desegregation plan; and (5) a reiteration by the Board of Education of its commitment to hire and promote blacks throughout all employment levels of the public school system.

The role of the magnet and Milliken II schools in the desegregation process is discussed below in detail. The other primary provisions of the Memorandum of Understanding are described generally to indicate how they relate to the desegregation program.

The implementation of the magnet-based desegregation order was to be overseen by an Advisory Council on Magnet and Compensatory Educational Programs (Council of 100) selected by the Board of Education with some input from the National Association for the Advancement of Colored People (NAACP). The memorandum provided "that the Advisory Council would be composed of four sub committees, one of which would be a Monitoring Subcommittee to monitor the development and implementation of the magnet school program and the compensatory/remedial educational program. It also stipulated that "eight of the 24 members of the Monitoring Sub-committee shall be selected from a list of 16 nominees provided by the plaintiffs, with the nominees being taken from the list of the entire Community Advisory Council".[11] The subcommittee chairman was to be jointly agreed to by the NAACP and the board. The subcommittee, which includes members from all sections of the county, represents the diversity of local opinion about school desegregation.

The subcommittee was given three primary functions: (1) to monitor the effectiveness of the desegregation plan; (2) to monitor the extent to which court orders were being followed; and (3) to monitor the extent to which financial commitments resulting from the desegregation order were met. To date, the Council of 100 has submitted two reports to the Board of Education.[12]

The mandatory backup plan that was developed by the board and sealed by the district court, could, according to the memorandum, include "the reassignment of student attendance areas; the provision of majority to minority transfers within specified geographic areas, with public school transportation provided and the provision of further Milliken II relief, or some combination of the above." The backup busing plan was to be maintained "from January 1, 1986, on a reasonably updated basis." Various alternative options for schools outside the court's guidelines were included, which followed the backup plan.

Notwithstanding the fact that the court found that the school board had not discriminated against blacks with respect to hiring, the Superintendent reiterated the commitment of the board to hire and promote blacks throughout the school system in the memorandum.[13]

With a citizens' group to monitor its implementation, a commitment to hire and promote more blacks, and an agreement to develop a backup busing plan, the board moved to develop and implement its Magnet and Milliken II desegregation program.

MAGNETS AND MILLIKEN II SCHOOLS AS DESEGREGATION TOOLS

The experiment with magnet and Milliken II schools in Prince George's County is important because it will indicate whether a magnet school program, with some involuntary busing, can: (1) successfully desegregate a large suburban school district that has a majority of black students and (2) provide the foundation for enhanced academic achievement for all students. The experiment takes on increased importance because the presence of the Milliken II schools will give an indication of the acceptability and effectiveness of single-race schools as desegregation tools when they receive compensatory educational resources. As the desegregation program has evolved, it has become clear that the success of the magnet schools is inextricably tied to that of the one-race schools.

The Magnet Schools

The school board's magnet school proposal to the court emerged as other school districts around the nation were experimenting with or reassessing their use of magnet schools as desegregation tools. Data had been offered to support the idea that school systems can desegregate quite comprehensively by relying on magnets in combination with paring, rezoning, two-way busing, and mandatory assignment.[14] Even the NAACP has indicated on a number of occasions that magnet schools should be attempted as an option that can be used to help with the desegregation of a public school system.[15]

Conversely, the research indicates that magnet school-based desegregation programs have been problematic. About the initial magnet program in St. Louis, Trombley wrote that "the magnet program is very expensive and it can desegregate learning for only a small part of the city's student population. They tend to work pretty well in small districts but not in large cities with big ghetto or barrio populations."[16] Observing the Chicago magnet school plan, Schmidt noted that the magnet program was creating a new kind of dual system of education. He pointed out that "on the one hand, the city maintains a handful of average, or in one or two cases, slightly above average, speciality schools where teachers and students have all the things needed for effective learning. On the other hand, the rest of the schools, 80 percent or more, are . . . generic."[17] Finally, because the developers of the Prince George's County plan relied heavily on Milwaukee's magnet school-based desegregation program, it is interesting to note that the Milwaukee program was found to have "unacceptable disparities between the educational opportunities and achievements of minority and non-minority students and a wide gap between the quality of city and suburban schools."[18]

During the 1985-86 school year, the county board approved a limited number of magnet schools, all located in black communities. Presently, ten different magnet programs operate at the elementary, middle, and high school levels:

- Extended Day Program—provides before and after-school care and selected academic instruction for students from both inside and outside the school's boundaries. Seven schools currently have this program.
- Talented-and-Gifted (TAG) Program—has an entrance test and teacher reference requirement and is designed for students identified as suitable for advanced instruction. Nine schools currently offer the TAG program.
- Science and Math Program—exists in nine schools; it is designed to give students specialized instruction in a rigorous science and math curriculum.

- Traditional Academies/Academic Centers—located in six schools; emphasis is placed on highly structured learning in a very disciplined environment.
- Foreign Language Immersion Program—organized in two schools with French as the immersion language.
- Montessori School Program—offered at three schools.
- Creative Arts Programs—in one school, ranging from Kindergarten through eighth grade.
- Humanities/Social Science Program—located in one middle and one high school.
- University High School—located at one high school, with emphasis on college preparation.
- Visual and Performing Arts Center—located at one high school; like the TAG program, there is a performance requirement to enter this program.

The issue of the equity of participation in the various magnet programs has been present since the Memorandum of Understanding was signed.[19] Table 1 shows the level of participation in the county's magnet programs by race as of September 30, 1987.

The table reveals that 11,745 students are currently participating in the programs. Blacks make up 58% of the students, whereas non-blacks constitute 42%. The black participation rate is only 3.2% below the percentage of black students in the total school system total population. The table also indicates that black students represent 45% of those enrolled in the elementary school TAG and 44% of those enrolled in the middle school TAG program. While these percentages are significantly higher than the initial 30% black participation rate in TAG, they are still well below the 62.6% representation in the total school system population.

Six of the thirteen magnet programs at the elementary, middle, and high school levels have black participation rates well below their percentage of the total school population. These programs include elementary school Talented and Gifted, Foreign Language Immersion, and Montessori; middle school Talented and Gifted and Traditional Academy and Academic Centers; and high school Humanities and Social Science.

At every stage of the development of the magnet school program, waiting lists for enrollment have consisted largely of black students. The waiting lists have caused great concern in the black community and raised questions about the overall fairness of the program.[20] As a result, the board is now considering proposals that would eliminate waiting lists.[21]

Table 1 data merely show the physical presence of blacks and other students in the magnet programs; it does not indicate level of performance or degree of involvement in the programs. To make such assessments, it is necessary to examine test scores and other indicators of achievement levels and consider the students' ability to continue in the programs to the next level. According to the school board, this type of information will not be available until the end of the current academic year (1987-88).

The board has suggested that the magnet schools have successfully helped desegregate the public schools. The September 30, 1987 pupil census indicated that 83,691 or 81%

TABLE 1
Participation in Magnet Programs by Race*

Magnet Program	Total Enrolled	Outside				Inside			
		Blacks		Other		Blacks		Other	
		No.	%	No.	%	No.	%	No.	%
Talented and Gifted-Elem.	1476	534	36	638	43	139	9	165	11
Science/Math & Tech-Elem.	2960	592	20	295	10	1179	40	894	30
Traditional Academy & Academic Centers Elementary	2477	326	13	198	8	1180	48	773	31
Foreign Language Immersion	107	14	13	53	50	33	31	7	7
Montessori	183	30	16	117	64	32	17	4	2
Extended Day	554	62	11	46	8	415	75	31	6
Creative and Performing Arts	593	366	62	227	38	0	0	0	0
Talented and Gifted Middle	531	201	38	277	52	30	6	23	4
Science & Math Middle	740	124	17	113	15	424	57	79	11
Traditional/ Classical Academy Academic Center	1299	163	13	69	5	525	40	542	42
Humanities/Social Science, Middle	224	3	1	20	9	160	71	41	19
Humanities High	182	57	31	94	52	30	16	1	.05
Univ. High School/ Visual & Performing Arts	419	140	33	141	34	115	27	23	5
Totals		2612	22	2288	19	4262	36	2583	22

*As of September 30, 1987

Source: Table compiled from data provided by the Department of Pupil Accounting and School Boundaries, Prince George's County Public School System, October 28, 1987.

of the total public school students attended schools that were within the 10% to 80% guideline. The board noted that this percentage was consistent with the requirements of the Memorandum of Understanding which mandated that "at least 80 percent of the elementary, middle and high school students should be attending schools between 10 and 80 percent black" by the commencement of the 1987-88 school year.[22]

However, the desegregation requirement states, "as of the commencement of school year 1988-89, at least 85% of the elementary, middle and high school students will be attending schools that are between 10% and 80% black." The Board has indicated that "it is unlikely that this precise standard will be attained at that time," and reminded the court of the memorandum provision that "the ultimate measure of the success of a magnet school program can be determined, at its earliest, in the third year." The board therefore suggested that the 1988-89 standard could be met shortly thereafter.[23]

The Milliken II Schools

In 1977, the U.S. Supreme Court authorized the use of a limited number of one-race schools where the enrollment of black students could not reasonably be brought below 80%.[24] To compensate for the violation of the constitutional rights of the black students attending such schools, the Court ordered that a program of compensatory education be instituted in those schools. The program of Milliken II schools in Prince George's County is based on this principle.

The county school board cited a number of considerations in proposing the Milliken II schools. Specific issues to be addressed were "the rapidly changing demographics of the population; the concentration of certain schools with black student enrollments over 80% in given geographic areas; a limited pool of white students and those of other races reasonably available for magnet programs without adversely affecting the racial composition of the schools they presently attend; and the long distance of some populations to the schools."[25]

With these concerns in mind, the board asked the district court to allow ten schools to remain over 80% black and for these schools to receive compensatory and remedial educational programs and equipment. The plaintiffs agreed not to propose any attendance area realignment for these schools for the 1985-86 school year. According to the memorandum, the plaintiffs did not contend that each of the ten schools had to fall within the court's flexible guidelines. Rather, they contended that the *Swann* standards had to be met "for the existence of a small number of one-race schools in later years."[26] In *Swann*, the Court held that "It should be clear that the existence of some number of one-race schools within a school district is not in and of itself the mark of a system that still practices segregation by law." The court indicated that it "would scrutinize such schools, and require school authorities to establish that these schools' racial composition was not the result of discrimination."

Many black organizational and political leaders (organized as the Ad Hoc Committee to Achieve Quality Education in Prince George's County) had expressed their views about the reforms needed to achieve uniformly higher-quality education. The committee argued that emphasis should be placed on desegregation to achieve high-quality education rather than to achieve integration. The Board was urged to examine the philosophical, educational, and cultural assumptions of the school system as part of a strategy to transcend busing as a remedy for segregation and unequal quality of education.

The Ad Hoc Committee's positions did not preclude the development of one-race schools. Instead, its concerns focused on what was required to make education work for black students, regardless of the racial composition of the schools they attended. The Committee recommended that the Board: (1) hire and promote more black administrators and teachers; (2) eliminate the unequal allocation of resources among majority black versus majority white schools; (3) address the disproportionate suspension of black students and negative effects of tracking and ability groupings; (4) remove the

TABLE 2
Milliken II Program Components
1985-86 School Year

Program Component	Major Goal(s)
Reduced class size	Increase average teacher-student instructional time.
Additional mathematics and reading materials	Increase scope and depth of mathematics and reading instruction.
Supplemental media resources	Increase educational opportunity to acquire knowledge.
Enriched cultural programs	Increase cultural enrichment.
Summer school for "at risk" students	Increase educational opportunities of students "at risk" of failure.
Comer School Development Process	Improve/enhance school climate, increase parental involvement, and improve academic achievement.

Source: Magnet and Milliken II Programs Evaluation Report 1985-86 School Year, Prince George's County Public Schools Department of Evaluation and Research, February 1987, p. 18.

built-in advantage of white students by enrolling in the initial magnet schools; and (5) increase the level of general funding for the school system. In reference to one-race schools the committee recommended that the board develop educational enhancement modules for use in schools falling outside the student ratio guidelines. These modules would then be evaluated by the community as part of its deliberation regarding whether to support one-race schools in designated parts of the county.[27]

Since the introduction of the initial ten Milliken II schools, the Board has added nine others. Among the nineteen present Milliken II schools in the county system, there are sixteen elementary, one middle, and two high schools.[28] The information in Table 2 summarizes the basic components of the Milliken II program and highlights its major goals.

These program components were conceptualized by the school system to implement the Milliken II program. The Memorandum of Understanding had only provided that in addition to their regular staffing and resources, these schools would receive the following: (1) a reduced instructional staff-to-student ratio, (2) a full-time guidance counselor, (3) a full-time library media specialist, (4) a full-time reading teacher, (5) full-day kindergarten, (6) fully equipped computer labs, (7) portable computers, (8) enriched instructional programs in reading, language arts, and mathematics, (9) a cultural arts program, (10) an after-school tutorial program, (11) a summer enrichment program, and (12) the Comer Development Program (see Comer, *et al.'s* article in this volume).

Opinions differ regarding the success of Milliken II schools in reaching their goals. For its evaluations, the board has relied on achievement test performance, provision of promised resources, and implementation of the Comer school management plan. Others measure success by factors that include academic achievement, resources, Comer's plan, curriculum enhancement, and staff development and diversification.[29]

One year after the Milliken Program was introduced, the school system reported improvements in the test scores of students at several of the Milliken II schools. Specifically, it noted that: (1) Milliken II students who took the October 1986 California Achievement Test increased average test scores for reading, mathematics, and language; (2) the rate of improvement in the Milliken II schools was greater than that of all students in the school district in third and fifth grade mathematics and language and third grade reading; (3) the Milliken II students' rate of improvement was greater than that for all black students in the school district in third and fifth grade mathematics and language, and in third grade reading; and (4) the rate of improvement for those Milliken II schools that were implementing the program most successfully was, on the average, several times the rate of improvement for all students in the school system.[30]

Questions have been raised, however, about whether the schools are "teaching the test" and thereby producing results that do not reflect improvements in educational quality. Those who voice these concerns believe that it is necessary to measure the success of Milliken II schools by examining their overall effectiveness in producing high-achieving students (as measured by national standards) by using a culturally-sensitive curriculum and featuring active parental participation. The board has demonstrated sensitivity to the need to use this more general measure of success and has appointed a full-time program implementation coordinator.

At this point it is not clear what the board's long-term plans are for the Milliken II schools. At least three options are currently being actively debated by board members and community leaders. Some would have the Milliken II schools converted to magnet schools to attract the requisite number of white students. Others would allow the Milliken II schools to remain mostly black and receive the compensatory resources. Many in the community support the idea of instituting an open enrollment policy to allow white students to enter, using the Milliken II status as a type of magnet. The basic question is whether it is better, educationally and developmentally, for black students to be in one-race schools throughout elementary and secondary school. Some contend that being in one-race schools may restrict black students' opportunities to receive the benefits of the magnet programs.

In many ways the Milliken II schools are the essence of Prince George's county's desegregation program. They reduce the pressure on the Board of Education to integrate schools in white majority communities and assist in creating racial stabilization, which is considered important by many to the development of real estate, the allocation of political power, and the control of population movement.[31] These are not necessarily positive developments because they often mean controlling the size of the black population, limiting its residential choices, and physically confining the blacks' base of political power.[32]

CONCLUSION AND CONTINUING CONCERNS

By adopting the magnet and Milliken II-based desegregation program, the school board indicated that it was willing to go a step beyond the physical desegregation of schools toward the achievement of higher quality education for all students. Many questions are now before the Board of Education, the answers to which will ultimately indicate whether it has been successful in achieving equal-quality education for all children using magnet and Milliken II schools. These questions include: (1) is the academic performance of children in Milliken II schools improving consistently at the same rate as those of children in the regular and magnet school programs; (2) which magnet program is having the greatest positive impact on academic achievement; (3) what is the comparative academic performance of magnet and non-magnet students in schools that have magnet components; (4) how is the academic performance of comprehensive school students affected by the departure of TAG and other magnet school students; and (5) are there significant differences between instructional staff qualifications and teaching experience, for magnet versus non-magnet and Milliken II schools?

Concerns about the Milliken II schools have received considerable attention in reports filed with the board by the Community Advisory Council. These concerns include maintaining the mandated student/teacher ratio, providing resource materials, and developing a multi-cultural curriculum are examples. Questions related to the full implementation of the Comer Program continue to be raised; some feel that the program has not been properly conceptualized or publicized widely enough, particularly among parents of Milliken II students.

Although these concerns continue, the school system has taken steps to address them. Several in-service workshops for staff have been held with Comer and members of his staff, a Milliken II coordinator was hired with responsibility for the Comer program, and additional information was developed to describe the different aspects of the program. Nonetheless, effective parental involvement with the schools remains a serious shortcoming.

Four basic developments have taken place in the county that are critical to the realization of a unitary public school system. The magnet and Milliken II program has evolved within the context of these larger developments: (1) A policy and institutional framework has been developed within which desegregation and effective education can be achieved. This framework has the potential to allow more effective community input and does not require direct involvement by federal courts. (2) There has been an increase in public understanding of the need to support public education, as demonstrated by the voters' 1984 decision to modify the property tax limitation (TRIM) legislation, which had previously limited the county's ability to fund public education. (3) Elected officials are more aware of the fact that school segregation, low academic achievement, and inequality in public education are continuing problems that cannot be pushed aside by premature assertions that unitary status has been achieved. (4) In addition, they have a better appreciation of the need to financially support public education and give it increased public relations support. At the core of these developments has been the realization that the quality of public education in the county cannot be improved without a basic improvement in the academic performance of black students, who make up almost two-thirds of the school population.

NOTES

1. *Report on Racial Composition by School*, Prince George's Public Schools, September 30, 1987, p. 10.
2. *The Business of Education*, A Report to the Board of Education of Prince George's County, prepared by Crosby International Group/Institute for Educational Leadership, October 1985, p. 1.
3. 347 U.S. 483 (1954).
4. 402 U.S. 1 (1971). The year the suit was filed black students comprised 22.4% of the school population, but there was only one black on the Board of Education. Today, there are two blacks on the nine-member board. The second black was initially appointed in 1981.
5. 355 F. Supp. 1034 (1972).
6. Vaughn, 355, F. Supp. 1051, 1064.
7. Vaughn, 574, F. 1230 (1983).
8. Green, Robert L., *Final Report on Desegregation of Prince George's County Public Schools*, submitted to Chief Judge Frank A. Kaufman, March 11, 1985.
9. See *The Challenge to Achieve Quality Education in Prince George's County, Maryland*, a report prepared by the Ad Hoc Committee on Quality Education in Prince George's County, April 30, 1985, for a summary of the concerns of the black community.
10. Memorandum of Understanding, Order of Chief Judge Frank A. Kaufman, U.S. District Court, June 30, 1985.
11. *Ibid.*
12. The initial council was chaired by John Slaughter, Chancellor of the University of Maryland, College Park. Presently, it is chaired by James Lyons, Sr., President of Bowie State College.
13. Shortly after the memorandum was signed, the top administration of the school system was reorganized, resulting in two black associate and two black assistant superintendents. However, little progress has been made in hiring black classroom teachers, notwithstanding the announcement of creative recruitment strategies.
14. See the "National Study of Magnet Schools," *A Chronicle* 5, no. 8 (June 1984).
15. Trombley, William, "Magnet Schools Costly in St. Louis," *Integrated Education* 15 (December 1977), p. 97.
16. *Ibid.*
17. Schmidt, George N., "Education Wonderland," *The Chicago Reporter*, December 28, 1983, p. 10.
18. Rose, Elizabeth, "Massive Milwaukee Study Reveals Quality Education Gap," *Education Week* 5, no. 18 (January 15, 1985), p. 25.
19. See Christine H. Rossell, "Magnet Schools as a Desegregation Tool," *Urban Education* 14, no. 3 (October 1979) for an analysis of some of the concerns about equity and magnet school programs.
20. See *Equity Issues in the Prince George's County School Desegregation Plan*, Equity Committee of the County Council of PTS's of Prince George's County, March 10, 1986, pp. 6-9.
21. See the recommendations of the Advisory Council on Magnet and Compensatory Educational Programs as transmitted by James Lyons, Sr. to the Board of Education on November 9, 1987.
22. Memorandum, p. 2.
23. *Semi-Annual Report to the Court*. Board of Education of Prince George's County, November 1987, pp. 7-8.
24. *Milliken v. Bradley*, 433 U.S. 267 (1977).
25. *Magnet and Milliken II Programs Evaluation Report: 1985-1986 School Year*, Program Review Office, Department of Evaluation and Research, Prince George's Public Schools, February 1987, p. 3.
26. Memorandum, p. 3.
27. *Challenge to Achieve Quality Education in Prince George's County*, p. 5.
28. *Report to the Court*, November 1987, pp. 6-7.
29. See testimony of Parent Adocates for Milliken II before the Board of Education, February 26, 1987, and a letter from Concerned Parents of John Bayne Elementary School to the Board, February 12, 1987, for examples of these concerns.
30. *Analysis of Milliken II Test Score Data After The First Year*, Staff Report to the Board of Education of Prince George's County, May 11, 1987. pp. 1-2.
31. Thornton, Alvin, "Milliken Schools Are Essence of Desegregation Plan," *The Prince George's Journal*, June 16, 1987, p. A-8.
32. See Paul E. Peterson, "School Desegregation and Racial Stabilization," in Stephen M. David and Paul E. Peterson (eds.), *Urban Politics and Public Policy: The City in Crisis* (New York: Praeger Publishers, 1976) for an analysis of the Chicago Board of Education's concern about the impact of school desegregation on racial stability, real estate development, and the development of political power among blacks.

15

The Consent Decree as a Tool for Desegregation in Higher Education

James J. Prestage and Jewel L. Prestage

Public policy has been defined as "a purposive course of action followed by an actor or a set of actors in dealing with a problem or matter of concern."[1] Several approaches to the study of public policy have been developed. One of these approaches focuses on *the process* by which public policy is formed; identifies six stages of activity. In order of occurrence, these stages are: problem formation, policy agenda, policy formulation, policy adoption, policy implementation, and policy evaluation.[2]

Within the basic framework outlined above, this study examines the 1981 Consent Decree (designed to deal with the problem of desegregation of public higher education in Louisiana) as part of a "purposive course of action." The specific stage of the policy process examined is the policy implementation stage, the point at which the adopted policy is put into effect. A period of almost eight years has elapsed since the Consent Decree was adopted as "public policy" in higher education in the state and it has not yet been fully implemented. This is a matter of grave concern because it is only through the application of the adopted policy, or policy implementation that the true meaning of the policy emerges.[3]

The consent decree is a legal mechanism that constitutes an official policy response to the lingering problem of racial segregation and gross resource inequities in state-sponsored systems of higher education. In concept, it is somewhat akin to the issues of busing and magnet schools. Indeed, it is a remedy, like other remedies utilized at the level of public secondary schools, encompassing efforts to equalize resources across all educational units affected, and attempting to selectively offer specialized programs at certain institutions in order to encourage a racial mix across institutions. The consent decree is, therefore, generally an ambitious and grand design to restructure higher education in states with particularly onerous separate systems.

The consent decree is also a federally imposed remedy, generally representing the result of years of unsuccessful efforts to obtain satisfactory voluntary compliance by the

*Originally published in the *Urban League Review*, Vol. 10, no.2 (1986–87) and was entitled "The Consent Decree as an Instrument for Desegregation in Higher Education."

target state. The consent decree thus tests the commitment of both federal regulators and state policy makers to dismantling the legacy and reality of separate and unequal treatment of blacks, prevalent since the earliest establishment of separate institutions of learning for blacks. As several southern states are currently under various court orders to restructure state systems of higher education, it is important that we understand the meaning and implications of a major policy initiative. This policy directly affects the life chances of hundreds of thousands of blacks who look to historically black state institutions for educational opportunities.

BACKGROUND TO THE LOUISIANA CONSENT DECREE

The predominantly white public institutions in Louisiana include the Louisiana State University System (LSU) under the LSU Board of Supervisors, eight of the nine institutions under the Board of Trustees for State Colleges and Universities, and two special schools under the Board of Elementary and Secondary Education. Louisiana's predominantly black public institutions of higher education include Grambling State University under the Board of Trustees for State Colleges and Universities and the three campuses of Southern University System (SU) under the SU Board of Supervisors. This higher education system had been challenged through a number of legal and extra-legal strategies, but remained principally intact even after the 1954 *Brown v. Board of Education* decision which outlawed forced racial segregation in precollegiate education. Efforts to alter the Louisiana system of higher education are documented through a series of court cases and other actions. The legal bases for the challenge to segregation that resulted in the Consent Decree on which this study focuses are the Fourteenth Amendment to the U.S. Constitution and Title VI of the Civil Rights Act of 1964.

On three separate occasions between 1965 and 1974, the U.S. Department of Health, Education and Welfare (HEW) notified officials of Louisiana that the state was in violation of both the 1964 Civil Rights Act and the Fourteenth Amendment by operating a dual system of higher education. In reaction of these notices, the governing boards of public institutions in the state had each public college and university prepare a document to substantiate the state's contention that it was in compliance with the law. These documents were compiled into a single document and submitted to HEW. The document was declared by HEW to be unacceptable and Louisiana was again directed to submit a plan to bring it into compliance or face the loss of federal funds.

However, the state made no effort to develop such a plan. In the absence of a plan or a good-faith effort to develop one, HEW referred this matter to the U.S. Department of Justice and on Thursday, March 14, 1974, a suit was filed in the U.S. District Court in Baton Rouge, claiming that Louisiana operated a dual system of higher education in violation of the 1964 Civil Rights Act and the Fourteenth Amendment. On September 8, 1981 (approximately seven and a half years after the suit was filed) a panel of three federal judges accepted a plan, hereafter referred to as the Consent Decree. The plan had been developed by representatives from the three managment boards for Louisiana's higher education (Louisiana State University Board of Supervisors, Southern

University Board of Supervisors and the Board of Trustees for State Colleges and Universities), the Louisiana Board of Regents, and the U.S. Department of Justice, in settlement of the suit.[4]

In September 1982, the U.S. District Court for the Eastern District of Louisiana accepted an addendum to the Consent Decree dealing with two-year collegiate offerings in the Caddo/Bossier Parishes area. The addendum specified the development of Southern University at Shreveport/Bossier (SUSBO) into a comprehensive community college. It also called for a specific cooperating arrangement between SUSBO and Bossier Parish Community College (BPCC).

The Consent Decree and addendum provided numerous elements of change to the policies of higher education in Louisiana. The elements of the Consent Decree selected for examination in this article are: (1) governance, (2) faculty development programs, (3) cooperative efforts of proximate institutions, (4) enhancement of predominantly black institutions, and (5) monitoring and reporting. The article concludes with a discussion of the relative successes of efforts to implement the decree in the above-mentioned five areas of analysis, as well as a brief discussion on the efficacy of the consent decree as a mechanism for policy implementation and for bringing about major transformations in black higher education.

GOVERNANCE

The Consent Decree provides for the increase of other-race representation on each of the four boards for higher education in Louisiana, so that the composition of the membership approximates the racial makeup of the population of the state. "Other-race" refers to blacks when the Louisiana Board of Regents, the Board of Supervisors of Louisiana State University, and the Board of Trustees for State Colleges and Universities are under consideration, and to whites when reference is made to the Board of Supervisors of Southern University.

Louisiana's population is approximately 70% white and 30% black. The Louisiana Board of Regents has a membership of fifteen, while each of the other three boards has a membership of seventeen. Each board has a student representative not included in the above figures. The Consent Decree requires that the state take affirmative steps to achieve an approximate 70% white, 30% black membership for the Louisiana Board of Regents, the Board of Supervisors for Louisiana State University, and the Board of Trustees for State Colleges and Universities as early as practicable, but within a period not to exceed six years. Further, composition of the Board of Supervisors for Southern University should be approximately 70% black, 30% white to reflect inversely the racial composition of the state. Board members are appointed by the governor and confirmed by the Senate. Except when appointed to fill a vacancy caused by death or resignation, board members serve six-year staggered terms with approximately one-third of the membership of each board appointed every two years.

The racial composition of Louisiana's four higher education boards for 1982 through 1985 is contained in Table 1. The table is taken from the *Fourth Annual Report of the Consent Decree Monitoring Committee.*[5]

TABLE 1
Racial Composition of Louisiana's Four Higher Education Boards

	1982				1983				1984				1985			
	White		Black		White		Black		White		Black		White		Black	
	N	%	N	%	N	%	N	%	N	%	N	%	N	%	N	%
Board of Regents	12	80	3	20	12	80	3	20	12	80	3	20	12	80	3	20
LSU Board of Super.	15	88	2	12	15	88	2	12	15	88	2	12	15	88	2	12
*SU Board of Super.	2	12	14	82	3	18	13	76	3	18	13	76	4	24	13	76
Board of Trustees	15	88	2	12	13	76	4	24	13	76	4	24	13	76	4	24

The above figures do not include the student representative. *Also, one American Indian served on the Board of Supervisors for Southern University 1982, 1983, 1984.

The data reveal that other-race representation on the Board of Regents and the LSU Board of Supervisors has remained constant over the four-year period, while on the Southern University Board of Supervisors, it increased from 12% in 1982 to 18% in 1983 and to 24% in 1985. Other-race representation on the Board of Trustees for State Colleges and Universities increased from 12% in 1982 to 24% in 1983 and has been maintained at that level. To achieve the six-year goal adopted by the state, another black person should be appointed to the Board of Regents, three more to the LSU Board of Supervisors, and one more to the Board of Trustees for State Colleges and Universities. Similarly, one more white person should be appointed to the Southern University Board of Supervisors. The state will have the opportunity to achieve the goals of other-race representation on the various boards when several terms on each board expire on or before December 31, 1986.[6]

FACULTY DEVELOPMENT PROGRAMS

The Consent Decree provides two programs to increase the number of terminal degree holders among incumbent faculty members of the state's colleges and universities: the Board of Regents' Graduate Fellowship Program and the Southern University and Grambling State University Faculty Development Program.

The Regents' Graduate Fellowship Program is domiciled with the Louisiana Board of Regents. Major guidelines governing this program are:

1. For a period of six years, ten persons selected to participate in the program by the Board of Regents on the advice of interinstitutional disciplinary faculty committees will be awarded $10,000 annual stipends for a maximum of three years. In the selection process, consideration shall be given to college-level grade point average, Graduate Record Examination score, letters of nomination and recommendation, and commitment to teach at an other-race public institution of higher education in Louisiana for three years.
2. Each predominantly white institution must identify and document up to three fields or disciplines in which its black faculty recruitment efforts have been unsuccessful due to lack of qualified applicants, and each predominantly black

institution must do the same in regard to its unsuccessful white faculty recruitment efforts. Each four-year predominantly white institution shall nominate three black persons, and the Southern University System and Grambling State University shall each nominate one white person to compete for one of the $10,000 stipends. Nominees must be from among advanced graduate students and faculty in a discipline specified by the Board of Regents as lacking a qualified other-race applicant pool.

3. All nominations for the Graduate Fellowship Program must be from the institutions, as individuals may not apply directly to the Board of Regents.

Each year the Board of Regents puts in place the mechanism to comply with the foregoing specifics. According to the *Fourth Annual Report of the Consent Decree Monitoring Committee,* as of June 30, 1985, thirty-two Graduate Fellowships had been awarded. Nine persons, all black, had completed the requirements for the terminal degree. Of the nine graduates, four were employed in accordance with the requirements of the Consent Decree. One was relieved of obligation to the state of Louisiana when efforts on the part of the recipient, Louisiana's public institutions of higher education, and the Board of Regents to identify suitable employment at a Louisiana other-race institution failed. Four were still either negotiating contracts with other-race institutions or actively seeking employment elsewhere. There are ten first-time recipients for the 1985-86 school term, bringing the total number of Graduate Fellowship recipients to forty-two. Thus, of the forty-two, to date nine (or 21%) have successfully completed doctorates. Less than half have been employed by Louisiana institutions, however.

The second program, the Southern University and Grambling State University Faculty Development Program, is administered by the respective institutions within approved procedures and criteria. The Consent Decree provides that "in addition to the Board of Regents' Graduate Fellowship Program, the state recognizes the need to provide advanced educational opportunities for faculty members at Louisiana's predominantly black institutions as one means of enhancing programs at Grambling State and Southern Universities." Under the program, faculty who have not earned terminal degrees at each institution may take paid leaves of absence in order to do so. For six years Grambling State University will receive $70,000 annually and the Southern University System will receive $230,000 annually. Southern University (including all three campuses), Grambling State University, their higher education boards, and the Board of Regents were directed to work together to develop a detailed plan for operation of the program. The Southern University and Grambling State University Faculty Development Program has been reasonably successful to date with thirty-three of the total fifty-five participants having begun advanced degree course work or having advanced to the dissertation stage; another nine have earned the terminal degree.

COOPERATIVE EFFORTS OF PROXIMATE INSTITUTIONS

The Consent Decree requires that the proximate public institutions in Lincoln Parish (Grambling State University and Louisiana Tech University), in Baton Rouge (Louisiana State University [LSU] and Southern University [SUBR]), and in New Orleans (Southern University [SUNO] and University of New Orleans [UNO]) develop cooperative plans to include (1) a faculty exchange program, (2) a student exchange program, (3) dual and/or cooperative degree programs, and (4) other cooperative efforts.

Goals for the proximate institutions for the period of 1982-83 to 1987-88 are set forth in the decree itself. Without exception, the proximate institutions met or surpassed the goals established for other-race faculty exchange for the period 1982-85. Moreover, the proximate institutions have achieved or exceeded the goals established for dual and/or cooperative degree programs. The goal of four dual and/or cooperative degree programs between Louisiana Tech and Grambling was achieved and exceeded by five during the 1982-83 academic school year, and has been maintained. The dual and/or cooperative program goal of five degree programs between SUBR and LSU was achieved in 1983 and has been maintained. With regard to other-race student exchange, only UNO and SUNO have met the established goals. Other-race student exchange efforts between the other affected institutions, as measured by credit hours completed, have lagged behind goals, but have shown gains since the initiation of exchange efforts.

ENHANCEMENT OF PREDOMINANTLY BLACK INSTITUTIONS

In addition to providing the opportunity for faculty members at the predominantly black institutions to pursue the terminal degree, the Consent Decree called for the enhancement of both programs and facilities of these institutions. With regard to programs, the Decree states that "the state shall strengthen and enhance the roles of its predominantly black institutions in the state system of public higher-education, and increase their capability to attract other-race students, by strengthening programs and by locating new academic programs at those institutions." The Decree further specifies that "the state shall provide additional funds in the amount of $1,000,000 per year for six years to be appropriated as follows: (1) $373,000 to Grambling State University; (2) $627,000 to the Southern University System. These funds are to be utilized for the general enhancement of the institutions, subject to the approval of the appropriate higher education board, the Board of Regents and the Governor or his designee."

While "the strengthening of programs" is not specifically addressed in terms of the precise means to be utilized in accomplishing it, it is surmised that such is expected to occur essentially through (1) the faculty development program and (2) the use of funds allocated for the general enhancement of the institutions. Participation in the faculty development program is open to all faculty members without regard to discipline. While the general enhancement funds may be used to assist in the strengthening of academic programs, it is within the purview of the institutions to use these funds to strengthen their support areas as well. Perhaps the only restraint in the use of these funds is that institutions were encouraged to refrain from using them for salaries for regular employees or for any activity requiring recurring expenditure.

Table 2 contains a listing of programs provided by the Consent Decree for Southern University-Baton Rouge, Southern University-New Orleans, and Grambling State Uni-

TABLE 2
New Academic Degree Programs Required by the Consent Decree
at Predominantly Black Institutions

Southern University-Baton Rouge

Program	Date Implemented
B.S. in Medical Technology (jointly with LSU Med. Ctr.)	Aug 1983
B.S. in Physical Therapy (jointly with LSU Med. Ctr.)	" "
B.S. in Cytotechnology (jointly with LSU Med. Ctr.)	" "
B.S. in Occupational Therapy (jointly with LSU Med. Ctr.)	" "
B.S. in Rehabilitation Counseling (jointly with LSU Med. Ctr.)	" "
B.S. in Cardiopulmonary Science (jointly with LSU Med. Ctr.)	" "
B.S. in Environmental Chemistry	" "
M.Ed. in Special Education (jointly with LSU-BR)	" "
Ed.S. in Special Education (jointly with LSU-BR)	Aug 1985
Ed.D in Special Education	" "
Ph.D. in Special Education	
M.S. in Computer Science	Aug 1983
Master of Public Administration (cooperatively with LSU-BR; School of Public and Urban Affairs)	" "
B.S. in Rehabilitation Counseling Psychology	" "
M.A. in Rehabilitation Counseling Psychology	" "
M.S. in Rehabilitation Counseling Psychology	" "
Center for Small Farm Research	Sep 1983
Master of Professional Accountancy (School of Accountancy)	Aug 1985
B.S. in Nursing (School of Nursing)	Aug 1986[1]
Doctor of Professional Accountancy	[2]

Southern University-New Orleans

Program	Date Implemented
A.S. in Computer Science	Aug 1982
B.S. in Substance Abuse	" "
B.S. in Medical Technology (jointly with LSU Med. Ctr.)	" "
B.S. in Physical Therapy (jointly with LSU Med. Ctr.)	" "
B.S. in Cytotechnology (jointly with LSU Med. Ctr.)	" "
B.S. in Occupational Therapy (jointly with LSU Med. Ctr.)	" "
B.S. in Rehabilitation Counseling (jointly with LSU Med.Ctr.)	" "
B.S. in Cardiopulmonary Science (jointly with LSU Med. Ctr.)	" "
B.S. in Criminal Justice	Aug 1984
B.S. in General Technology	Aug 1983
B.A. in Print Journalism	" "
Master of Social Work	" "
B.A. in Urban Studies	Aug 1984
B.S. in Transportation	" "

[1]Projected date for implementation.
[2]Date for implementation is undecided, perhaps after expiration of Consent Decree (December 31, 1987).

TABLE 2 (Continued)

Grambling State University

Program	Date Implemented
B.S. in Medical Technology (jointly with LSU Med. Ctr.)	Aug 1983
B.S. in Physical Therapy (jointly with LSU Med. Ctr.)	" "
B.S. in Cytotechnology (jointly with LSU Med. Ctr.)	" "
B.S. in Occupational Therapy (jointly with LSU Med. Ctr.)	" "
B.S. in Rehabilitation Counseling (jointly with LSU Med. Ctr.)	" "
B.S. in Cardiopulmonary Science (jointly with LSU Med. Ctr.)	" "
M.S. in Developmental Education	" "
M.A. in Liberal Studies[3]	" "
M.A.T. in Social Sciences	Jan 1984
M.A.T. in Natural Sciences	Aug 1983
Ed.D in Developmental Education	Aug 1984
B.S. in Nursing (School of Nursing)	" "
M.S. in Criminal Justice	" "
Master of Business Administration with Options in General Administration and Computer and Information Systems (in cooperation with Louisiana Tech)[4]	Aug 1985
Master of Social Work	Aug 1986[1]
Master of Public Administration	Aug 1986[1]
Ed.D. in Developmental Education	Aug 1986[1]
M.S. in International Business and Trade (in cooperation with Louisiana Tech)	Aug 1986[1]

Southern University-Shreveport/Bossier City[5]

Program	Date Implemented
A.S. in early Childhood Education	Aug 1984
A.A. in Day Care Administration	" "
A.S. in Small Business Administration	" "
A.S. in Surgical Technology	" "
Certificate in Nurse's Assistant	Aug 1986[1]
A.A. in Legal Assistant	Aug 1985
A.A. in Mental Health/Mental Retardation	Aug 1986[1]
A.S. in Computer Science	Aug 1985
A.A.S. in Banking and Finance	Aug 1986[1]
A.A.S. in Electronics Technology	" " [1]
A.A. in Tourism Travel Management	" " [1]
A.S. Hotel/Restaurant Management	" " [1]

Southern University-Shreveport/Bossier City and Bossier Parish Community College[2]

Program	Date Implemented
Associate in Occupational Studies in Data Processing	Aug 1984
A.A.S. in Medical Records Technician	Aug 1985
A.A.S. in Respiratory Therapy	" "

[1]Projected date for implementation.
[2]The Addendum to the Consent Decree requires SUSBO and BPCC to offer at least three but no more than five dual or cooperative programs.
[3]Substituted for M.A.T. in Humanities with approval of U.S. Dept. of Justice.
[4]Substituted for Options in Administration, Computer Science, and Information Systems with approval of U.S. Dept. of Justice.
[5]Although the Consent Decree does not prescribe programs for SUSBO, the Addendum does require the implementation of no fewer than twelve exclusive new programs at SUSBO.

versity and the date each was implemented. Where programs have not yet been implemented, projected dates are given. This table also contains a listing of programs for Southern University-Shreveport/Bossier (SUSBO), dates of implementation, and a listing of dual or cooperative programs between SUSBO and Bossier City Community College (BCCC).

The Consent Decree provides for twenty new programs for Southern University at Baton Rouge, fourteen for Southern University at New Orleans, and eighteen for Grambling State University. The addendum to the Consent Decree stipulates that "as part of the institutional development plan, the assisting agency shall recommend and assist in the preparation and implementation of no fewer than twelve exclusive new programs at SUSBO." In addition, it requires SUSBO and BPCC to offer at least three but no more than five dual or cooperative programs. The twelve programs have received the necessary approvals.

Of the twenty programs designated for SUBR, only two remain to be implemented. These are the Bachelor of Science in Nursing and the Doctor of Professional Accountancy. The offering of the latter and the Ed.D. and Ph.D. in Special Education represents the first time that programs at the doctoral level have been offered by this institution.

All fourteen programs designated for SUNO have been implemented. The offering of the Master of Social Work degree represents the first time this institution has offered a program above the bachelors level.

Fourteen of the eighteen programs designated for GSU have been implemented. GSU has obtained the necessary approvals to commence offering the Ed.D. in Developmental Education. For the first time GSU, like SUBR, will offer a program of study at the doctoral level. Six of the twelve programs approved for SUSBO have been implemented.

To date, most of these programs have not been subjected to on-site reviews by external consultants. In the absence of such reviews, there is no basis for addressing the quality of these programs. In most cases, the programs must be in operation for three or more years before a bid for accreditation can even be initiated. However, the programs in Rehabilitation Counseling Psychology at SUBR have received initial accreditation as well as the Social Work program at SUNO.

One expected outcome from the enhancement of predominantly black institutions was an increase in other-race enrollment at these institutions. Tables 3, 4, 5, and 6 provide information regarding enrollment in the new programs organized by major and race. In the main, the new programs have been well-received by students. However, there are continued efforts to disseminate information regarding these programs with the view of recruiting more, especially other-race students. Of concern also are those undergraduate programs which have low enrollments.

In Table 4, all eight of the new programs at SUNO show the enrollment of some other-race students. Of particular interest is that for the past two years the Substance Abuse program has had more other-race students than black students.

The Master of Education in Special Education offered by SUBR has the largest overall enrollment of students and other-race students, as revealed in Table 3. However,

TABLE 3
Majors by Race in New Academic Programs 1982-86[1]

| | Southern University-Baton Rouge[2] | | | | | | | | | | | |
| | 1982-83 | | | 1983-84 | | | 1984-85 | | | 1985-86 | | |
Program	B	W	O	B	W	O	B	W	O	B	W	O
Environmental Chemistry (B.S.)	—	—	—	2	0	1	4	0	1	6	0	1
Special Education (M.Ed.)	—	—	—	51	22	4	89	13	1	95	11	0
Special Education (Ed.D.)	—	—	—	—	—	—	—	—	—	0	0	1
Special Education (Ph.D.)	—	—	—	—	—	—	—	—	—	0	0	1
Computer Science (M.S.)	—	—	—	33	1	17	17	3	45	29	0	61
Public Administration (MPA)	—	—	—	12	0	6	29	1	25	36	2	42
Rehab. Counseling Psychology (B.S.)	—	—	—	5	0	0	19	0	0	37	1	0
Rehab. Counseling Psychology (M.S., M.S.)	—	—	—	8	0	0	14	1	0	26	4	0
Professional Accountancy (MPA)	—	—	—	—	—	—	—	—	—	8	0	14

[1]Allied Health programs and those that have not been implemented are omitted.
[2]Fall semester enrollments are given.

TABLE 4
Majors by Race in New Academic Programs 1982-86[1]

| | Southern University-New Orleans[2] | | | | | | | | | | | |
| | 1982-83 | | | 1983-84 | | | 1984-85 | | | 1985-86 | | |
Program	B	W	O	B	W	O	B	W	O	B	W	O
Computer Science (A.S.)	47	0	3	167	0	3	323	0	10	374	10	32
Substance Abuse (B.S.)	31	26	2	35	27	0	59	60	2	64	65	2
Criminal Justice (B.S.)	—	—	—	—	—	—	36	5	0	40	10	0
General Technology (B.S.)	—	—	—	0	0	0	22	1	15	17	2	3
Print Journalism (B.A.)	—	—	—	3	1	0	24	0	0	45	5	5
Social Work (MSW)	—	—	—	25	3	0	57	19	0	60	22	0
Urban Studies (B.A.)	—	—	—	—	—	—	16	1	0	18	2	0
Transportation (B.S.)	—	—	—	—	—	—	39	2	1	46	3	1

[1]Allied Health programs and those that have not been implemented are omitted.
[2]Fall semester enrollments are given.

based on the large number of inquiries made regarding the program in Nursing, it is anticipated that it will have the largest overall enrollment and the largest other-race enrollment of all new programs initiated on that campus. This pattern has already developed at Grambling according to Table 6. That institution's Bachelor of Science in Nursing has the largest overall enrollment of students among all consent decree programs at all institutions. The graduate programs, except for one, have been well received at Grambling according to enrollment figures. Several programs at SUNO, SUBR, and GSU have already had their first graduates.

Funds appropriated to the predominantly black institutions by the Louisiana Legislature for the support of the academic degree granting programs mandated by the Consent Decree for the period of 1982-85 are shown in Table 7. For the four years in question, a total of $20,088,124 was appropriated to initiate and sustain fifty degree-granting programs. As expected, the data reveal that for each of the four years the amount appropriated to each institution was increased. The increases coincided with

TABLE 5
Majors by Race in New Academic Programs 1982-86[1]

| | Southern University-Shreveport/Bossier[2] | | | | | | | | | | | |
| | 1982-83 | | | 1983-84 | | | 1984-85 | | | 1985-86 | | |
Program	B	W	O	B	W	O	B	W	O	B	W	O
Early Childhood Education (A.S.)	—	—	—	—	—	—	32	2	0	40	2	0
Day Care Administration (A.A.)	—	—	—	—	—	—	13	1	0	19	0	0
Small Business Administration (A.S.)	—	—	—	—	—	—	3	0	0	6	0	0
Legal Assistant (A.A.)	—	—	—	—	—	—	—	—	—	1	0	0
Surgical Technology (A.S.)	—	—	—	—	—	—	—	—	—	12	4	0
Computer Science (A.S.)	—	—	—	—	—	—	—	—	—	40	3	0

[1]Allied Health programs and those that have not been implemented are omitted.
[2]Fall semester enrollments are given.

TABLE 6
Majors by Race in New Academic Programs 1982-86[1]

| | Grambling State University[2] | | | | | | | | | | | |
| | 1982-83 | | | 1983-84 | | | 1984-85 | | | 1985-86 | | |
Program	B	W	O	B	W	O	B	W	O	B	W	O
Developmental Education (M.S.)	—	—	—	17	2	0	25	2	0	30	1	0
Liberal Studies (M.A.)	—	—	—	16	0	0	27	0	1	33	2	0
Social Sciences (M.A.T.)	—	—	—	—	—	—	15	0	0	35	0	0
Natural Sciences (M.A.T.)	—	—	—	5	0	0	6	0	2	8	0	3
Developmental Education (Ed.S.)	—	—	—	—	—	—	42	3	1	38	5	0
Nursing (B.S.)	—	—	—	—	—	—	264	11	0	203	19	0
Criminal Justice (M.S.)	—	—	—	—	—	—	19	2	0	25	0	1

[1]Allied Health programs and those that have not been implemented are omitted.
[2]Fall semester enrollments are given.

TABLE 7
Funds Appropriated to Predominantly Black Institutions by the Louisiana Legislature
for Academic Programs Mandated by the Consent Decree

Institutions	1982	1983	1984	1985	Total
Grambling	—0—	$ 356,963	$1,677,635	$ 3,276,355	$ 5,310,953
Southern Baton Rouge	$184,743	2,032,658	2,692,733	4,516,058	9,426,192
Southern-New Orleans	380,467	972,221	1,098,950	1,984,965	4,436,603
Southern-Shreveport	—0—	—0—	106,153	808,223	914,376
Total	$565,210	$3,361,842	$5,575,471	$10,585,601	$20,088,124

the introduction of new programs and the further development of those implemented during prior years.

With regard to the enhancement of facilities, the Consent Decree stipulates, "The state shall improve existing facilities and construct new facilities at its predominantly black institutions such that their physical plants will be comparable to those available at comparable predominantly white institutions. The parties agree that the new programs approved for each of the predominantly black institutions at New Orleans, Baton Rouge, and Lincoln Parish will require the construction of one or more new facilities."

TABLE 8
Consent Decree Facilities Development Funding 1983-1988 (Five-Year Plan)

Institution	New Construction	Renovation	Demolition	Master Plan	Total
Grambling	$14,831,608 (n = 4)	$16,681,772 (n = 16)	$ 52,109 (n = 12)	$ 80,000	$31,645,489
SUBR	$24,118,706 (n = 6)	$24,646,503 (n = 32)	$112,338 (n = 25)	$150,000	$52,027,437
SUNO	$ 6,271,155 (n = 1)	$ 1,772,634 (n = 5)	None	None	$ 8,043,789
SUSBO	None	$ 116,889	None	None	$ 116,889
Total	$48,221,469	$43,217,798	$164,447	$230,000	$91,833,714

The Decree also directed that the state provide $148,000 through the Board of Regents, for a study to be completed within six months, in order to determine the nature and extent of continuing deficiencies in the physical plants of Grambling State University and Southern University. A facilities plan was stipulated to identify capital outlay projects necessary to upgrade the physical plants of both colleges, consistent with their newly-defined missions and the goals of attracting other-race students.

The Board of Regents was directed to adjust its five-year capital outlay plan by January 1, 1983, to incorporate the recommendations of the facilities study. The Board was to assign the highest priority to correcting deficiencies identified by the study by providing necessary capital outlay funds. Capital outlay requirements identified in the adjusted five-year capital outlay plan and any new facilities for predominantly black institutions were to be funded and constructed as near as practicable within six years of entry of the decree. The Facilities Study Panel submitted its final report to the Board of Regents in August 1982.

The Board of Regents' adjusted five-year capital outlay plan (1983-88) for Consent Decree projects for the predominantly black institutions is summarized in Table 8. The projects may be placed in four categories: new construction, renovation, demolition, and master planning. Master planning includes landscape, facilities, and utilities planning. As revealed, the five-year plan for GSU provides for planning, constructing, and equipping four new buildings at an estimated cost of $14,830,608, renovating sixteen buildings at an estimated cost of $16,681,772, demolishing twelve buildings at an estimated cost of $52,109, and $80,000 of landscaping and facilities master planning. The estimated cost for all GSU projects is $31,645,489.

For SUBR, the five-year plan provides funds in the amount of $27,118,706 for planning, constructing and equipping of six new buildings, $24,646,503 for renovating thirty-two buildings, $112,338 for demolishing twenty-five buildings, and $150,000 for the utilities and landscape master plan. All SUBR projects are estimated at $52,027,437.

With regard to SUNO, the plan provides $6,271,155 for constructing and equipping of a multi-purpose building and $1,772,634 for renovating five buildings. The projected total for SUNO is $8,043,789. At SUSBO, only $116,889 is provided for computer

TABLE 9
Status Facilities Development at Predominantly Black Institutions

Institution	Total Projects Scheduled	Projects Completed	Projects Underway	Projects not Yet Begun
Grambling State Univ.	32	1	1	30
Southern Univ.-B.R.	63	6	8	49
Southern Univ.-N.O.	6	0	0	6
Southern USBO	1	1	0	0
	(Computer Equipment)			

equipment. A total of $91,833,714 was proposed by the Board of Regents for the predominantly black colleges.

There is a major controversy regarding one facilities enhancement question. Grambling State University has taken and continues to take the position that a Health, Physical Education, and Recreational Building was included in the Consent Decree settlement. The project was listed in the Board of Regents 1984-85 Consent Decree recommendations. However, the Board of Regents contends that the building is not a Consent Decree project, and the fact that it was listed in its 1984-85 recommendations was a "typographical" error. Table 9 presents a summary of the status of facilities development at these predominantly black institutions.

Of the four new construction projects at Grambling State University, not one has yet been initiated. At Southern University in Baton Rouge, only one of the six has been started while at SUNO, problems of land acquisition have delayed initiation of the work on the one building to be constructed. Among Grambling's sixteen renovation projects, only one has been completed and one is underway. Only one of the thirty-two projects at Southern University-Baton Rouge has been started, and at SUNO none are underway. Of the twenty-five demolition projects at Southern University-Baton Rouge six have been completed and none are currently underway. At Grambling State University, no projects have been started to date. The Master Planning work at Southern University-Baton Rouge has been completed and work is underway at Grambling. Acquisition and installation of computer equipment in existing buildings at SUSBO has been completed.

MONITORING AND REPORTING

As mandated in the Consent Decree, a Consent Decree Monitoring Committee (CDMC) was established. This nine-member committee is made up of a minimum of two representatives from each of the four higher education boards and one member appointed by the governor, who serves as chairman. It is specifically charged to "establish procedures for effectively monitoring compliance with the requirements of this Decree, for collecting data and filing all reports required thereunder and for making recommendations to assist in the achievement of the goals and objectives thereof."

Regular meetings of the CDMC are held bimonthly. Representatives of colleges and universities and other state agencies make presentations in response to requests made by the CDMC. A subcommittee visits the various public colleges and universities on alternate months to examine institutional activities called for in the Consent Decree. On or before August 15 of each year, the CDMC is required to file an annual report with the Court and the U.S. Department of Justice. This report describes the actions taken by the defendants to fulfill the commitments set forth in the Consent Decree. Initially the CDMC membership was 44% black. Since 1982, however, the racial composition has been maintained at one-third black.

A review of annual reports and minutes of the monitoring committee reveals that during the first year of operation, the committee was organized and adopted by-laws and procedures, was appropriated a $250,000 budget, initiated the requirement that each higher education board submit a bimonthly report on Consent Decree activities, and dealt with a variety of issues and actions inherent in initiating the Decree.

In the second year, a long-term staff member of the Board of Regents was selected to staff the committee. The committee successfully recommended that Consent Decree activities be exempt from budget cuts required in an executive order by the governor. It also accepted the conditional approval of a Ph.D. program in Computer Science at LSU-BR over objections of Southern University and the University of Southwestern Louisiana. Finally, the committee recommended that all Consent Decree items recommended by the Board of Regents be included in capital outlay funding. During 1983–84, its third year, the CDMC decided to invite affected institutional representatives to its meetings and to initiate visits by a subcommittee to the various campuses with Consent Decree responsibilities. This practice was continued through 1984-85. Other concerns handled by the CDMC included investigating complaints lodged by Grambling State University and Southern University at New Orleans regarding denial of access to recruit students by certain high schools, as well as the level of funding for new programs. Overall, it seems that the Consent Decree Monitoring Committee engaged in intensive examination of bimonthly reports and the disposition of problems and issues arising therefrom.

CONCLUDING DISCUSSION

The Consent Decree, including the addendum, was scheduled to terminate on December 31, 1987. However, under the "Term of Decree" it is stated that "if any party, prior to December 31, 1987, has commenced proceedings either to seek compliance with this Decree or to seek other relief necessarily implicating this Decree, this court shall retain jurisdiction over this action until all issues relating to such proceedings have been resolved." As of this writing, the plaintiff has not issued a public statement of its assessment of the implementation of the decree by the defendants. Nor is there information to suggest if one or more of the defendants will initiate action to seek further relief or to bring about further compliance prior to the expiration date. In the absence of legal action by any party, the decree will automatically terminate on the above-referenced date.

Governance mandates in the Consent Decree are perhaps the easiest of all to accomplish. In order to satisfy these mandates, there must be a net gain of one black person on the Board of Regents, three on the Louisiana State University Board, and one on the Board of Trustees for State Colleges and Universities. One more white is needed for the Southern University Board. The governor of the state could appoint and the Senate approve the necessary members as vacancies occur between now and the expiration date for the Consent Decree.

The faculty development programs designed to increase doctorate degree holders at both black and white universities have been implemented with good responses. The nine black doctorate recipients (from predominantly white institutions) under the Regents' Fellowship Program, however, have not been effectively placed in over half of the cases reported. This is particularly disturbing since these individuals had to be nominated by predominantly white institutions in order to get the grants for their terminal degrees. This fact, coupled with the extreme shortage of black doctorate holders in almost all fields, and the financial investment that the state has made in educating these doctorates makes the failure to place them even more critical. Because no white nominated by a black institution has completed a doctorate, there is no basis for judging the placement of white doctorates at predominantly black institutions.

In the faculty development program at Southern University and Grambling State University, 60% of the recipients are still pursuing doctorates and 17% have completed their degrees. The 23% attrition rate is perhaps typical of doctoral programs generally.

Faculty development support for predominantly black institutions has extended only to the receipt of the doctorate. If these institutions are to experience optimum development of their graduate level programs, provisions for sabbatical leaves for postdoctoral study and research must be provided along with fundings for centers, institutes, and other developments essential to high-quality graduate programs. Especially essential is the adequacy of data processing facilities and staff available to serve the needs of faculty and graduate students in research and publication efforts. Faculty development must be more liberally interpreted and financially supported at predominantly black institutions. The needs of these institutions must be regarded as equivalent to those of similarly situated institutions in American higher education.

Cooperative faculty exchange efforts have been very successful in reaching and exceeding goals at all universities involved. Student exchange goals have been met for at least one year at all institutions except LSUBR and SUBR. One possible explanation for this situation might lie in the fact that LSUBR is the "flagship" university of the state. This special status and the plethora of strong academic programs at all degree levels may lessen the attraction of a predominantly black university for LSUBR students, especially at the graduate level. In addition, special efforts should be made to create a more hospitable environment for exchange students on each of the involved campuses in Baton Rouge. Such efforts might include a survey of student attitudes regarding problems and concerns associated with the exchange program. For example, ease of access to the other campus, dealing with unfamiliar settings, and coordination of course scheduling are concerns that are widely discussed by some students. Moreover, to the extent that the differences in university missions are more pronounced between the Baton Rouge institutions (because of the flagship status of one) the relative difficulty in meeting student exchange goals might be expected. On the other hand, the identification of specific courses for students from one campus to pursue on the other campus, as in the UNO-SUNO student exchange program, might be a viable strategy, even for the flagship university.

Enhancement of predominantly black institutions through new programs and upgrading of facilities by demolition, renovation, and construction provides some special problems. The majority of the new programs are now in place. However, recruitment of faculty and the development of courses are still ongoing in most institutions. There has been little or no opportunity for systematic internal assessment of these new programs and most have not been in place long enough to meet time requirements for accreditation bids. Building of library resources consistent with graduate-level program needs, setting up internships and clinical relationships, and development of placement strategies are long-term activities that will need extraordinary financial support long after the established date for the expiration of the Consent Decree. Unless such support is continued, the new programs are destined not to reach the level of quality necessary for them to be competitive.

In the case of dual and cooperative programs, the arrangements between the institutions, which are accountable to different management boards in two of the three sites affected, are enforced by the Consent Decree. The interdependence built into the programs would seem to be jeopardized by the termination of the decree, especially because the programs will have been structured (course offerings) and financed (library and equipment funds) on the assumption of access to the cooperating institutions' facilities and resources. The end of such access and the newness of the programs could cause irreparable damage to their development. A strategy for "independent/stand-alone status" for these programs prior to the end of the term of the Consent Decree would seem a judicious move—even if it entails action to extend the decree beyond December 31, 1987.

The adequacy of the funding of the Consent Decree programs at predominantly black universities is a matter of continuing dispute. In most cases, the programs were established without the prior faculty release time and other resources characteristic of development of new programs at colleges and universities. University requests for funds for library acquisitions, equipment, travel, and computer support were drastically pared and no effort has been made in the Decree toward parity in faculty salaries at predominantly black and white institutions.

When an institution is entering the doctoral degree offering stage, it requires substantial infusion of new financial resources in order to improve library holdings, increase faculty research time through lowering teaching loads, increase graduate assistantships, increase travel funds to support participation in professional associations and meetings, and upgrade support equipment such as word processors, computers, and research laboratories, recruit graduate students, and provide input from expert consultants. Representatives of programs at predominantly black institutions have offered testimony as to the inadequacy of funding. Also, the requirement of special permission from the Board of Regents to transfer funds between line items in consent decree budgets, a requirement which does not apply to non-consent decree budgets, poses problems for maximizing the resources allocated.

With regard to facilities enhancement, the data on demolition, renovation, and construction indicate problems in complying with the decree deadline. The enhancement of facilities has lagged behind the implementation of the new academic programs, many of which are to be housed in the promised new buildings. Because it routinely takes two to three years from appropriation of funds to completion of a building, it seems reasonable to expect the mandated renovation and construction to extend well into the 1990s.

It is clear that many of the programs and facilities will not have achieved the level of quality prior to December 31, 1987 to make them "viable and capable of attracting students of all races" as required by the Consent Decree. Thus, it stands to reason that the continuation of special support for these programs and facilities is absolutely essential if the spirit and letter of the decree are to be met. The notion that these could be sustained out of regular formula-generated dollars is faulty, as even the implementation of the formula at 100% would not provide the total resources necessary to attain and maintain the desired quality. In retrospect, during the negotiations of the decree, officials of predominantly black institutions sought, without success, to have the decree in effect for a minimum of ten years. They contended that the personnel of their respective campuses would be overwhelmed with the volume of work required to meet the many mandates of the decree in a six-year time frame while carrying on other normal activities. The findings reported in this study would seem to confirm their reservations.

Monitoring and reporting for the Consent Decree is lodged with the CDMC, which is staffed by and accountable to the Board of Regents. This arrangement sets up a monitoring and reporting process that is somewhat less than independent, given the role and authority of the Board of Regents in the overall operation of state higher education. The aggressiveness of the monitoring process as it affects the actions taken by the Board of Regents is likely to be strongly impacted by the client relationship that institutions represented on the CDMC have with the Board of Regents.

The Louisiana Consent Decree is ripe with promise, and has great potential to significantly transform the quality of educational programs and resources at the state's historically black institutions. Full implementation of the decree is imperative to any such transformation, and it will likely require a continuation of the federal imposition and an ongoing spirit of commitment and cooperation on the part of state officials. Much is at stake both for the state, and the nation.

However, the Louisiana case and others like it in Alabama and Georgia (which ensued from the *Adams* vs. *Richardson/Califano* case of 1973) are reflective of the circumstances that have surrounded implementation of explicitly racially-oriented public policies. In short, there has been little sense of urgency, and unending delaying tactics on the part of responsible officials at both the state and federal levels. Moreover, the Louisiana Consent Decree is the culmination of a policy initiative begun in an era of relatively strong support for desegregation initiatives. It has survived over an extended period, during which federal support for such initiatives has waxed and waned under the varying commitments of several administrations, widely vacillating public support, and the exigencies of untold political calculations.

The acceptance of the Louisiana Consent Decree in 1981 to dismantle the longstanding system of dual, unequal, and discriminatory higher education in the state is in essence the second phase of an extended policy implementation process. It shows the vulnerabilities and limitations of the consent decree as a policy implementation mechanism. The plantiff in this case is (now) the U.S. Department of Education. With a forceful and continuing federal role, the decree may well realize its transforming potential. However, in the likely event that the expiration date of the decree is not extended beyond December 1987, the result will be a shift of responsibility for implementation and enforcement of the terms of the decree to the state level; a veritable "fox watching the chickens" situation. Such a shift would undoubtedly require an enormously well-organized and well-directed mobilization effort on the part of blacks within the state of Louisiana to ensure elimination of the historic vestiges of racial inequality in higher education.

NOTES

1. Anderson, James E. *Public Policy-Making* (New York: Praeger Publishers, 1975), p. 3.
2. Bullock, Charles S., III, Anderson, James E., Brady, David W. *Public Policy in the Eighties* (Monterey, California: Brooks, Cole Publishing Co., 1983), p. 5.
3. Anderson, James (ed.), *Cases in Public Policy-Making*, 2d ed. (New York: Holt, Rinehart and Winston, 1982), p. 153.
4. *United States of America versus State of Louisiana, et. al. Consent Decree*, Civil Action N. 20-3300, Section "A" (September 8, 1981).
5. August 1985.
6. A news release of June 6, 1986 indicates that the governor nominated three blacks for the LSU Board of Supervisors which will result in four black members for 1986 and bring the total to that required in the Consent Decree. Confirmation by the state senate is required.

16
Elements of Effective Black Schools

Charles D. Moody, Sr. and Christella D. Moody

Effective black schools are not a new phenomenon in the American educational system. Faustine Jones, in *A Traditional Model of Educational Excellence: Dunbar High School of Little Rock, Arkansas*, discussed the adult roles and status of graduates of an all-black high school. A quote of Edgar Epps from Jones' book provides a clue as to why this school has been, and perhaps other urban black schools can be, effective educational institutions:

> [T]hese big city Black schools generally had viable programs, highly qualified and the best paid teachers, better facilities, and higher ratings than they are now accorded . . . Dunbar of Greater Little Rock and many other schools in the North and South produced hundreds of leaders of contemporary Black society. Teachers and students in the community were mutually and emotionally involved in the community development. Extra effort was expended to make all proud of the school. The school was inseparable from the community and they proceeded together.[1]

Other documentation attests to the existence of many other effective black schools across this nation. This article presents the practical components that work together to comprise effective schools. It further provides some prescriptive guidelines and initiatives for those practitioners who are committed to educational equity and excellence for black students.

GROWTH OF THE EFFECTIVE BLACK SCHOOL MOVEMENT

The late Ronald Edmonds once exhorted that "We can, whenever and wherever we choose, successfully teach all children whose schooling is of interest to us; we already know more than we need to do that; and whether or not we do it must finally depend on how we feel about the fact that we have not so far."[2] This quote undergirds Edmonds' contention that all students are educable. Edmonds further reasoned that a student's family background neither causes nor precludes school effectiveness. The myth that family background determines academic achievement, Edmond contended, has the effect of absolving educators of their professional responsibility to be instructionally effective. With these convictions, Edmonds launched his effective school research and movement.

In 1970, while serving as an Assistant Superintendent of Schools for the state of Michigan, Edmonds developed the concept of effective schools. The state of Michigan was developing desegregation guidelines, and Edmonds wanted exemptions from deseg-regation for black schools that were achieving at a satisfactory level. In the late 1970s, Edmonds left Michigan for Harvard, where he continued to work on effective schools in urban settings. The need for such schools, he believed, was crucial, as 75% of the total U.S. population resided in urban areas.

Edmonds reasoned that the lack of achievement of some students is a political rather than a genetic issue in that the schooling of some students is not important to us as a nation. He believed politics was the substantive and procedural basis for determining the distribution of educational resources, defining the use to which schools operate, and establishing the criteria by which school personnel are evaluated. Edmonds concluded that schools taught only those that they thought they must teach. The research on ascription, mobility, power, and social status has indicated that one of the major func-tions of education has been to socialize students to willingly accept the adult roles that are ascribed to them. Some students, so to speak, are educated to assume high status and leadership positions. Other students, however, are educated to assume low-status positions in society.[3]

Studies by James Coleman and Christopher Jenks[4] have led many educators to er-roneously believe that schools cannot be effective for low socioeconomic status (SES) urban black students. Both Coleman and Jenks reasoned that schools could not over-come the disadvantages implied by such low-income status. However, studies by Ed-monds, Weber, Sizemore, Benjamin[5] and Moody have uncovered evidence that urban schools serving poor black students can be effective in preparing black students for all walks of life.[6] Weber, in particular, was an early contributor to the literature on the school determinants of achievement. This author proposes a debunking of the thesis of such researchers as Arthur Jensen,[7] who had contended that low achievement among poor children was derived principally from their innate mental limitations, particularly for blacks.

ELEMENTS OF EFFECTIVE SCHOOLS: SELECTED RESEARCH FINDINGS

Edmonds searched for schools where poor and black children were achieving at the same level as middle-income white children. His research identified several correlates in schools where poor and black students were achieving minimal mastery of basic skills. He discovered that those schools shared the following characteristics:[8]

- A principal who is a strong instructional leader.

- A climate of high expectations in which no children are permitted to fall below minimal levels in an atmosphere that is orderly without being rigid or oppressive.
- An emphasis on the teaching of basic skills in a well-prepared classroom where students spend most of their time on clearly-defined tasks.
- A means of frequent monitoring of pupil progress.

Instructional Leadership: Role of School Principals

The attributes of an effective principal involves a set of professional behaviors, rather than describing a single type of individual. These behaviors include:[9]

—taking initiative in identifying and articulating goals and priorities.
—setting instruction as the first priority and communicating this to staff.
—spending half of the time in classroom and halls.
—caring more about the school's academic progress than about human relations or informal, collegial relations.
—attempting to handpick the staff.
—finding ways to reward excellent teachers with greater responsibilities.
—setting a consistent tone of high expectations.

The research on effective principals indicates that there is little relationship between a principal's personal characteristics, such as age, gender, training, and personality, and his or her behavior in the role. Instead, effective principals have strong educational backgrounds in reading and/or curriculum development. They know their school's educational programs well and are willing to go into the classroom and teach for demonstrational purposes.[10]

In 1978-80, Sizemore and his associates studied three black elementary schools. Two of the schools had high student achievement, while the third did not. Sizemore found the following differences among the targeted schools:[11]

- In the two higher-achieving schools, there was mid-range consensus among the school officials around high achievement as the highest-priority goal; in the other there was low consensus.
- In the two higher-achieving schools, principals assumed the responsibility for student discipline and parental conflict, generating loyalty among their teachers through the sense of obligation engendered by the principal's actions. In the third school, a secret battle, generally led by veteran teachers, was created by the principal's failure to assume this responsibility.
- In the two higher-achieving schools, the principals monitored student progress and pacing, supervised teacher performance consistently, and evaluated teachers promptly. In the third school, the principal relied on her supervisory spe-

cialist for assistance in evaluation and in-service and on external sources for help in supervision.

- In the two higher-achieving schools, the principals persuaded unsatisfactory personnel to transfer by threatening an unsatisfactory rating rather than by terminating them through the long tortuous process prescribed by the Board of Education and the Federation of Teachers (FOT). In the third school, the principal was restricted by the presence of an FOT official on her faculty and forced to submit to the process.

- The third school also had higher rates of faculty and student mobility and student absenteeism, a lower student population, a larger number of extra programs, more loosely-structured classrooms, and fewer lower income students. Because of the students' higher socio economic status, the investigators thought achievement would be higher, but this proved not to be the case, in fact, the data show a school in transition.

- The principals of the two higher-achieving schools spent a great deal of their work time interacting with students; the third principal spent more time with faculty and staff from the central office and the university regarding the extra programs housed in her school.

The importance of leadership has been clearly demonstrated in the cases of Dr. J. Jerome Harris, District Superintendent in District 13, Brooklyn, NY, and George J. McKenna, Principal, Washington Preparatory High, Los Angeles Unified School District. Both are administrators in districts where there are large numbers of poor, black children. These individuals have clear, specific goals and high expectations; maintain high standards for students, teachers, and parents; visit classrooms on a regular basis; have homework policies; publish data about achievement and absenteeism; and provide in-service training for staff. Their efforts have been richly rewarded. For example, in 1974 in District 13, the students performed at the twentieth percentile on the average. By 1985, the students were performing at the sixty-second percentile. Currently, not one school in District 13 has an average reading rate below the national norm.[12] At George Washington Preparatory High School, 70% of the students go on to college. Absenteeism dropped from 33% in 1979 to less than 10% in 1985.

School Climate/Atmosphere

Climate has been defined as "a set of measurable properties of the work environment, perceived directly or indirectly by people who live and work in this environment and assumed to influence their motivation and behavior."[13] In effective schools, the climate is conducive to learning; it is safe, orderly, and relatively free of discipline and vandalism problems. Emmer, Evertson, and Anderson[14] have suggested that teachers set the stage for the entire year early in the term. These authors pointed out that:

[H]ighly rated teachers used the first class day for orienting and climate setting, whereas new teachers jumped right into content more quickly. Highly rated teachers also dealt more with student feelings, had less off-task behavior, smiled and joked more than new teachers on the first day.[15]

Observations made later in the year led these authors to conclude that the very first day of school was crucial for setting the pattern for the year. The more effective teachers clearly established themselves as classroom leaders. They worked on rules and procedures until the students learned them. The teaching of content was important for these teachers, but they initially stressed socialization into the classroom system. By the end of the first three weeks, their classes were ready to concentrate on learning for the rest of the school year.

A significant part of school climate is related to the effectiveness of the teacher's instructional management. Emmer Everton and Anderson further noted that:

> Many of the instructional problems faced by the less effective teachers grew out of their difficulties in behavior management. Likewise, the instructional management of the better [teachers] was facilitated by their good management practices . . . The better [teachers] tended to have better procedures for institutional activities, just as they had for their overall classroom organization. They generally managed time well, . . . gave clear directions and instructions, . . . held students accountable for their work, . . . monitored student seat work frequently . . . and kept track of students' progress on assignments.[16]

The school's climate is affected greatly by the teacher's managerial behavior and the establishment of clear-cut rules for student behavior. Much of what has been described or characterized as discipline problems stem from instructional management problems, although some discipline problems are initiated by a peculiarity of individual students.

Programs exist to assist schools in improving their climate. An excellent example of such a program is the Rational Application of Practical School Discipline (RAPS) Program developed and conducted by Trevor Gardner of Eastern Michigan University. RAPS facilitates training and structure in a school district so that schools can maintain ownership, direction, and purpose after the program is implemented. The staff is trained to help students internalize appropriate social behaviors and teachers are provided with a basic framework by which discipline can be effectively managed. School rules and policies are reviewed and developed so that there is consistency for all students and staff.

Teacher Expectations

In 1968, Rosenthal and Jacobson reported the results of research on the effects of teacher expectation on student achievement in the book *Pygmalion in the Classroom*.[17] This work created a great deal of interest in how teachers interact with both low and high-achieving students. Rosenthal and Jacobson revealed four classroom behavior categories associated with teacher performance expectations. These researchers found that high-achievement students received:

1. a supportive socio-emotional climate
    —more smiles, head nods, forward body-leaning, eye contact, support, and friendliness.
2. more verbal inputs
    —opportunities to learn new material and
    —difficult material.
3. more verbal outputs
    —clue giving, repetition, and rephrasing
    —opportunities to respond.
4. more effective feedback
    —more praise
    —less criticism.

What, then, do other research findings indicate? In what specific ways have teachers been found to vary their behaviors toward high and low-achieving students ("lows")? They do so in a variety of ways:[18]

- Seating slow students farther from the teacher or in a group (making it harder to monitor low-achieving students or to treat them as individuals).
- Paying less attention to lows in academic situations (smiling less often and maintaining less eye contact).
- Calling on lows less often to answer classroom questions or make public demonstrations.
- Waiting less time for lows to answer questions.
- Not staying with lows in failure situations (providing clues, asking follow-up questions).
- Criticizing lows more frequently than highs for incorrect public responses.
- Praising lows more frequently than highs for incorrect public responses.
- Providing low-achieving students with less accurate and less detailed feedback than highs.
- Failing to provide lows with feedback about their responses more frequently than highs.
- Demanding less work and effort from lows than from highs.
- Interrupting the performance of low-achievers more frequently than that by high-achievers.

Thomas Good has remarked that:

One myth that has been discredited by classroom observation is that schooling is a constant experience with teachers behaving in similar ways and pursuing similar goals within a common curriculum. [Some researchers have] illustrated that it is possible to find teachers (at the same grade level in the same school) who differ notably in their classroom behaviors and goals.[19]

Teaching Process

Effective schools are characterized by a strong emphasis on academics. Teachers and administrators of such schools emphasize reading, writing, and math in a businesslike environment. Homework is given and graded regularly. Student success is built into lessons by teaching at the appropriate level. Standards are high but reasonable. Several instructional models have been developed for different aspects of the teaching process. Among them are Mastery Learning (Bloom),[20] Direct Instruction (Good & Grouws),[21] and Diagnostic/Prescriptive Teaching (Hunter).[22]

Mastery Learning involves a group of students learning certain strategies that are organized into a series of units or chapters. Students are expected to achieve a preset performance level at the end of each unit. Students who do not attain this level are usually given additional time and help in the form of alternate learning materials, small group study, or peer tutoring; they are then retested.[23] Studies of Mastery Learning have shown that when students are given extra time and appropriate help, and when they are motivated to learn, 80% or more can ultimately attain the preset mastery level on each learning unit.[24]

During the 1970s, numerous research studies examined the "direct instruction" approach to teaching. As the name implies, this strategy attempts to identify the specific teacher behaviors that produce student learning. Leinhardt, Zigmond, and Colley[25] examined the behaviors and characteristics of teachers that lead to high rates of engagement in reading activities by students. Their research question was simply What do teachers do that enables students to do things that help them learn?

Leinhardt and his associates found that the teacher behaviors that contributed markedly to student attention and engagement were teacher instruction, reinforcement, and "cognitive press." According to these authors, "Instructional behaviors included model presentations, explanations, feedback, cuing, and monitoring." Consistent with the rest of the study, teaching was measured by how much time teachers spent performing these instructional activites. A second important teacher behavior was reinforcement of student learning. This was measured by counting the number of reinforcements, that is, praises, acknowledgments, written kudos, and the like, received by each child daily.

The measure of "cognitive press" assessed how fully the teacher was supporting and encouraging student orientation to academic material. This effect should be underscored because Leinhardt also found an increase of five minutes per day of silent reading produced a one-month gain in achievement.[26] Time on task has indeed proven to be a simple and pragmatic way to raise academic achievement, improve the instructional leadership of principals, and provide teachers with techniques for more effective instruction. Simple as it is, however, it is not a simplistic solution.

Researchers in cognitive psychology have approached the task of educational success by examining black Americans' cognitive style. Shade has examined the adaptational/survival premise that suggests that:

> Afro-Americans developed a parallel culture in response to their isolation through discrimination, slavery, and ghettoization. Using the various elements of African culture patterns they were able to retain while acquiring others from the Europeans with whom they had contact, Afro-Americans developed an approach to life that assisted in their survival.[27]

This theory also maintains that Afro-Americans developed a culturally-specific method of organizing and processing information. While this method was effective in social situations, Shade and others have concluded that this strategy differs from the one required for success in the typical educational setting.[28] Proponents of this thesis found that the cognitive strategies of many black Americans are described as holistic, intuitive, and person-oriented. However, a review of the literature suggests that successful functioning within the typical school context requires the cognitive strategies that are described as sequential, analytical, or object-oriented.[29]

Hollins has proposed that the following conditions should be present in schools to help black students achieve:[30]

1. The process and content of the learning should be related in a meaningful way and should be familiar to the learner.
2. The content should be communicated in a way that is acceptable and comprehensible to the learner.
3. The learner should be provided adequate time to access, process, and apply the content.
4. An affective environment ought to be such that the learner feels comfort and support so that he/she will take the risks necessary for learning.

Cognitive research has identified other key instructional variables. Teachers should:[31]

- Communicate the objectives of the lesson. Students need to be told what they will learn, how they will learn it, the behavior needed for mastery, and how the new learning is related to prior knowledge.
- Establish routines and structures in the classroom.
- Use a variety of approaches: e.g., discussion, inquiry, concept development, peer tutoring.
- Make presentations more oriented toward active involvement.
- Include the culture of the students as much as possible by incorporating pupils' interest, experience, and language.
- Make the material relevant to the learner. When new learning is linked to what the student already knows, success is more likely.

- Plan activities so students have a high rate of success. Students develop a better self-concept when their existing abilities are emphasized rather than their inadequacies. Teachers should estimate where the student is and build on that base.

Monitoring Student Progress

The principal is the key to the final correlate: frequent monitoring of student progress. Indicators of effective monitoring are:

1. school records that clearly document student performance and achievement;
2. The use of formal and informal measures;
3. The use of test data when placing students;
4. The use of the principal's careful monitoring of student achievement;
5. The use of evaluation data are used to improve the school's program.

The purpose of monitoring is to ensure that low- and high-income students, males and females, and whites and nonwhites demonstrate mastery of the basic skills. Unfortunately, some schools monitor progress, but if some students are not achieving, no changes are made to the program. Monitoring also dictates that if something is not working, it may be time to try something different. Inadequate performance is a cause for restructuring and redesigning educational programs and support and supervision systems. Monitoring should have an impact on school climate, teacher expectations, and the teaching process.

CONCLUSION: SOME INITIATIVES FOR EFFECTIVE SCHOOLS

Although Edmonds died in 1983, the legacy of his work is growing. For example, Congressman Augustus Hawkins of California convened a group of educators whose goal was to develop a *Blueprint for Action*. This effort on the part of Congressman Hawkins is consistent with Edmonds' commitment to the Effective Schools movement. Hawkins sponsored The School Improvement Act (HR 5), which was passed by Congress in 1987. The Blueprint for Action II also outlines some action items and implementation activities.[32]

In 1984, the National Alliance of Black School Educators (NABSE) commissioned a Task Force on Black Academic and Cultural Excellence that resulted in the publication of *Saving the African American Child: A Report of the National Alliance of Black School Educators, Inc., Task Force on Black Academic and Cultural Excellence.*
The Task Force concluded that:

[A]cademic excellence cannot be reached without cultural excellence. We expect African Americans to meet academic standards of excellence. We also know that African American history and culture will be unavoidable if truth and quality scholarship form the basis of what is taught and respected in public schools, not as an appendage to subjects but as an integral part.[33]

This statement means that there must be cultural congruence in the implementation of the teaching and learning process. The expectation that black students can learn and that their culture and contributions are to be respected must also exist. NABSE has translated the principles espoused in the document into action through its Task Force II efforts: establishing a NABSE Foundation, A Documentation School Project, and the NABSE/Charles D. Moody, Sr. Research Institute of African American Education.

At least thirty-five states have mandated school improvement plans. A substantial number of these programs utilize the effective schools research correlates. Programs using these correlates have been adopted in Milwaukee, Wisconsin (Project Rise); New York City, New York (The New York City School Improvement Project (SIP); Jackson, Mississippi; Norfolk, Virginia; Ann Arbor, Michigan; Flint, Michigan (Beecher (SITE)); and Tallahassee, Florida.

Given the demonstrated effectiveness of some inner-city black schools, there is no longer any valid justification for other similar schools to fail. The benefits that accrue to society by such schools' success are too great to allow schools to perpetuate demonstrably ineffective approaches while refusing to institute the characteristics of success. Every urban public school, regardless of its percentage of poor and/or minority children, must educate its students to the national standards already achieved by many schools or at least adopt the characteristics of successful institutions.

Moreover, these characteristics must be couched in the context of equity. Such an equity-based education is four-dimensional. The dimensions are:

—Access: As it relates to schools classes, programs, and activities.

—Process: As it relates to the fair, equitable, and humane treatment of students, parents, and staff.

—Achievement: As it relates to graduation rates, dropout rates, test scores, awards, rewards, and recognition.

—Transfer: As it relates to additional educational opportunities, but eventually into jobs that will provide equal pay, privilege, power, and prestige.[34]

Each of these dimensions is fundamental to an effective school approach, but until all students believe that they can transfer their achievements into an improved quality of life, too many students will continue to fail. Indeed, no child starts kindergarten wanting to become a failure. To help prevent failure, children must not be written off as helpless casualties. To be sure, well-researched instructional methods, strategies, and tools are now available, but they cannot replace a caring teacher who will help children develop a sense of personal responsibility. "We know enough to teach all children. The question is, Do we want to teach all children?"[35]

NOTES

1. Jones, Faustine, *A Traditional Model of Education Excellence: Dunbar High School of Little Rock, Arkansas* (Washington, D.C.: Howard Univ. Press, 1981).

2. Edmonds, Ronald, "Effective Schools for Urban Poor," *Educational Leadership* 36 (Oct. 1979), p. 23.

3. Ogbu, John U., "Caste and Education and How They Function in the United States," Chapter I of *Minority Education and Caste: The American System in Cultural Perspective* (New York: Academic Press, 1978).

4. Cited in Hawkins, Augustus, *Report of the Committee on Education and Labor House of Representatives. Increasing Educational Success: The Effective Schools Model* (Washington, D.C.: Government Printing Office, 1987).

5. Benjamin, Robert, *Making Schools Work: A Reporter's Journey Through Some of America's Most Remarkable Classrooms* (New York: Continuum Publications, 1981).

6. Hawkins, *Report on Education*.

7. Jensen, Arthur R., "How Much Can We Boost I.Q. and Scholastic Achievement?" *Harvard Educational Review*, 39 (1969), pp. 1-23.

8. Edmonds, "Effective Schools."

9. Cross, Ray, "What Makes an Effective Principal?" *Principal* 22, Mar. 1981.

10. Ibid.

11. Sizemore, Barbara A., Carlos Brosard and Berny Harrigan, "An Abashing Anomaly: The High Achieving Predominantly Black Elementary Schools," National Institute of Education, Pittsburgh, PA: (Univ. of Pittsburg, 1982).

12. Harris, J. Jerome, Presentation made at the NABSE/Ron Edmonds Effective Schools Summer Academy, Ann Arbor, MI, July 15, 1987.

13. Emmers, Edmonds T., Carolyn M. Evertson, and Linda M. Anderson. "Effective Classroom Management at the Beginning of the School Year," *The Elementary School Journal* 80, no. 219 (1985).

14. Ibid.

15. Ibid.

16. Ibid.

17. Rosenthal, Robert and Lenore Jacobson, *Pygmalian in the Classroom: Teacher Expectations and Pupils' Intellectual Development* (New York: Holt, Rheinhart and Winston, 1968).

18. Good, Thomas L., "Teacher Expectation and Student Perceptions: A Decade of Research," *Educational Leadership* 38, no. 416 (1979).

19. Ibid.

20. Bloom, Benjamin, *All Our Children Learning* (New York: McGraw Hill, 1981).

21. Hawkins, *Report on Education*.

22. Hunter, Madeline, *Mastering Teaching* (El Segundo, CA.: T I P Publishers, 1982).

23. Bloom, Benjamin, *Human Characteristics and School Learning* (New York: McGraw Hill, 1985).

24. Ibid.

25. Leinhardt, G., N. Sigmon, and W.W. Cooley, "Reading Instruction and Its Effects," *American Educational Research Journal*, 18 (1981) pp. 343-61.

26. ERIC Clearinghouse on Educational Management, Research Action Brief #4,Eugene, OR: Univ. of Oregon, July, 1979.

27. Shade, Barbara, Presentation given at the NABSE/Ron Edmonds Effective Schools Summer Academy, Ann Arbor, MI, July 17, 1986.

28. Shade, Barbara, "Afro-American Cognitive Style," *Review of Educational Research* 52 (Summer 1982), pp. 219-44.

29. Ibid.

30. Hollins, Etta Ruth, Presentation given at the NABSE/Ron Edmonds Effective Schools Summer Academy, Ann Arbor, Mi. July 17, 1987.

31. Shade, "Afro-American Style."

32. National Conference on Educating Black Children, A Blueprint for Action II, Washington, DC: (The Washington Urban League 1987).

33. National Alliance of Black School Educators, *Saving the African American Child: A Report of the National Alliance of Black School Educators, Inc. Task Force on Black Academic and Cultural Excellence* (Washington, D.C., Nov. 1984).

34. Moody, Charles, D., "Breakthrough," Univ. of Michigan School of Education 10, no. 2 (Winter 1982).

35. Edmonds, "Effective Schools."

17

School Power: A Model for Improving Black Student Achievement

James P. Comer, Norris M. Haynes, and Muriel Hamilton-Lee

During recent years, the status of public education in America has been severely criticized. The Coleman Report[1] stated that Catholic schools had significantly higher achievement levels than public schools and that private schools were better able than public institutions to narrow achievement gaps that exist among children of different socioeconomic backgrounds. This report attributed the superiority of Catholic schools to higher academic demands and greater discipline. The National Commission on Excellence in Education[2] also issued a scathing report on American schools, finding that 13% of all 17 year olds and 40% of minority youth were functionally illiterate. This latter point is crucial because it underscores the serious underachievement and other school-related problems facing black children in public schools.

West[3] reported on the results of a 1982 Gallup poll in which a national sample of citizens were asked their opinions on the state of public schools. Whereas in 1974, 48% of individuals interviewed rated public schools "A" or "B," in 1982 only 37% gave public schools an A or B rating. Further, seven out of ten individuals indicated that discipline was a serious problem in schools. West also cited data from the U.S. Law Enforcement Administration's national crime survey of public schools, which indicated that 68% of robberies and 50% of assaults against young people occur in schools. A National Institute of Education report[4] indicated that students in public schools had a fairly high probability of being robbed and attacked.

Thus within the past ten years a lack of discipline and the presence of both vandalism and violence have been identified as serious problems that plague public schools. These problems appear to exist at a disproportionately high level in urban inner-city public schools where black and minority children often comprise the majority of the total student population.

Parker[5] presented rebuttals to these beliefs made by several distinguished educators who criticized the negative reports of American schools as being too pessimistic and unbalanced. Ernest Boyer, president of the Carnegie Foundation for the Advancement of Teaching, faulted the National Commission on Excellence in Education for not reporting that reading and math scores had improved since the 1970s. Boyer accused the commission of oversimplifying the data and presenting too grim a picture. Ben J. Wattenberg of the American Enterprise Institute chastised the commission for omitting significant information. He indicated that preschool attendance rose from 37% to 57% between 1970 and 1983. The high school dropout rate fell from 39% to 14% between 1960 and 1983; and the percentage of young people graduating from college doubled in 20 years. Patricia Graham, Dean of the Harvard University School of Education, attributed the reported declines in American schools to the fact that educators were being asked to perform too many nonacademic tasks. Myron Atkin, Dean of the Stanford University School of Education, reminded critics of the considerable amount of improvement that has taken place in American education.

SCHOOL REFORM MOVEMENTS

Despite the recognized gains made by American schools in recent years, there is general agreement that public schools still need considerable improvement, both in terms of academic achievement and social climate. In fact, the insidious and perfidious threat to the well-being of children posed by widespread drug use and the escalating incidence of adolescent pregnancy, especially in inner-city schools, has created a new urgency for school reform. School reform movements of both past and present have failed to deal with the root causes of school failure and disaffection with education among black youth; such reform movements have made only cosmetic educational changes with limited beneficial effect. Following is a brief chronology of school reform movements identified by Bruce:[6]

1. Academic Reform Movement (early 1960s). This movement gained impetus after the Russians' success with Sputnik in space. Concerned citizens wanted to know "why Johnny could not read" while "Ivan" could. The result was the development of new curricula such as new physics and new math.
2. School Reorganization Movement (early 1960s). Concurrent with academic reform was an attempt at school reorganization. Schools were regarded as centers of inquiry. Teachers were encouraged to try new methods of teaching. In-service education was stressed and team teaching was popular.
3. New School Designs Movement (mid 1960s). The architectural design of schools was based on specific teaching philosophies. For example, Bruce noted that "some schools were built around concepts of multimedia storage and retrieval systems with flexible learning spaces built throughout their environments. Other school designs stressed the learning center concept which could be reoriented as philosophies changed." The open classroom structure was a good example of this movement.
4. Social Reform Movement (mid 1960s to early 1970s). Multi-cultural education emphasized. The major purpose was to help expose students to diverse cultures and promote respect for and tolerance of cultural differences.

Two other important school reform movements that Bruce did not identify, the Compensatory Education Movement and the Effective Schools movement, are discussed below:

Compensatory Education:

Compensatory education strategies were based on specific assumptions regarding the causes of chronic underachievement among minority children. Three of the most significant and well-known programs initiated were Head Start, Follow Through, and ESEA Title 1. The basic thrust of compensatory education was the identification of deficiencies in basic skills such as reading and writing and the provision of remedial assistance to slower children.

Many educators and psychologists felt that compensatory education programs were not responsive to the demand for successful and meaningful education of large numbers of schoolchildren. Programs for enrichment, remedial reading, ungraded classrooms, team teaching, and special education teachers were found to have no relationship to the management of the educational system and thus had limited impact. Their effectiveness was usually dependent upon the ethos of the school community into which they were introduced. Preschool programs, while perhaps themselves useful, frequently had debatable longitudinal effects. Insofar as they had only limited parental involvement, while such programs may have reduced parental alienation from their childrens' educational experience, they did not involve parents in school management and operations in a meaningful way. Additionally, too many participants in such programs were unfamiliar with the communities in which they served. It has become increasingly evident that too few parents of black children are intimately involved in their children's educational experience and that ways must be found to involve them.

Effective School Movement

The most recent thrust in school reform is the growing call for effective schools. Proponents of effective schools identify exemplary schools that they believe are effective based on criteria they establish, and describe the characteristics of these schools that make them effective.

Edmonds[7] defined effective schools as those which are "sufficiently powerful to raise otherwise mediocre pupils to levels of instructional effectiveness they might not ordinarily have though they could aspire to." In his study of 1,300 public schools in New York, this author classified those schools as effective if they demonstrated the ability to deliver basic school skills to all students, regardless of race or socio-economic status for at least three consecutive years. A needs assessment was done for each school to identify its strengths and weaknesses with respect to five characteristics, and technical assistance was offered to make schools effective. The five characteristics of effective schools identified by Edmonds are:

- Style of leadership.
- Instructional emphasis.
- Climate.
- Implied expecations derived from teacher.
- Presence and use of and response to standardized instruments for increasing pupil progress.

Bosert et al.[8] identified essentially the same characteristics of effective schools as did Edmonds. Bossert listed the following:

1. School climate conducive to learning, free of disciplinary problems and vandalism.
2. A school-wide emphasis on basic skills instruction.
3. Expectations among teachers that all students can achieve.
4. Clear instructional objectives for monitoring and assessing students' performance.

For both Edmonds and Bossert, a positive school climate, an emphasis on the achievement of basic skills, high expectations for students, and clear instructional objectives with efficient mechanisms for monitoring student progress distinguish effective schools from other schools. Coleman[9] noted that a consensus appears to be emerging that effective schools differ from other schools in significant ways that can be reliably associated with student achievement. One of the key differences between effective and ineffective schools is the instructional climate discussed in the literature, Rutter et al.[10], McDill, Rigsby and Meyers,[11] and Brookover et al.[12] Effective schools are seen as having environments that foster academic success on the part of students.

A significant flaw of the effective school movement is the limited value given to parental involvement. For this movement, school administrators and teachers are primarily responsible for creating the environment conducive to achievement, while the role of parents is minimized. However, in the model presented by the present authors, parental involvement is a key component. It is viewed as particularly essential to the improvement of school climate and the enhancement of academic achievement among black children, who may perceive home and school as being separate entities more than do other students.

Achilles[13] provided a thorough review and summary of the effective school literature. He identified school climate and administrator and teacher behaviors that correlated significantly with school outcomes. These climate and behavior variables include: coordinated instructional programs, emphasis on basic skills achievement, frequent evaluations of pupil progress, orderly learning environments, specific instructional strategies, high expectations for students, task-oriented classrooms, structured direct instruction, use of a variety of reward systems, involvement of administrators and teachers in curriculum planning, and preventive rather than punitive discipline discussed by Weber,[14] Edmonds,[15] Goodlad,[16] Clark et al.,[17] and Venezky, et al.[18]

Critique of the Effective School Movement

Proponents of effective schools have developed, as it were, a laundry list of positive characteristics that make schools "effective." Their approach has been to establish certain effectiveness criteria, to identify schools that meet these criteria, and then observe the processes within these schools to demonstrate the operation of an effective school in a qualitative manner. The consideration given to climate is really only superficial, in the sense that only such surface operations as discipline and rules are emphasized. Deeper and more basic concerns, such as school organization, decision sharing, and parental involvement are not highlighted.

Purkey and Smith[19] faulted the effective schools literature on the following grounds: (1) research on effective schools utilized small and narrow samples that severely limited their generalizability; (2) only one study was longitudinal, preventing conclusions being drawn concerning the staying power of effective schools over time; (3) the studies are mostly correlational, thus begging the question on cause and effect, a problem exacerbated by their lack of a theoretical model; (4) the definition of effective schools masks the fact that most of the inner-city schools identified as effective still have lower mean scores than do more affluent schools within the same district; and (5) there is a tendency for studies in effective schools to compare exceptionally bad schools (negative outliers) with exceptionally good schools (positive outliers); this approach risks missing those characteristics that differentiate the majority of average schools from both extremes.

Thus, Purkey and Smith viewed research on effective schools as being weak and simplistic. They suggested that research into educational innovation should look more at school organization and school culture, as did studies by Berman McLaughlin,[20] Meyer and Rowan,[21] Miles,[22] Sarason,[23] and Weick.[24] Indeed, the work of O'Toole[25] on workplace culture is seen as having provided a useful framework for examining the effectiveness of schools. Selby[26] noted that the "ethos" of a school or any learning environment has a significant influence on the quality and quantity of learning that takes place in that school or learning environment. The School Development Program described below reflects the sentiments and ideas of those who support systemic organizational changes in schools to meet the unique needs of black and other disadvantaged children.

THE SCHOOL DEVELOPMENT PROGRAM (SDP): A MODEL FOR MEANINGFUL CHANGE

The School Development Program (SDP) Model is not new. It was initiated by Dr. James P. Comer, the senior author, and his colleagues, in collaboration with the New Haven (CT) Public Schools System in 1968. The model was refined from 1973 to 1975. Since 1975, the effectiveness of the model in this school system has been evaluated and documented.[27] This documentation has led to adoption of the model by several other school systems around the country.

The School Development Program (SDP) was not derived from a specific theory, but is based on a theoretical formulation that combines elements from several models. These include the population adjustment model by Beck, Wyland & McCourt,[28] and Hartman,[29] and the social action model by Reiff.[30] The SDP contains components of the adjustment model that apply intervention strategies to groups identified as having psycho-educational problems. Further, it seeks the best possible adaptation of children (particularly those of minority groups) to the school environment through the implementation of child development and systems management principles.

The SDP resembles a social action model in that it attempts to serve children through social change. More specifically, it seeks to open social structures to a variety of inputs, build parent involvement, and empower the community. While the intervention resembles the adjustment and social action models, it is best conceptualized as an example of the ecological approach to prevention as discussed by Kelly.[31] The intervention is designed to change the human interactions—ecology—within the social system of a school. The improved interaction promotes the development of an ethos or social climate which, in turn, facilitates desirable management, teaching, and student learning and behavior. In this regard, it contains elements of Lewin's[32] social psychology: The adoption of the ecological approach in intervention and research programs has been urged by many mental health professionals, such as Weinstein & Frankel[33] and Wilkinson & O'Connor.[34]

School Planning and Management Team

An essential characteristic of the model is to move the school from a bureaucratic method of management to a system of democratic participation in which parents play a key role. The purpose of this team is to establish a representative body within each school to address the governance and management issues of the school.

The Governance and Management Team is comprised of 12 to 15 individuals and is representative of all adults involved in the school. It is led by the school principal, and also includes two teachers selected by their colleagues at each grade level, three or four parents selected by the parent organization, and a Mental Health Team member from the school (the Mental Health Team is described below). This group meets on a weekly basis.

The function of the governance and management group is to: (1) establish policy guidelines to address the curriculum, social climate, and staff development aspects of the school program; (2) carry out systematic school planning, resource assessment and mobilization, program implementation, and evaluation and modification in the curriculum, social climate, and staff development areas; (3) coordinate the activities of all individuals, groups, and programs in the school; and (4) work with the parent group to plan an annual social (activity) calendar. The governance and management group systematically structures and coordinates these activities to improve the climate of the school.

Mental Health Team

The team is usually composed of the school principal, assistant principals, school psychologist, social worker, special education teacher, guidance counselors, nurse, and other pupil personnel staff within the school.

The team provides input to the work of the governance and management body, integrating mental health principles with the functioning of all school activities. The team also serves individual teachers by suggesting in-classroom ways to manage early and potential problem behaviors. It trains school personnel in providing a variety of child development and mental health-sensitive services.

The Mental Health Team meets on a weekly basis to respond to referrals from classroom teachers. The referrals are presented and managed like a clinical case conference. The Mental Health Team's responses to the referrals include a variety of services including immediate consultation with the classroom teacher, observations and extensive consultations, and direct counseling for students. An alternative in some cases is that children are referred to the Discovery Room (described below).

The activities of the Mental Health Team sometimes suggest school policy and practice changes that are then communicated to the governance and management group and reviewed and implemented if approved (e.g., the Discovery Room).

The Mental Health Team differs from the usual pupil personnel teams in that it serves both a preventive as well as a treatment function in schools. In its preventive role it identifies potential problem situations and acts to prevent them from developing into full-blown crises. Further, it brings together the mental health professionals in the school in a unique way that affects the entire school climate. In its treatment function, it works with individual teachers to address specific classroom problems and deals directly with individual student problems. The concept of the discovery room and the transfer orientation program are examples of activities instituted by Mental Health Teams in some schools as prevention and intervention measures.

The discovery room program was designed and directed by a resource teacher/research assistant and was created to meet the needs of children who have difficulty adjusting to school. Such adjustment difficulties frequently stem from shyness, withdrawal, acting out, or low self-esteem. These children tend to be of normal intelligence and exhibit no serious learning problems, yet they are not able to cope with the demands of the classroom.

Children are referred to the discovery room teacher by both the mental health team and the classroom teacher: The standard referral procedure is through the classroom teacher, while referrals are made by other members of the core mental health team via the school's internal Pupil Personnel Services. Groups of three or four children spend two or three hours a week in the discovery room throughout the academic year.

The discovery room was designed to be an attractive setting that draws children out of their defensive postures of negative ways of handling fears and anxieties. The materials and teaching methods are individualized to help children establish more positive ways of thinking about themselves as learners and behaving in school. Activities are structured to allow the discovery room teacher and the children to discover their interests and strengths. Within the small groups, the children's behavior is directed toward positive social interaction and their attitudes influenced in the direction of learning.

The transfer orientation program was designed to decrease the anxiety and acting-out behavior often associated with transfer. All students transferring out of the intervention school were prepared by their teachers and the mental health team members. Students transferring into the school were assigned a guide who took the student around the school. The guide introduced the transfer student to every aspect of the school and instructed him or her on what to do if the new student had an academic or social problem. Placement testing was conducted in mathematics and reading so that children were not frustrated or understimulated in the classroom. Teachers developed a classroom introduction. New students were assigned to one of the most successful students in the class for guidance during the initial weeks.

Parent Participation Program

This component of the model consists of three sequential levels of parent participation. The first level is concerned with structuring broad-based activities for a large number of parents. At the second level, approximately one parent per professional staff member works in the school as a classroom assistant, tutor, or aide. At the third level, highly-involved parents participate in school governance. The project provides consultation and material resources to operationalize parent participation at all three levels.

Level I. Broad-Based Participation. This level of broad-based participation is designed to include most or all of the parent body. The school builds a cultural bridge into the community through the formation of a parent-staff organization. Activities include general meetings, potluck suppers, gospel music nights, children's pageants, report card conferences, school newsletters, fundraising events, and other functions culturally compatible with the community.

Level II: Parent Participation in Day-to-Day School Affairs—The Parent Stipend Program. At the second level of participation, parents become active in the ongoing life of school and classroom. A range of parent education activities are offered that focus both on parenting skills and teaching methods. The key component at this level is the parent stipend program. About fifteen parents from each school are employed as classroom assistants, tutors, and clerical and cafeteria aides. Parents are paid the equivalent of minimum wage for about fifteen hours a week. In addition, parents function as unpaid volunteers for an average of five hours per parent per month.

Level III: Parents in School Governance. The third or most sophisticated level of the parent program is the participation of parents in school governance. In this intervention model, parent-staff collaboration is stressed and therefore parents tend to participate in the school's regular governing body rather than in a separate parent advisory group. Training in participatory skills is provided by the intervention staff, principal, and parent coordinator on an issue-by-issue basis. Techniques for letter-writing, telephoning, follow-up with the central office, and mobilizing the larger parent-staff community are taught as needed to solve specific problems. For example, in 1979, in the Brennan New Haven elementary school, parents were assisted in completing a community survey that formed the basis of their recommendations to the Superintendent of Schools for a change in the physical plan. Similarly, they documented a high level of community and school support for the parent stipend program, which was reflected in a successful application to the school system to utilize Title I funds to continue the stipend program after the project ended. Finally, Brennan parents joined with staff to initiate a selection procedure for a new building principal.

Curriculum and Staff Development

This component provides instruction, direction, and support to teachers to enhance the quality of education received by children. The aims of this component are carried out in curriculum planning, which integrates a mental health approach into curriculum activities, and in the provision of resources to teachers to enhance their effectiveness in the classroom. Teachers review achievement data, determine needs for each grade level, and bring in curriculum specialists on a consulting basis.

Monthly seminars are based on building level objectives. Consultants are selected by the teachers and instructed to address areas where they feel they need skill development. This approach differs from traditional in-service education, in which central office curriculum specialists impose district staff development activities on school staff, whether or not they are relevant for the school.

Curriculum development takes two forms. First, teachers are expected to plan and organize basic skills instruction. Second, they are encouraged to submit individual or group "social skills curriculum" proposals. Social skills projects incorporate both social and academic skills in a series of "units" designed to improve students' self-concepts and enable children to more successfully negotiate mainstream American society.

Basic Skill Instruction. Skill instruction is usually undertaken in response to teacher requests for help with learning-disabled students. A reading-learning disabilities consultant works with teachers around these specific requests and he or she is increasingly utilized to assist staff with the organization of the reading program for all students.

Intervention staff and consultants meet to prepare individual programs for each child classified as "high risk" based on the results of diagnostic tests. Areas of strengths and weaknesses in both reading and math are identified and individualized programs are prepared. In order to facilitate administration of individual programs, subgroups (by domain areas) of the high risk children are formed. These groups include Verbal Ability, Perceptual Performance, Quantitative Ability, and Motor Coordination. "Stations" or centers are set up around the classroom. Each station is designed to aid children in a particular area and contains educational materials chosen collectively by consultants and school personnel. Additional materials that encourage acquisition of reading skills are made available to the class as a whole. Parent aides are trained to teach at different stations and work closely with the children. Each child is rotated among the stations according to a schedule most relevant to his or her needs.

The Social Skills Units. Social skills curriculum units are innovative teaching strategies designed to fuse social and academic skills development as an integral part of the regular curriculum. Social skills include relating to others in a mutually acceptable caring way, developing social amenities, and learning the skills necessary to deal successfully with social institutions such as banking, the political process, and securing employment. The process of engaging teachers in the development of the units (i.e., identifying curriculum needs, utilizing consultants and resources, and developing appropriate teaching programs) is stressed.

The School Development Program, then, is based on the assumption that educational improvement can be achieved more efficiently and effectively at an institutional level. The entire school must be the focus of attention. All aspects of school functioning must be part of an ecological approach to educational improvement, curriculum planning, social and psychological services, extracurricular activities, classroom management, and the myriad of personal interactions that take place between and among staff, parents, and students on a day-to-day basis.

Like the Effective School Movement, the School Development Program emphasizes the importance of school climate but in a more basic sense. While Effective School literature defined climate in terms of rules, discipline, and teacher expectations, the SDP model defines it in terms of an 'ethos' or profound organizational structure in which groups of individuals engage in collaborative decision making. While the Effective Schools approach minimized the role of parents, the SDP model emphasizes the importance and essential nature of parental involvement. The parent program is a key element of a model.

PROGRAM ASSESSMENT STUDY

Essential to the implementation of an intervention such as the School Development Program is some evaluation or assessment of its impact. An important aspect of these authors' work is an ongoing assessment of the program's operation and effects. A report of a study conducted by the authors' research staff conducted to assess program impact follows.

The study sample included 306 randomly-selected black students in grades 3-5 who attended 14 different elementary schools. Of the total sample, 176 attended 7 experimental schools, 91 attended 4 control schools, and 39 attended 3 special schools. All schools were located in low socioeconomic areas. The control schools were very similar to experimental schools in terms of achievement, behavior, and attendance: Those schools had no specially-structured activities but followed a regular schedule and curriculum. The special schools were schools in which specially designed curricular activities occurred. The three special schools included a creative arts academy, a gifted and talented program, and a Montessori program.

The sample also included 98 teachers who taught the children in the sample, and 276 parents of those children. Of the 98 teachers, 56 were from experimental schools, 29 from control schools, and 13 from special schools. Of the 276 parents, 155 were from experimental schools, 85 from control schools, and 36 from special schools.

The dependent measures used in the study were:

Classroom Climate—Measured by the Classroom Environment Scale (CES) (Trickett and Moos, 1974).[35] This scale requires children to assess the climate of their classroom along nine dimensions: (1) Involvement; (2) Affiliation; (3) Task Orientation; (4) Competition; (5) Rule Clarity; (6) Innovation; (7) Teacher Control; (8) Order and Organization; and (9) Teacher Support. A two-point rating scale was used.

School Climate—Measured by a scale called the School Climate Survey (SCS), developed by the School Development Program staff for this study. It was completed by both teachers and parents. The wording on the parent's version is slightly different from the wording on the teacher's version, but the content of both versions is essentially the same. A three-point rating scale was used.

Attendance—Measured by the percentage of days students were absent during the study period.

Achievement—Measured by classroom grades on reading and math.

To design the study, pretest data on the above measures were collected in the fall of 1985. Posttest data on the same measures for the same sample were collected at the end of the school year (spring 1986) after a full year of the School Development Program was in effect.

Written consent was obtained from the parents or guardians of all children who participated in the study. Procedures were instituted to protect the confidentiality of participants. Teachers and parents were also required to provide written assent prior to their participation in the study.

The analysis consisted of t-test procedures for repeated measures to examine whether significant changes occcured between pretests and posttests on the dependent measures among the three groups. The level of significance for rejecting the null hypothesis was set at .05.

Results were prepared according to the respective dependent measures.

Assessment of classroom climate by children in the experimental schools showed significant improvement along the following dimensions: Involvement, $t(175) = 6.98$, $p.000$; Affiliation, $t(175) = 4.3$, $p < .000$; Innovation, $t(175) = 8.2$, $p < .000$; Order and organization, $t(175) = 10.0$, $p < .000$; Teacher support, $t(175) = 10.0$, $p < .000$, Total Scale, $t(175) = 4.3$, $p < .000$. A significant negative change was noted on the competition dimension, $t(175) = 2.8$, $p < .000$. Assessment of classroom climate by children in control schools showed significant positive improvement on task orientation, $t(90) = 3.6$, $p < .001$ and competition, $t(90) = 1.8$, $p < .05$. Assessment of classroom climate by children in the special schools showed no significant change of any dimension.

The assessment of school climate by teachers in experimental schools and control schools showed no significant change. However, a significant positive change occurred in special schools, $t(12) = 3.2$, $p < .002$. The assessment of school climate by parents in experimental schools showed a significant positive change $t(154) = 6.8$, $p < .000$. The assessment of school climate by parents in control schools, $t(84) = 5.9$, $p < .000$ and special schools, $t(36) = 1.9$, $p < .053$, showed significant negative changes.

The percentage of days absent among children in experimental schools declined significantly, $t(175) = 2.0$, $p < .047$. No significant change occurred among children in control and special schools.

Children in the experimental schools showed significant improvement on classroom reading grades, $t(175) = 3.3$, $p < .010$, but not in math. The control and special children showed no significant changes.

Generally, children who were selected from schools where the School Development Program was implemented showed significant improvement in attendance and achievement in classroom reading grades. In addition, significant improvements were noted in children's assessments of their classrooms and parents' assessments of the climate in their children's schools. The control and special sample showed considerably less positive changes in these areas and in some instances showed significant negative changes. These results indicate that the School Development Program had a positive effect on school climate, as well as on student behavior and achievement. Because the SDP targets the entire school for change, it was expected that in the short term the most significant changes would occur in school climate, followed by significant positive changes in student behavior and achievement.

The lack of significant change in teachers' perceptions of their school climate in experimental schools may be explained by the fact that teachers' expectations for climate change were quite high and were not met within the study period. However, it is important that a significant positive change in their perceptions of school climate occurred among parents in the experimental schools, while no such significant changes occurred among parents in the control and special schools. This appears to indicate that the meaningful involvement of black parents in their childrens' schools began to bridge the gap between home and school and that it had a beneficial impact on school climate.

CONCLUSION

The task of educating America's youth rests mainly with the public schools. Coleman and Hoffer[36] reported that over 90% of all children in America are educated in public schools. Black children are disproportionately represented among this group because very few of them attend private schools. Yet, it appears that the black students who do attend private schools tend to do better academically than their peers in public schools. Dropout rates among students in public schools also repeatedly exceed that of students in private schools. Thus, the picture that emerges is one in which the large numbers of children in public schools, and especially black children, fail to achieve the levels of academic performance demonstrated by their peers who attend private schools.

Coleman and Hoffer attribute the apparent superiority of private schools to what they call the "social integration" provided by Catholic schools. This social integration stems from the human and social capital fostered by Catholic schools. Human capital is the development of skills and capabilities in individuals. Social capital is the relationship that exists among individuals. Comer[37] made this point many years ago, implicating the lack of an integrated and synergistic human service delivery system sensitive to the unique needs of black children in the failure of public schools to motivate such children. The School Development Program builds "human capital" through its emphasis on staff development training, which equips teachers and staff to deal with instructional and socio-cultural issues with competence and flexibility. SDE builds "social capital" through its emphasis on school management philosophy in which administrators, teachers, and parents work together to determine the climate, priorities, and objectives within their schools.

For black children in particular, school climate plays a significant role in their adjustment to school and the ability to perform well. Other research by these authors[38] has reported significant correlations between achievement and perceptions of classroom climate among black children. Other researchers[39] have reported similar results. Thus, the School Development Program, with its strong emphasis on changing attitudes, values, and ways of interacting among the adults and children in schools, seeks to create a climate, an ethos if you will, that is sensitive, challenging, and conducive to high academic achievement among black children in public schools.

Private schools are not inherently better than public schools. They appear to be better because they are organized differently and promote different attitudes and values. Public schools can succeed just as well and even surpass private schools. With active involvement by parents, local communities can work with educators to improve the quality of education in public schools and thereby enhance the achievement of the majority of black children who attend these schools.

NOTES

1. J. Coleman, T. Hoffer, & S. Kilgure, *High school achievement: Public, Catholic and other private schools compared* (New York: Basic Books, 1982).

2. National Commission on Excellence in Education, *A nation at risk: The imperative for educational reform* (Washington, DC: 1983).

3. E.G. West, *Are American schools working: Disturbing cost and quality trends. Policy analysis No. 26.* (ERIC Research Document No. 235 885), 1983.

4. National Institute on Education, *Violent schools—safe schools* (Washington, DC: HEW, 1977).

5. F. Parker, *Behind a nation at risk: The imperative for educational reform* (ERIC Research Document No. 238-797), 1983.

6. J. Bruce, *The continuous process of school improvement: Learned from the past* (Reston, VA: Association of Teacher Educators, 1980).

7. R.R. Edmonds, "Improving the effectiveness of New York City public schools," in *The minority student in public schools: Fostering academic excellence* (Princeton, NJ: Educational Testing Service, Office for Minority Education, 1981), pp. 23-30.

8. S.T. Bossert, D.C. Dwyer, S. Rowan & G.V. Lee, "The instructional management role of the principal," *Educational Administration Quarterly*, no. 3 (1982), pp. 34-64.

9. P. Coleman, *Elementary school self-improvement through social climate enhancement* (ERIC Research Document No. 251 961), 1984.

10. M. Rutter, B. Maughan, P. Mortimore, J. Ouston, & A. Smith, *Fifteen thousand hairs: Secondary schools and their effects on children* (Cambridge, MA: Harvard Univ. Press, 1979).

11. E.L. McDill, L.C. Rigsby, E.D. Meyers Jr., "Educational climates of high schools: Their effects and sources," in D.A. Erickson (ed.), *Educational organization and administration* (Berkeley, CA: McCutchen, 1977).

12. W.B. Brookover, L. Beamer, H. Efthim, D. Hathaway, L.W. Lesotte, S.K. Miller, T. Passalacqua, & L. Tornatsky, *Creating effective schools* (Holmes Beach: Learning Publications, 1983).

13. C. Achilles et al. Development and use of a replication and evaluation model to track the implementation progress of effective schools elements in an inner city setting. Paper presented at the annual meeting of the Mid-South Educational Research Association, New Orleans, LA, 1982.

14. G. Weber, *Inner city children can be taught to read: Four successful schools.* Council for Basic Education, Vol. 18 of Occasional papers, 1971.

15. R.R. Edmonds, "Programs of school improvement: An overview," *Educational Leadership* 39 (1983), pp. 4-14.

16. J.I. Goodlad, "Can our schools get better," *Phi Delta Kappan* (Jan. 1979), pp. 342-47.

17. D. Clark et al., "Factors associated with success in urban elementary schools," *Phi Delta Kappan*, 61, no. 3 (1980), pp. 467-70.

18. R.L. Venezky & L. Winfield, *Schools that exceed beyond expectations in teaching reading* (Dover, DE: Univ. of Delaware Studies on Education, 1979).

19. S. Purkey & M.S. Smith, *School reform: The policy implications of the effective schools literature.* (ERIC Research Document No. ED 245 350), 1983.

20. P. Berman & M.W. McLaughlin, *Federal programs supporting educational change: Factors affecting implementation and continuation* (Santa Monica, CA: Rand Corp. 1977).

21. J.W. Meyer & B. Rowan, "The structure of educational organizations," in Meyer et al (eds.). *Environments and Organizations* (San Francisco: Jossey-Boss, 1978).

22. M.B. Miles, "Mapping the common properties of schools," in R. Lehming and M. Kane (eds.), *Improving schools: using what we know* (Beverly Hills: Sage Publications, 1981).

23. S.B. Sarason, *The culture of the school and the problem of change* (Boston: Allyn and Bacon, 1971).

24. R.E. Weick, "Educational organizations as loosely coupled systems," *Administrative Science Quarterly*, 21 (1976), pp. 1-19.

25. J. O'Toole, *Making America work* (New York: Continuum Publishing Co., 1981).

26. C.C. Selby, Need for top down and bottom up leadership. Address delivered at the Forum on Excellence in Education, Indianapolis, IN, 1983.

27. J.P. Comer, *School Power* (New York: The Free Press, 1980).

28. A. Beck, L. Wyland & W. McCourt, "Primary prevention: Whose responsibility?, *American Journal of Psychiatry*, 128 (1971), pp. 412-17.

29. L. Hartman, "The preventive reduction of psychological risk in asymptomatic adolescents," *American Journal of Orthopsychiatry*, 48 (1979), pp. 121-35.

30. J. Reiff, "Mental health manpower and institutional change," *American Psychologist* 21 (1966), pp. 540-48.

31. J.G. Kelly, "Ecological constraints on mental health services," *American Psychologist* 21 (1966), pp. 535-39.

32. R. Lewin, *Principles of topological psychology* (New York: McGraw Hill, 1936).

33. M. Weinstein & M. Frankel, "Ecological and psychological approaches to community psychology," *American Journal of Community Psychology* 2 (1974), pp. 43-52.

34. E.G. Wilkinson & W.A. O'Connor, "Human ecology and mental illness," *American Journal of Psychiatry* 139 (1982), pp. 985-90.

35. E.J. Trickett and R.H. Moos, "The Classroom Scale," *American Journal of Commonity Psychology* 2 (no. 1), pp. 1–12.

36. J.S. Coleman and T. Hoffer, *Public and private high schools: the impact of communities* (New York: Basic Books, 1987).

37. J.P. Comer, *School Power*.

38. N.M. Haynes, J.P. Comer & M. Hamilton-Lee, "The effects of parental involvement on student performance," *Journal of Research in Childhood Education* (in press).

39. C. Woods, "The efffects of parent involvement on reading readiness scores," in A. Henderson (ed.), *Parent participation—student achievement: The evidence grows* (Columbia, MD: National Committee for Citizens in Education).

18
Reintegration for Education: Black Community Involvement with Black Students in Schools

Asa G. Hilliard III

Some years ago the late Ronald Edmonds of Harvard University initiated what has come to be known as the Effective Schools Movement. Professor Edmond was among the first to popularize research on education, looking specifically at schools that would normally have been expected to fail. Edmonds identified many schools in the U.S. where students were achieving far beyond what would have been predicted. He went further and examined the successful schools to determine the factors that they had in common.

Since Edmonds' initial work, many other researchers have also developed lists of factors associated with successful schools. One of these factors is strong leadership on the part of the principal, who is expected to set the tone and to establish a systematic way of monitoring progress toward goals that are mutually agreed upon and become the shared mission of school faculty. Most later school effectiveness researchers have tended to emphasize the importance of community involvement in the schools. Yet interestingly enough, in Ron Edmonds' early work, parent or community involvement in the schools was *not* found to be a major factor associated with school success. In other words, it was possible for schools to help students to achieve academically solely on the basis of what the schools themselves did.

There are two ways to help students attain academic achievement. First, it is possible for schools alone, independent of the type of community support available, to organize and to offer effective instruction that can overcome many negative factors in a child's environment. In other words, such things as low family income, divorced parents, or poor nutrition are important factors in the learning environment for children; however, they are not the determining factors. Second, when schools fail to provide the education that students require, there are examples to show that communities, operating independently of schools, can take the steps necessary to overcome the failure of schools. For example, parents may provide tutorials for their students, become involved in the school as tutors, or offer supplementary educational experiences or even private school education for their children.

The fact that schools or communities can do the job alone does not mean that either one should. What it does mean is that the rationale for parent involvement in the school must be based on something other than the necessity of parents to become involved for the purpose of producing achievement in traditional academic areas. Academic achievement is only a small part of schools and the educational process: general socialization is of equal importance. Moreover, in thinking about academic achievement, it is important to keep in mind that it is usually discussed in very narrow terms, meaning academic achievement as measured by basic skills tests. Another level of academic achievement is even more important: the academic achievement in school curricula such as the college preparatory curriculum. There are few, if any, tests that measure achievement in these areas. Therefore, such test results are not normally a part of school effectiveness research. It is unnecessary to develop checklists of activities for African American community members to become involved in the schools, because particular ways are less important than the rationale and the goals. Means become clear when ends are articulated.

ACADEMIC AND CULTURAL GOALS

Education for the African American child includes at least two specific things. First is academic content like that currently offered in the college preparatory curriculum. As indicated in the report of the National Alliance of Black School Educators, *Saving the African American Child,* it is reasonable to expect that the masses of African American children can attain these goals if appropriate instruction is provided. Second and equal in importance to these high-level academic goals, is the matter of socialization. The African American community has a vital stake, not only in whether African American children master academic content and skills, but in the outlook, values, and behaviors that they develop through the process of socialization, be it formal or informal. It is through this process that children come to develop a sense of coherence about their experience, a sense of time and of space. They are able to locate themselves on the map of human history. They develop an orientation and a set of values and perhaps, most of all, they come to seee themselves as part of a larger community that has its own cohesiveness, and to which the child *belongs.*

The academic and socialization goals must always be kept in mind when discussing the education process for our children. Answers to questions about these two components will and should determine the aims, the content, and the method of education.

The African American population has suffered slavery, segregation, racism, and other forms of group oppression. Such suffering has been, perhaps longer than that of any other group with the possible exception of the American Indian. Many immigrant groups have come to the U.S. and have advanced in the socioeconomic structure within a few generations. Yet the experience of African Americans has been like being on a roller coaster, with extreme ups and downs. Presently, African Americans appear to be falling behind others in the general march for improvement that characterizes the experience of other groups in the U.S.

African Americans traditionally have depended upon the formal educational process to serve as a vehicle for social mobility. To a large extent, this has worked for many; however, a large number of African Americans remain below the poverty line and have low levels of educational achievement. Worst of all, throughout the long history of struggle, it appears that African Americans have come to rely less upon ability, instinct, and initiative in determining the nature of the education that their children should receive, and instead, trust in alien systems and leadership to make decisions for them.

At times it appears that African Americans have been so happy to overcome deprivation in education that the mere access to whatever exists in the standard educational process is accepted with enthusiasm. African Americans have been far too complacent and far too silent in criticizing the fundamental character of the educational process itself. As the many reform reports in education show, that process has not been adequate even for the European American majority; and certainly not for African Americans.

What is it that is meant by community involvement in the schools? It is not enough merely to assume that African Americans comprise a community or that there is agreement about what is meant by community. What actually is and what ought to be regarding community must be clarified.

THE REALITY AND NECESSITY OF PLURALITY

In his recent book, *Plural But Equal*,[1] Dr. Harold Cruise has done a brilliant job of tracing and analyzing the experience of African Americans throughout the years. The very title of this book, *Plural But Equal*, is a take-off on the legal slogan "Separate But Equal." Neither Cruise, nor anyone, could accept the evils of a separate but equal system of segregation that has been fought so vigorously. That system was one in which the highest laws of the land mandated segregation, preventing access of African Americans to the benefits of U.S. citizenship. The remedy for such a separatist ideology and legal practice has been achieved through a series of court actions outlawing the legal basis for discrimination. However, this dismantling process was accompanied by the emergence of a new ideology of "integration" and was accepted by many black and white Americans. It was an ideology produced by those who apparently failed to recognize the fact that the U.S. is now, always has been, and in the near future will remain, ethnically and racially a culturally plural society. Society is made up of ethnic groups.

At the same time, African Americans saw in the concept of integration something that would actually mean the disintegration of the African American community and the cultural assimilation of that community into the mainstream. However, no clear sense of this mainstream was apparent. To the extent that assimilation is seen as a goal and a way of life for African Americans, the very meaning of "the community" becomes ambiguous. Under true assimilation, there would be no "African American" group at all, but instead, individuals whose historical roots were in African America and who functioned as culturally indistinct individuals within a much larger and more diverse group. Yet, as Harold Cruise points out, the idea of the mainstream is pure fiction, since ethnic groups survive and exert power in many ethnic power centers around the nation.

If we are to talk community, then we must be clear about what we mean by the African American community. Such a community should have a concept of itself and be rooted in a true cultural reality, with an historical foundation. Further, to be a true community, its existence must be manifest through institutional structures that have continuity, focus, and purpose. A carefull look at the history of African Americans over the past four hundred years shows that the primary struggle, has been to maintain a sense of group cohesiveness and unity based upon group identity. More than anything else under racism and oppression, this cohesiveness and unity have been under attack. The result is that while some African Americans continue to feel a sense of cohesiveness, many others feel no sense of group cohesiveness at all. Many are confused and even doubtful about whether such cohesiveness exists or ever existed.

African Americans have been slow to perceive the true, culturally plural structure of American society. The general belief in or assumption of U.S. cultural homogeneity has led to a general embarrassment about things suggesting the assertion of the individual's cultural identity. The recognition and acceptance of this identity is made more difficult by the fact that neither the educational nor the socialization process for African Americans contributes in any sustained way to an understanding of African American cultural identity. Formal, structured, systematic cultural education and socialization activities are necessary if persons are to recognize, understand, appreciate, and above all, have access to an individual culture for use in a plural society.

The foundation of such a pluralistic posture in the African American community is rooted in the reality of U.S. society. The cultural base of the broad African American community is African. Despite the fact that the vast majority of African Americans participate in, exhibit, and typify African cultural forms, few have had the formal training to know Africa and to know of the parts of African culture that are still manifest in the behavior of Africans throughout the diaspora and especially, Africans in the U.S. As a result, much of the behavior of African Americans is not well understood. Nor will it be understood by professionals who seek to solve the kinds of school problems we have identified such as the appropriate kind of community participation in the schools.

The study of African culture is absolutely essential to the understanding of African American people. Moreover, the study of African American culture is also important as those cultural forms can then be utilized for unity and cohesiveness in order to make group mobilization possible.

These statements are true even though many African Americans have been taught to reject their Africanness, or have been taught in such a way that they fail to recognize their Africanness. Some not only reject their own Africanness, but are hostile to any suggestion that their own behavior may manifest residual African cultural forms. Perhaps there will always be divisions within the African American community on this issue. That leaves us in something of a quandry in that if the cultural base is rejected or ignored, the group identity of African Americans is based upon either poverty or oppression. Neither poverty nor oppression is a sufficient basis for the development of a positive group identity.

When a group has cultural cohesiveness, that cohesiveness is unavoidably manifested through the use of its institutional structures to socialize its children. Social organizations such as fraternities and sororities, community service agencies such as the YMCA and Boy Scouts, and religious organizations such as churches all support the cultural socialization of African American children. One of the major reasons that the current generation of young people seem so lost is that many have never been touched by any structured form of systematic socialization under the leadership of African American adults. Peers and the mass media become the major socializing influences of African American children.

Once the fact is accepted that African Americans exist as a group with a cultural foundation that is meaningful and essential, the question of black community involvement in the educational process takes on a special character and meaning. Such involvement becomes obligatory. A cohesive community would have a clear sense of direction for education and systematic ways of working to ensure that education takes place. In fact, the family must see itself as the primary educator. Formal public schools would then be an offshoot of group activities toward self-education.

There are certain things that, by nature, public schools are able to do most efficiently. For example, they can teach basic skills to masses of children very economically and efficiently. However, because public schools serve a culturally plural society, they are very inefficient and probably incompetent to carry out the broader socialization process for all of the diverse cultural groups that such institutions serve. Consequently, each group must forge linkages with the public schools to help them to do what they can do best, and to ensure the greatest degree of harmony between the school's efforts and those of the community to educate and socialize African American children.

COMMUNITY FUNCTIONS IN THE EDUCATION AND SOCIALIZATION PROCESS

Several important functions that can and must be performed by the African American community in the education and socialization process. First, the community must play a key role in setting the goals for the education of its children. When this author attended the Denver public schools, virtually all of the community's African Americans attended one of Denver's five high schools: four academic and one manual training high school. Goals for the African American community were set by the city's school boards. Naturally, the manual training high school was located in the middle of the African American community. This was a clear example of goal-setting that did not rely upon community input, nor was the community at any time effective in influencing the establishment of new goals.

Second, the African American community can and ought to provide models for its children. This modeling should be offered through a formally-designed process. For example, in traditional African culture, formal preparation and initiation were vehicles through which children were exposed to community models. To a large measure, for the current masses of African American children, the community appears to have abandoned this responsibility. The remnants of such activities can be seen in such things as debutante parties for the children of a small, elite group, but these parties are not linked to a systematic socialization process. Further, the masses of African American children have no systematically-presented models for future behavior.

Third, a community that is conscious of itself should systematically take steps to carefully monitor the progress of the masses of its children. At present, the responsibility for doing this has been abandoned to society's formal educational institutions. This means that African Americans are dependent upon others and that the only part of the process that is treated in even a cursory way is the formal academic process. Those outside African American communities do not monitor the broader socialization process for African American children at all.

Fourth, a community that is conscious of itself provides systematically for activities that express the community's concern about what is legitimate and what is illegitimate. The existence of the community as the primary legitimation agent is essential to the development of a sense of orientation in its children.

Finally, a conscious community provides fiscal support for the socialization and educational processes. This is done to a limited extent through the variety of fund-raising activities that produce small scholarships for a few students; however, a more responsible and responsive approach, is to establish structures to augment the work that goes on in public schools for African American children. These structures, as indicated above, may be community centers or organizational programs that have a relative degree of permanance.

Such a conscious community is pro-active in matters of education and socialization. A community cannot function in this way unless it is conscious of itself, is properly oriented in time and space, has the capacity to generate collective effort, and has institutional structures dedicated to the educational and socialization processes.

These things are not unique to the African American community. In fact, what has been said can be used as a framework for evaluating the effectiveness of any group and for comparing the relative effectiveness of many groups. For example, the most successful cultural minority groups in America exhibit careful control over the school and socialization processes of their children. Groups including the Chinese, Japanese, Jews, and Mormans do not leave such things to chance. In most of these communities, parents are clearly and deeply involved in the design of the education and socialization processes for their children. All of these groups have made full use of the public educational system, yet none have allowed themselves to become totally dependent upon it.

CONCLUSION

The African American community should and indeed must be fully involved in the total educational process of African American children. However, this involvement must be predicated upon a great deal of work done to revive and enhance the capacity of the community to perform these functions appropriately. A careful evaluation of the current situation must be conducted, and the results of such an evaluation shared widely within the community. The many organizations within the African American community must develop an educational mission, and there must be some degree of unity of purpose within the broader community in order to provide guidance and contribute to the education and socialization of African American children. If African Americans intend to compete upon the world stage, it is unthinkable that the education and socialization of their children can be left to chance. Such processes cannot be left to others, merely demanding that children have access to schooling processes over which parental and community control is minimal.

Therefore, African Americans must come to terms with their ethnicity. They must, if possible, strengthen it. This does not mean a loss of respect for others. It means that plurality is recognized as a fact and utilized for the benefit of African American adults and children. The African American community must, as others do, give systematic attention to the recognition, study, and practice of its own cultural creativities.

African American people need a new concept of integration. Currently, they are "disintegrated" or fragmented, and must re-integrate the community. This in no way should be considered a call for segregation; it is a call for a conceptual model of pluralism—a pluralism that accepts the idea of cultural families. After accepting pluralism, it becomes possible to speak of "black community involvement in the schools."

Research results are clear. We know how to produce excellent student achievers. However, the question of community cohesiveness is not a matter of research so much as it is a matter of philosophy. Once there are strong, cohesive communities, the question of community involvement in the schools will be *pro forma,* because strong communities oversee, support, and collaborate with helping agencies.

In the final analysis, thinking about community involvement with African American children in the schools is really a matter of thinking about the assumption of primary responsibility for the direction of the children's education and socialization.

NOTE

1. H. Cruise, *Plural but Equal:, A Critical Study of Blacks and Minorities and America's Plural Society* (New York: William Morrow, 1987).

REFERENCES

Blyden, J.W. *Christianity, Islam and the Negro.* Edinburgh Univ. Press, 1967.
Diop, C.A. *The Cultural Unity of Black Africa.* Chicago: Third World Press, 1978.
DuBois, W.E.B. *The Negro American Family.* Cambridge: M.I.T. Press, 1970.
Erny, P. *Childhood and Cosmos: The Social Psychology of the Black African Child.* New York: Black Orpheus Press, 1973.
Hare N. and J. Hare, *Bringing the Young Black Boy to Manhood: The Passage.* San Francisco: Black Think Tank, 1985.
Hilliard, A.G. "Pedagogy and Ancient Kemet." In M. Karenga and J. Carruthers, *Kemet and the African worldview.* Los Angeles: University of Sankore Pess, 1986.
Hilliard, A.G. "Kemetic Concepts in Education." In *Nile Valley Civilizations,* edited by I. Van Sertima. *Journal of African Civilization, Ltd.* 1985, pp. 153-62.

National Alliance of Black School Educators. *Saving the African American Child.* Report of the National Alliance of
   Black School Educators, Inc. Task Force on Black Academic and Cultural Excellence, Nov. 1984.
Nobles, W. and L. Goddard, *Understanding the Black family: A Guide for Scholarship and Research.* Oakland, Ca.:
   Black Family Institute, 1984.
Powell, G.J. *Black Monday's Children: A Study of the Effects of School Desegregation on Self-concepts of Southern
   Children.* New York: Appleton Century-Crafts.
Woodson, C.G. *The Miseducation of the Negro.* Washington, D.C.: The Associated Publishers, Inc., 1977.

19
Memphis Inner-City Schools Improvement Project: A Holistic Approach for Developing Academic Excellence

Willie W. Herenton

Our society has failed dismally to adequately educate black students in our urban public schools. This failure has been amply documented. While some academic achievement gains have been noted in a few school districts, far too many black students are receiving an inferior education. The educational outcomes for black students continue to cause major concerns about the future economic, social, and political stability of the black community.

Public school systems across the nation are under intense pressure to substantially improve the educational performance of their low-achieving students. In response to this condition, school systems are restructuring delivery systems, revising curriculum, retraining teachers, and imposing higher standards. The attainment of the hopes, dreams, and aspirations of black students are largely dependent on the quality of education received in our public schools.

It is clear that the growing rate of poverty among our children must be addressed by our society before we can expect any dramatic changes in the urban condition. We desperately need some public policy initiatives that can address poverty among our youth.

The causes, symptoms, and effects of urban poverty as they relate to the academic achievement of significant numbers of inner-city students are many, varied, and complex. Because they are societal in nature, these problems must be acknowledged and addressed in order to move students beyond basic skills achievement to academic excellence and personal enhancement. Among the problems facing inner-city residents are: unemployment and underemployment, generational welfarism, poor academic achievement, high absenteeism, suspension and dropout rates, a rising incidence of teenage pregnancy, drug and alcohol abuse, crime and delinquency, and lack of access to community resources.

INNER-CITY SCHOOLS IMPROVEMENT PROJECT

In an effort to address the myriad of problems that confront black students in the Memphis city school system, the Inner-City Schools Improvement Project was initiated in the fall of 1987. This project was unique in the history of education because it purports to deal with the causes, symptoms, and effects of urban poverty in a comprehensive manner. It combines the elements of the Effective Schools Movement with the strategies of a holistic community-based intervention/prevention approach. Without denying the need to focus on internal school improvements, the project acknowledges that the schools do not exist in a vacuum and that it is appropriate to view urban education in the context of "community schools," with the community including the students and their families, neighbors, and friends.

The Inner-City Schools Improvement Project also aknowledges the responsibilities of other institutions within the community with which students and their parents interact. Such institutions include: social service, welfare, and health care systems, churches, civic organizations, businesses, government agencies, and the criminal justice system. Within this framework, the community is seen both as a resource to be tapped and a point of intervention/prevention. The Inner-City Schools Improvement Project will, therefore, address educational, vocational-technical, personal enrichment, and social service needs of a target group of inner-city residents in the Memphis community ranging from preschoolers to adults.

The Project is designed to provide a coordinated and holistic approach to improving academic achievement among minority inner-city students in the Memphis city school system. Central to this effort is a community-based approach that recognizes that all aspects of personal, community, and school life can impact the learning potential of students.

Parent Education and Training Programs

Parents are their children's first and most important teachers. The things parents do with and for their children and the time and manner in which these things are done affect children indefinitely and indelibly, and can be positive or negative. Recently, national attention has been focused on the need to train parents to become more effective. More affluent parents are aware of available community resources and have access to them. Parents in the target communities, however, have more limited awareness of such resources and the means to procure them.

The Parent Training Program will develop and implement programs that are designed: 1) to increase parental awareness and understanding of the educational process; 2) to help parents understand their roles in influencing the success of their children in school; 3) to develop basic fundamental skills and abilities of parents to help their children experience success in school; 4) to provide parents with a set of tools and strategies for helping their children achieve academic success; and 5) to increase parents' understanding of policy implications.

The New Parents as Teachers Project is designed to share child development and educational information with parents of children under three years of age. This program will provide private visits with a parent educator, group meetings with other parents, access to a resource center and toy lending library, screening of children's vision, hearing, and physical development, and activities designed to help children learn.

The Model Community in the Schools Program is an early-intervention program designed to identify those problems in the target communities that impede the children's education. Project personnel will develop and demonstrate successful strategies that remediate or eliminate such problems. While this project will initially function in a problem identification/resolution mode, its primary functions will subsequently become the planning, coordination, and mobilization of community resources, as these functions address the needs of the target communities.

Home-Based Early Childhood Education Program

Authorities generally agree that the first three to four years of a child's life are the most important from a developmental perspective. Therefore, it is essential that parents possess adequate parenting skills in order to enable their children to flourish and acquire the kinds of skills and abilities necessary for subsequent success. However, many of the parents in the target communities lack the kinds of parenting skills necessary to give their children a good head start in life.

The Home-Based Early Childhood Education Program is predicated on the premise that the earlier appropriate developmental, educational intervention begins for inner-city students with identified cognitive, social, psychomotor, or language weaknesses, the better the chances of ameliorating these problems and improving the student's potential for success in school. The program is based on the concept that the parent is the first and most important teacher and that the home is the child's first school. Parents of the participating students will be taught how to become actively and positively involved in the education of their children.

After-School Tutorial Program

Increased academic standards, as well as the requirements for promotion and retention necessitate that marginal or "at-risk" students receive additional instructional assistance. The need for such additional assistance is compounded for students in the target schools who have cumulative academic deficits. Because these students do not have the option of hiring private tutors, and their parents are unable to intervene, the lack of alternative assistance may cause many of them to fail.

Students in the target schools who are experiencing considerable academic difficulty in core curriculum courses will be eligible to participate in the After School Tutorial Program. The program will be operated by experienced teachers who will tutor students in their areas of difficulty.

After-School Homework Center

Educators have historically recognized the value of homework as a supportive learning activity. When it is appropriately designed, homework reinforces and extends skills previously taught. To be effective, however, homework should be done in an environment that is conducive to studying. The facility should be quiet, well-lighted and ventilated, and free of clutter and other physical distractions. Study aids such as a good dictionary, a set of encyclopedias, an atlas, and an almanac should be available. Unfortunately, many of the students in the target schools do not have access to such instructional aids and study environment. Consequently, homework assignments are frequently not completed or are completed poorly. Assignments requiring the use of a dictionary, encyclopedia, atlas, almanac, or other references may simply go undone because students do not have access to them.

An After School Homework Center will initially operate at the Martin Luther King, Jr. Center. Staffed by successful and experienced teachers, the center will operate four days a week. Study aids as well as limited school supplies will be available for students in order to enhance homework completion and subsequent academic success.

Non-Tuition Elementary Remedial Summer School Program

Research suggests that students who do poorly in school during the regular school year tend to forget newly-acquired skills, information, and applications during their summer vacations. This is especially true of significant numbers of students in the five target elementary schools. Over a period of time and without viable intervention strategies, these students acquire cumulative academic deficits in reading and mathematics. Moreover, this problem will escalate with the implementation of performance standards as the basis for promotion or retention.

A non-tuition remedial summer school program will be provided for students in grades one through six in the target schools who are in greatest need of assistance in reading and mathematics. Priority consideration will be given to students who are retained because of failure to meet promotion/retention standards. The overall purpose of this program will be to raise the academic achievement levels of participating students in reading and mathematics.

Peer Self-Help Substance Abuse and Teen Pregnancy Program

Peer pressure is a major motivating force in the lives of teenagers. Any strategy that takes advantage of peer pressure in a positive way has great potential for success. Teens helping teens is one way of harnessing such peer pressure as a positive force.

A specialized self-help program that makes use of peer pressure will be implemented. A corps of student leaders will be identified and trained in leadership skills. Under the supervision of a mental health professional and a trained faculty sponsor, student leaders will develop specific action plans designed to prevent and counter substance abuse and teenage pregnancy. This peer self-help program will be well structured and closely supervised.

Role Model Component

It is generally agreed that many black youth are deprived of the opportunity to interact with positive role models. Unfortunately, too many inner-city youngsters are influenced by negative role models. It is, therefore, imperative that blacks who have emerged from disadvantaged backgrounds and succeeded despite obstacles help black students in this way.

Thus, a large mobilization effort will be launched to attract black professionals, skilled workers, sorority and fraternity members, and other individuals and organizations to the program. The purpose will be to motivate successful blacks in the broader community to reach back and devote some of their time and expertise to helping inner-city youth. The expected outcome of this component will be the enhancement of the students' self-concepts, levels of aspiration, and motivation to achieve in life.

Adult Education

Many of the residents in the target communities lack the education necessary to obtain and retain viable employment. They are also unable to assist their children with homework and other related school assignments. This lack of education traps the residents and their children in a vicious and self-perpetuating cycle of poverty, frustration, and despair from which there is little opportunity or hope for escape. Yet, an increasingly technologically driven economy demands that citizens possess at least basic skills and understanding in the areas of reading, writing, and arithmetic if they are to function effectively.

Adult basic education classes will be available to parents and residents who have attained less than an eighth-grade education. Pre-general education development and general education development classes will be offered to residents who have more than an eighth-grade level of education, but do not possess a high school diploma. An adult high school program will be available to those residents who want to pursue traditional courses of study. Each program will be available at no cost to the residents except for a refundable textbook deposit fee.

Adult Vocational-Technical Courses and Services

Statistics indicate that the American economy is rapidly changing from a manufacturing and industrial base to a scientific, technological, and service-oriented one. Meanwhile, business, industry, and government are concerned about the capability of the work force and the country's ability to compete in world markets. The overwhelming majority of the residents in the target communities are unemployed or under-employed. Many lack the knowledge, skills, abilities, training, and work habits that will enable them to secure and retain viable employment. A significant number of these residents also lack the financial means to pay for vocational-technical training or re-training. Consequently, their opportunities to improve economically are very limited.

Still other residents have few opportunities to participate in personal development courses that will enrich their lives and the lives of their children.

Adult vocational-technical education classes and services will be available in three major areas: 1) trade, industry and occupational courses; 2) personal development courses and services; and 3) services for special populations. Available trade, industry, and occupational courses will include automotive technology, general building trades, office occupations, health occupations, and cosmetology. Personal development courses will include such areas as woodworking, ceramics, sewing, cake decorating, and upholstering. The services component will include child care, career counseling, job placement, and transportation vouchers for eligible residents who are acquiring or upgrading job skills. These courses and services will be available to residents at no cost.

Computer Education Program

Computers are commonplace in business, industry, government and education, and will become even more common in the future. Citizens who fail to understand this technology and who do not know how to use computers will be denied access to opportunities and benefits in the worlds of work and education. Students in the target schools have some knowledge of computers and computer applications, but many of their parents have little or no understanding of this technology, its benefits, and its power. Microcomputers are not present in the homes of these students as they are in the homes of more affluent students. Consequently, parents and other residents have limited, if any, opportunities to develop or sharpen computer skills.

The Computer Education Program will comprise a microcomputer laboratory with fifteen Apple IIE Systems, a printer, and a variety of software. Through this program, parents and community residents will be able: 1) to understand the computer and the roles it plays in society; 2) to become computer literate; and 3) to utilize a microcomputer for selected applications skills. Additionally, the lab will provide students in the target community with increased opportunities to use computers for instructional purposes.

Martin Luther King, Jr. Library and Research Center

Recent studies indicate that vast numbers of blacks have limited knowledge of and lack access to information about their ethnic, cultural, and historical origins. Blacks are generally uninformed about the significant contributions that African Americans have made to western civilization. This lack of knowledge and information, along with the myriad of problems that have historically afflicted black people, results in a low self-concept and lack of self-esteem in far too many African Americans.

The Martin Luther King, Jr. Educational and Cultural Center will house a library and media and research facilities that will contain an extensive collection of books, documents and audio and visual media about African Americans past and present. The collection will contain materials written on various reading levels to appeal to a broad readership. Inner-city residents, students, and the broader community will be encouraged to utilize library and research center materials to become familiar with the accomplishments and contributions that African Americans have made to civilization. As students and residents become more knowledgeable about these past and present achievements, their feelings about themselves and what is possible for them to achieve should improve.

Coordination of Social, Welfare, Human, and Medical Services

A preponderance of the residents in the targeted communities rely on existing governmental and/or volunteer community agencies to provide needed social, welfare, human, and medical services. Many lack adequate knowledge of available services and programs. Others do not have the means and wherewithal to access referenced services in a timely manner. Often residents become confused, frustrated, disgusted with the bureaucracy or perceived bureaucracy attendant to these agencies and thus fail to pursue needed services or assistance. Although such aid is available, residents often have difficulty coping with a demoralizing system whose referral, certification, and verification processes frequently send them from one agency to another.

The Inner-City Schools Improvement Project will request providers of the social, welfare, human, and medical services most frequently needed by the target communities to coordinate their services and programs. Such coordination should eliminate duplication, replication, and fragmentation of services, reduce the frustration of clients, and provide services in a more timely and cost-effective manner. The school system will also provide office space within the Martin Luther King, Jr. Center for these agencies so that a "one-stop social services shop" is available to eligible residents.

System-Wide Achievement Team (SWAT)

The seven target schools involved in the Project are characterized by low student achievement, including poor performance on the Basic Skills First, State Proficiency, California Achievement, and Stanford Achievement Tests as well as by low retention rates and high absenteeism, suspension, and dropout rates. Though some progress has been made in resolving these problems, much remains to be done.

The System-Wide Achievement Team will analyze and use existing data to pinpoint problems and to formulate and implement comprehensive plans for improvement. These plans will be designed to achieve the following:

- to improve the instructional leadership in the targeted schools;
- to increase the academic focus in the schools;
- to improve the schools' climate in terms of orderliness, discipline, safety, and cleanliness;
- to raise expectations for teachers, students, and parents;
- to provide continuing assessment of student performance;

- to increase engaged time of students;
- to improve home-school relationships;
- to improve the overall administration, supervision, and operation of the target schools.

CONCLUSION

The Memphis School System's Inner-City Schools Improvement Project represents a comprehensive approach toward ensuring that all children will be adequately educated in a majority black school district. The major premise that undergirds these efforts is that black children can and must be expected to learn. This premise must be embraced by teachers, administrators, parents, and students themselves if excellence is to be achieved. It is imperative that the public schools do a better job of educating minority students. The creation of a permanent underclass largely comprised of blacks and other minority groups must not be allowed to form. The Inner-City Schools Improvement Project will help put Memphis on the road to ensuring that all children will receive equal educational opportunities.

20

A Community Initiative: Making a Difference in the Quality of Black Education

William A. Johnson, Jr., Betty Dwyer, and Joan Z. Spade

Since its founding in April 1965, the Urban League of Rochester has placed a high priority on the improvement of educational opportunity for blacks and other minority students in the Rochester public schools. This concern has been actualized over the past twenty-two years through direct services and advocacy activities as diverse as the offering of adult basic skills classes, recognition for students with high academic achievement, and a detailed proposal for reducing racial isolation in urban schools. In stressing the necessity for top-quality education, it is the League's position that black and other minority youth will not be able to achieve in the economic mainstream without the necessary skills. Mindful of this belief and recognizing that a crisis in educational opportunity was on the community's doorstep, the League launched an activity of tremendous magnitude that, looking back two years later, has had a profound impact on the entire community.

In 1985, as it entered its twentieth anniversary year, the Urban League launched its Community-wide Initiative to Improve the Quality of Education in the Rochester Public Schools. This initiative was based on mounting evidence which indicated that Rochester was failing to meet the educational needs of its youth, the majority of whom were black (59%) or Hispanic (11%). Of the 14,038 secondary school students enrolled in the Rochester City School District in 1983-84, 941 students were dropped or "kicked" out of school. By comparison, 1,273 graduated. Furthermore, only 35 of the black graduates in the class of 1984 had a "B" or higher average. Coaches reported that one-third to one-half of all students who went out for team sports were disqualified because of their failure to maintain a "C" average as required by School District policy.

The Urban League of Rochester realized that education is the responsibility of the total community, and any serious attempt to address this crisis must involve the whole community. Therefore, the Rochester Education Initiative was launched with two primary objectives: (1) to inform the total community of the crisis of low academic achievement within the public school system; and (2) to involve the total community in a set of strategies to correct this problem.

THE ROCHESTER EDUCATION INITIATIVE

The plan to achieve the objectives stated above included five phases of activity. In Phase I, meetings were held to solicit the support of key individuals and groups within the community. As a result of this phase, sixty-two organizations endorsed the initiative by becoming co-sponsors, including religious, neighborhood, fraternal, business, human service, and govermental organizations. These groups participated in planning and implementing activities in the later phases of the educational initiative.

Phase II involved the organization of three speakouts to solicit the views and concerns of the "key players" in the educational process: students, parents, and educators. Participants in the speakouts were invited to speak to the question "What can be done to improve the academic performance of Rochester's students?" A key element of cooperation was achieved with personnel at WXXI-TV, the local public television station, which agreed to videotape each speakout in its entirety, and from these hours of footage, to prepare excerpts that most dramatically focused on the concerns of key players. The edited video was used at the leadership conference in June and the October Town Meetings.

Approximately 200 students from 11 secondary schools attended the Youth Speakout in April 1985. Prior to addressing the central question, students used the platform to describe grievances they felt had often been ignored. This was a rare opportunity for the students to talk candidly with the hope of getting a response to their concerns. The youth addressed topics such as magnet vs. comprehensive schools, student-teacher communication, conflict resolution, and counseling. The Parent Speakout was held in May 1985. Prior to the event, volunteers canvassed neighborhoods to survey parents' attitudes toward the schools and to encourage parents to attend the speakout. News releases and flyers were also distributed through the churches and schools. Approximately 250 parents participated in a four-hour session that raised many concerns and possible solutions. The Educators Speakout also was held in May. Educators from the City School District took the lead in organizing and implementing this program, and the nearly 100 participants made a diligent effort to focus on solutions rather than recriminations.

In Phase III, a conference, jointly sponsored by the Urban League and the University of Rochester, was held in June, 1985. Its purpose was to involve a broad cross section of community leaders in developing an action plan to address the problem of the large and growing number of young people who were failing in city schools. About 150 key community leaders attended the conference. The conference charge was given by the president of the University, Dr. G. Dennis O'Brien; the president of the Urban League, William A. Johnson, Jr.; and the superintendent of the Rochester city school district, Dr. Laval S. Wilson. Statements of concern were presented by the mayor, the president of the teachers' union, the president of the board of education,the executive director of the local anti-poverty agency, and a prominent business leader. Sol Hurwitz, senior vice president for the Committee for Economic Development in New York City, was the keynote speaker, and he focused on education collaboratives undertaken in other communities. Videotaped highlights of the three speakouts were shown. At the conclusion, most conferees stated that they had a greater sense of urgency about the educational crisis in the city's schools.

In Phase IV, twelve town meetings were held throughout the city on October 29, 1985. Neighborhood organizations and settlement houses were enlisted to act as lead agencies in setting up the meetings in areas of the city they serve. Prominent leaders from all sectors of the community made spot announcements that were used by local television and radio stations to help promote the meetings. In addition, the evening daily newspaper and a prominent weekly paper ran featured series of articles on public education issues.

The twelve town meetings built upon the momentum generated and brought those issues identified in earlier phases to the publisher's attention. Videotaped highlights of the earlier speakouts and conference were used to stimulate group discussions. Participants were also given data about student achievement, broken down by elementary and secondary enrollment. The initiative proposed "school-based action committees" to be comprised of parents, educators, clergy, businesspersons, community residents, and where appropriate, students to serve as a vehicle for addressing and resolving the issues of performance and accountability. Participants were encouraged to join neighborhood-based Action Committees at the 45 schools within the city. Over 1,000 persons participated in the town meetings and close to 600 registered for school action committees.

Phase V involved the convening of the school action committees (SACs) by a school principal and a community volunteer. SACs were charged with the task of launching at least one identifiable project that they felt would substantially improve academic achievement in their schools. Fact sheets listing suspensions, attendance data and academic information for each school were provided to help committees identify specific areas of weakness in their schools and determine what type of project they would initiate. By the end of the first year, 35 of the 45 city public schools had selected, implemented, and reported on school projects for the 1985-86 school year.

A city-wide steering committee was convened by the Urban League in April 1986. The committee meets periodically and serves as a vehicle for SACs to share information about projects, to advocate for the replication of effective projects, and to assist in the identification of resources that committees may need to implement school-based projects.

COMMUNITY RESPONSES

As a result of the Rochester Education Initiative, a variety of activities were developed to address the problem of improving student achievement in the city's public schools. These activities were generated from a variety of community sectors and involved various strategies. Oversight, advocacy, and programs to improve academic performance occured at all levels including school action committees, a city-wide task force, and a business task force. In addition, businesses, human service agencies, churches, colleges, foundations, and other community groups looked for ways they could improve the educational achievement of city youth. The following sections describe in greater detail the activities that are occurring.

School Action Committees (SACs)

As previously discussed, the Urban League and its education initiative co-sponsors promoted the formation of building-based action committees at all city schools as an effective strategy to improve the academic achievement of students of each school. This strategy emphasized the importance of focusing attention at the school level and inviting all members of the school community to participate. It also acknowledged that needs and circumstances differ from school to school and that the neighborhoods and individuals who constitute each school community should determine what actions can have the greatest impact on the academic achievement of students in the individual schools.

The first SAC meetings were convened in December 1986. The development of SACs varied by school. There was a diversity of participants, with some SACs composed primarily of parents, and others primarily of school staff. Most were a combination of both parents and staff with participation from residents, businesspersons, and/or community leaders. In some cases SAC volunteers joined already-existing school improvement activities and parent groups. SACs developed their own unique organizational structures. Several formed subcommittees or task forces to work on particular issues. Some met as frequently as twice a month, while others met only three times during the school year. In order to provide ongoing encouragement and technical support, the Urban League obtained funding from several local foundations and corporations for a staff coordinator.

SAC projects reflected a variety of strategies designed to help improve academic achievement. For example, SACs in two elementary schools developed projects to increase the reading skills of students. Three different approaches for improving achievement through tutoring were initiated in elementary schools, while another project provided motivational activities for students achieving below their potential. Other projects focused on reducing student suspensions, improving attendance, increasing student and staff participation, raising school spirit, or facilitating communication among staff, parents, and community through special events, workshops, or newsletters.

The league staff coordinator monitors SAC activities. Some of the projects have been folded into ongoing school activities, either through the administration or parent group, while others have remained autonomous. The SAC initiatives are beginning to show some positive effects. In 1986-87, average daily attendance rates went up at least 1.5 percentage points in one school. This improvement in attendance occured through a series of incentives that were subsidized by local businesses, such as gift certificates from restaurants and plaques for classes with the highest attendance. Another school has reduced the number of suspensions by 78% through the implementation of a plan developed by the School Action Committee. League staff members have conducted a survey of teachers and school administrators to evaluate the process by which the reduction in suspensions has occurred, and their report will be disseminated to other schools and interested parties.

City-Wide Task Force

In August 1985, as a result of the leadership conference at the University of Rochester, a task force comprised of representatives from area colleges and universities, city government, schools (including the board of education), the media, churches, parents, fraternal organizations, and human service agencies was convened by the Urban League and the local Center for Educational Development. In March 1986, the task force issued its "Call to Action" report to the Community. The report acknowledged that there was an education crisis in the community: "all of us share responsibility for the problem, and all of us can contribute to finding solutions." The task force recommended specific actions to be taken by the city school district, teachers, parents, students, the business community, community groups, human service agencies, cultural and service agencies, religious institutions, colleges and universities, libraries, the city Department of Recreation and Community Services, and the media.

Recommendations were not restricted to programmatic approaches to problems, but included changes or new directions in institutional policies and attitudes. Students were told: "take control of your education . . . ask for help of teachers after school, of tutors, of parents." Teachers were called on to "raise their sights about what they expect of their students" and "be willing to make home visits." Each governing body of a human service, cultural, educational, and service organization was called on to "examine what it can do to enhance public education in Rochester, and work cooperatively to do so." More specific actions or program approaches were also recommended, such as internship programs for new teachers and administrators, elimination of social promotions by the school district, and the provision of student interns by local colleges and universities to serve as classroom assistants.

A plan to oversee the implementation of the recommendations, presented in the report, included the formation of a Community Roundtable. The roundtable aids in communication and coordination of activities initiated in response to the Call to Action; the group is comprised of representatives from all major community groups.

Under the heading, "We Call this Community to Action," the *Times Union* (the daily evening newspaper) published the entire test of the Call to Action report on the day it was released. Both television and radio stations also gave extensive coverage, which saturated a large part of the metropolitan area with news of the Education Initiative. This high media profile generated a significant amount of interest and activity by organizations and individuals.

Business Task Force

In September 1985, the business community, through the Industrial Management Council and the Chamber of Commerce, formed a Business Task Force to "determine how business can best participate in the community-wide effort to assist Rochester's students to become productive participants in the community." After several months of study of and visits to cities where major efforts had been launched to involve the business community in addressing the problems of education, the task force released its report as part of the call to action. This report acknowledged the importance of total community involvement in the initiative and defined "areas of opportunity" for community members to participate and help students improve academically. The report identified five tasks as the most effective responses the business community can make to those "areas of opportunity." The tasks included providing:

1. job placement opportunities as incentives for student performance;
2. partnerships between businesses and schools that would provide opportunities for interaction between employers/employees and students, faculty, and administrators at the school building level;
3. the marketing of education to raise the community's awareness of the importance of education and encourage participation in schooling by parents and others in the community;
4. assistance with staff development in the city school district;
5. consultants from the business community to help with management/problem-solving issues in the city school district.

Other Community Groups

The Rochester business community's response to the Education Initiative and its call to action has been extremely positive. The business community established the Edu/Action Project in May 1986 with a full-time director to oversee the implementation of the recommendations made in the task force report. A Jobs Collaborative Program was initiated at five secondary schools during the 1986-87 school year to provide students with pre-employment training, counseling, and part-time employment. The program will expand to a sixth secondary school in the 1987-88 school year.

Under the auspices of the Ad Council of Rochester, a two-year marketing effort was launched. A Marketing Education task force, including some of the community's top communicators drawn from the public relations and marketing divisions of local corporations, will oversee the advertising campaign. In addition, an umbrella advertising agency will take the lead in developing and coordinating the implementation of a comprehensive marketing plan. The ad campaign is visible with "Rochester runs on brainpower—Better education is everybody's job" billboards, and a television spot done in rap emphasizing the value of staying in school.

Several businesses have developed their own responses to the "Call to Action." Wegmans, a large local supermarket chain, began a Work-Scholarship Connection program under which the stores hire fourteen or fifteen-year old city junior high school students to work part-time as cashiers or clerks at one of their twenty-five Rochester-area stores. Because most of the stores are located outside of the city, Wegmans provides transportation to and from work. Students have mentors who are store employees and sponsors (school employees) to monitor their progress both in school and on the job. When participants graduate from high school, they are eligible for up to $5,000 per year for college tuition. As of the fall of 1987, 50 students have participated in this program.

Marine Midland Bank has established a partnership with a secondary school that has a Business Magnet program. The program will provide jobs for students after school and during the summer in areas such as check processing, word processing, and bank tellers. Other parts of the program will include college scholarships for graduates, speakers for school classes, "shadowing" programs in which a student follows a bank employee for a day at work, field trips, and training materials for teachers. Another bank, the Rochester Community Savings Bank, has granted $10,000 to the city school district to finance field trips to cultural institutions and events.

The Eastman Kodak Company has been a most prominent and active supporter of the initiative and the call to action from the beginning of these efforts. Kodak has contributed more than $35,000 to the league to underwrite some of the staff and program costs of the initiative, and has encourged several of its key staff to work on programmatic efforts. Additionally, the company has produced two high-quality video presentations that have been used locally and around the country to graphically illustrate the initiative's success.

The Center for Educational Development (CED) has facilitated the establishment of numerous partnerships between schools, businesses, and other agencies and organizations that serve the Rochester area, including colleges, a health consortium, and state, county, and city parks departments. The Center for Educational Development is a not-for-profit organization set up to bring the resources and skills of the community-at-large into the process of educating city youth.

CED has also administered a mini-grant program designed to fund "innovative and enriching supplemental teaching efforts and learning activities that directly benefit students in Rochester's public schools." CED administered grants from local foundations that totaled approximately $34,000 in mini-grants during the 1985-86 school year and $27,750 in 1986-87. In 1987-88, CED will administer a $150,000 grant from the Gannett Foundation to support projects sponsored jointly by elementary and secondary schools to meet the needs of at-risk youth. CED has also assumed responsibility for staffing the Community Roundtable on Education, which has been charged with overseeing the implementation of recommendations made in the "Call to Action" report.

Over 180 United Way-supported human service agencies that manage programs influencing clients' "readiness to learn" banded together under Partners in Education to provide more cohesive services for Rochester area youth and to better link these agencies and the schools. Among the activities which have been initiated are a workshop by the Girl Scouts of Genesee Valley entitled "Successful Strategies for Involving Parents in Education," and an effort by a neighborhood group to involve parents in the development of an early childhood magnet at a local high school.

Religious institutions have responded to the call to action in a variety of ways. One church sponsored a series of workshops under the heading of "Christian Parent Involvement in Education." Other churches have initiated tutoring or enrichment programs that extend beyond their own congregations to other youth in need.

Several area colleges have initiated programs that offer tutoring and counseling services to students in secondary schools. Others have become involved in efforts to improve teacher training, both for students entering the profession and for practicing teachers. In addition to hosting the leadership conference, the University of Rochester sponsored a conference on methods to improve the teaching profession and its workplace.

Local foundations have been major factors in the success of the initiative. More than $50,000 has been given to the League since 1985 to underwrite some of the staff and programmatic costs of the initiative. The Gannett, Daisy Marquis Jones, the Gleason Memorial Fund, and Rochester area foundations have actively participated. Additional funding was received from the Rochester-Monroe County Youth Bureau and Project Hometown America, a national competitive grant.

The city school district has acted on a number of the recommendations made in the call to action report. For example, a mentor teacher program was implemented in the 1986-87 school year, with 22 experienced teachers assigned to help 150 new teachers develop their classroom skills. Proposals to serve at-risk students were solicited from all secondary schools in the district and funds were made available for delivery of proposed services during the 1986-87 school year. The 1987-88 school budget responded to the concerns of the call to action report by including $2.5 million for programs to increase the ability of schools to meet students'needs, implement standardized district-wide curricula, and develop grade-level standards for students. The lobbying efforts of local officials including the mayor brought additional budget dollars to the district for the expansion of services. In addition, the 1987 Rochester Teachers' Association contract incorporates several of the ideas advocated in the call to action report including: (1) home-based guidance, which involves more counseling activities by teachers and more communication with parents; (2) elimination of the seniority system as a basis for teacher assignments, so that more experienced teachers can be assigned to the students with greater need; and (3) more in-service time for teachers at the beginning and the end of the school year.

There have been numerous other responses to the call to action by large and small organizations and individual citizens. It is impossible to keep track of all of those responses and difficult to know all of the plans being made or new approaches being explored. The city school district itself is large and complex; it includes 45 schools and serves over 30,000 students. As demonstrated by the examples above, however, it is safe to say that the Education Initiative has achieved its objective of involving the total community in addressing the crisis we face in educating Rochester's youth.

REFLECTIONS

As we look back over the past two years, it is worthwhile to try to identify those factors that may have contributed most significantly toward achieving broad community involvement in the Education Initiative. The first factor to consider is leadership. The Urban League is respected by a broad section of the community and has an extensive history of addressing community issues. The personal involvement and commitment of key board and staff members to the Education Initiative was a significant factor in its success. Two vice-chairs of the board took leadership roles in the initiative: one was instrumental in the League's efforts to mobilize the community from the inception of the initiative through the town meetings; the other chaired the task force that developed the "Call to Action" report and the Community Roundtable. It is not an exaggeration to say that a massive staff effort was also involved in the initiative. In addition to League staff contributing in ways from assembling packets to hosting at speakouts and conferences, six top managers comprised a work group which operated throughout the first year to ensure the success of every phase of the initiative.

In addition, the involvement of business executives, including the presidents of several large corporations in Rochester, was undoubtedly a factor in the successful involvement of the business community. The cooperation and commitment of the two school superintendents who have served since the initiative got underway, the school board, and the president of the teachers' union have also been crucial in involving other community institutions. Opposition or obstruction by the school district or the union would have made the broad mobilization of the community extremely difficult, if not impossible.

Another important factor in convincing the community that there was a crisis in education in Rochester was the availability of clear-cut data on student performance from the city school district. The district's system of collecting, compiling, and publishing data on student characteristics and performance has provided and will continue to provide a strong tool for the community to use in evaluating student achievement. Additional data available through the Urban League's Black Scholars program served to dramatize the problem even more and is an additional evaluative check on the progress of the initiative.

The final factor is the concerned effort that was made by community leaders and educators not to point fingers of blame at each other or other community groups for the crisis that existed. Instead, attention and energy was directed to responding to the questions "What can I do?" and "What can we do to improve the academic achievement of students?" This approach to the problem has helped reduce some of the barriers and tensions that often make it difficult for school staff, parents, and other community groups to work together for the benefit of the students.

IMPACT OF INITIATIVE ON STUDENT ACHIEVEMENT

In October 1986, the Urban League had a second town meeting; a third was scheduled for 1987. These meetings will report the status of student achievement in the city school district to the community and provide an opportunity for SACs to display and share information about the projects they implemented during the school year. Updated fact sheets with indicators of student achievement at the end of the first year did not show significant improvement in student achievement levels. At the time this article was prepared, the fact sheets were not available for the 1986-87 school year; however, there have been some signs of success. The number of Black Scholars who graduated from city schools has increased: from 35 in the class of 1984, 23 in 1985, 32 in 1986, up to a total of 62 in 1987. In addition, the number of black students identified by the Urban League's Early Recognition Program (students who have B or higher averages in the ninth, tenth, and eleventh grades) went from 226 in 1986 to 346 in 1987.

The task of improving the quality of education for our youth is not a short and easy one. The success that has been achieved in raising the consciousness of the community about the current crisis in education and in involving such a broad section of the community in activities designed to resolve the crisis is obvious. Although it will take several years to determine the impact of these activities on student achievement, the data on the Urban League's Black Scholars and Early Recognitition students are hopeful signs.

As of this writing, Rochester was one of ten cities competing for five grants from the Annie E. Casey Foundation of $10 million per city, to be spread out over five years. These grants provide an inducement to communities to effect new intervention strategies targeted to "at-risk" youth. Because of the collaborative activities that have already taken place through the Education Initiative, Rochester is ideally situated to compete successfully for this grant. All of these experiences bode well for a community that is seriously committed to improving the quality of education for all of its students.

21

Black School Pushouts And Dropouts: Strategies For Reduction

Antoine M. Garibaldi and Melinda Bartley

While tremendous gains have been made by black Americans in the attainment of a quality education over the last quarter of a century, serious problems still persist. Much of the emphasis today has focused on improving the academic achievement of all children and on the accountability of teachers and administrators. But lost in the debates of the educational reform movements that have swept this nation are two critical issues that have disproportionately affected black children since the early 1970s. These issues are the increased numbers of students who drop out, and those who are "pushed out" of school through suspensions and expulsions before they obtain a high school diploma. This article will discuss those issues as well as highlight several ongoing efforts designed to abate the early departure of black students from America's public schools.

SCHOOL SUSPENSIONS AND EXPULSIONS

If black children are to take full advantage of the educational access and opportunities for which Civil Rights organizations such as the National Urban League (NUL) and the National Association for the Advancement of Colored People (NAACP) fought so fervently in the 1950s and 1960s, they must first attend school everyday. However, data have clearly shown that most metropolitan school districts, where the majority of these children are enrolled, have average daily attendance rates of only 80%, compared to a national average of 92%.[1] This issue was first brought to the attention of most Americans by a 1974 report of the Children's Defense Fund (CDF), *Children Out of School in America.*[2]

CDF highlighted the importance and severity of this problem by releasing another report in 1975 on school suspensions, where it reanalyzed data collected by the federal government's Office for Civil Rights for the 1972-73 school year.[3] In the latter report, CDF found that of approximately 24 million students enrolled in the schools surveyed, almost 37,000 had been expelled and slightly more than 930,000 had been suspended at least once for an average of four days each. Non-white students comprised only 38% of the total enrollment in this survey but accounted for 43% of the expulsions, 49% of the suspensions (black students accounted for 47% of this total), and more than half of the 3½ million days lost by suspension. Moreover, non-white students were suspended for an average of 4.3 days per suspension, compared to 3.5 days for white students.

The apparent inequities in the disciplinary systems of most schools across the country prompted many administrators to investigate the causes and dispensation of suspensions and expulsions more closely, as well as the development of alternative programs and in-school strategies to keep these young people in school. Fifteen years later, however, suspensions and expulsions continue to have an adverse impact on the numbers of young people, particularly blacks and Hispanics, who leave school before graduation. The situation is even more grave, because the majority of urban public school systems are predominantly non-white and more than half of all suspensions, expulsions, and dropouts in metropolitan school districts are black.

Incidences of suspensions cannot be separated from expulsions and dropout behavior because statistics clearly show that disciplinary problems are strongly related to a student's probability of being expelled and/or subsequent propensity to drop out. CDF's earlier analyses of the reasons for student suspensions are very similar to the infractions that lead to suspension in most schools today. In the CDF report, almost two-thirds of all suspensions were administered for non-violent offenses such as truancy, tardiness, and "class cutting." Insubordination was also included in their findings to cover such things as classroom disturbance, disrespect for authority, use of profane or obscene language, or other similar violations of school rules where the physical safety of students or teachers is not threatened.

As more consistent record-keeping and school system studies were conducted, concerned educators and citizens quickly recognized the severity and impact of out-of-school suspensions on students. Suspended students not only lost credit for missed school work, but also missed valuable instruction time. They generally were left unsupervised for the remainder of the day and many parents, in fact, never knew that their children had been suspended from school. Moreover, because these same students had "free time," they were more susceptible to become involved in acts that would result in misdemeanors (e.g., shoplifting, loitering, disorderly conduct, or minor acts of vandalism)—thereby bringing them into contact with the juvenile justice system. Students suspended from school were also castigated by their peers and stigmatized or labeled as troublemakers by their teachers.

Alternatives to Suspension

Those negative effects prompted school systems to immediately look for alternatives to out-of-school suspensions so that students would neither fall behind academically nor miss school during their suspension period. (This latter rationale also benefits the school system because its revenue is based on daily attendance.) The in-school alternatives, many of which are still used today, include: (1) time-out rooms for short-term referrals such as class period; (2) in-school suspension centers, designed as full-day alternative programs located on the school campus, where "master teachers" could assist students with the daily classwork assigned by their regular teachers; and (3) counseling/guidance centers where students were required to meet on a regular basis with a counselor during or after the school day to discuss infractions.[4]

Many of these programs, begun through various federal, state, local, and private sources still exist. The majority of such programs have been very successful not only in reducing the numbers of out-of-school suspensions but also encouraging teachers to handle school or classroom disruptions themselves, rather than referring the student for an out-of-school suspension. The latter point is particularly important because skeptics of these programs not only feared that these alternative placements could become "dumping grounds" used by teachers who preferred not to work with students who had chronic disciplinary problems, but that the alternatives could become mechanisms for circumventing the usual due process of a fair and impartial hearing. Many programs that have survived this scrutiny have carefully taken precautions so that students' and parents' rights are always protected through the development of systematic referral systems. Thus, the needs of students who commit less serious offenses can be taken care of through some other means, e.g., a parent conference or behavior modification contract signed by the student and the parent.

SCHOOL DROPOUTS

While the high school graduation rates of blacks have steadily improved over the last two decades, 30% of eighteen to twenty-four-year old blacks are still not graduating from high school, and even that figure may be a conservative estimate. There are two analytic procedures used for calculating dropout statistics, but neither of them can precisely determine the actual American high school dropout rate. Nevertheless, the procedures are useful barometers for gauging the extent of the problem. Rumberger has recently described these methods, used by the Census Bureau and Department of Education, in a 1987 article.

> The U.S. Census Bureau computes the dropout rate as the proportion of a given age cohort that is not enrolled in school and has not completed high school. The latest figures, available, for October 1984, show a dropout rate of 6.8% for persons 16 and 17 years old and a dropout rate of 15.2% for persons 18 and 19 years old. The other widely-cited national data is based on attrition data, which shows the proportion of a given entering high school class, usually the ninth grade, that graduates four years later. The latest figures show an average attrition rate of 29.1% for the high school class of 1984, with state level attrition rates varying from a low of 10.7% in Minnesota to a high of 43.3% in Louisiana.[5]

Rumberger reminds the reader that both procedures' results vary considerably because their methodologies were designed for different purposes. Census data are chiefly used for determining the number and proportion of persons from a given demographic cohort who are dropouts; the state attrition data are used to judge how well an educational system is doing in graduating students. Neither method is clearly better because census data, for example, do not classify students with a G.E.D. as high school dropouts; state attrition data do not take into account students who have dropped out of school prior to ninth grade.

Regardless of the methodological problems, the fact is clear that at least 20-30% of students drop out of school annually and the majority of these students are black or Hispanic. The National Foundation for the Improvement of Education, an affiliate of the National Education Association, which has developed a national Operation Rescue program to combat the rising numbers of school dropouts, cites some alarming information on the problem in their program brochure:

—approximately 700,000 students drop out of high schools each year and another 300,000 are chronically truant;
—nationally, one of every four students entering the eighth grade will drop out before graduating; the ratio increases to two of four in the inner cities; and,
—dropout estimates for Native American, Hispanic and Black youth range from 35 to 85 percent.[6]

Reasons for Dropping Out

In large city school districts, dropout rates exceed 40% and in some areas more than 50%. As has been reported earlier, the dropout rate is higher among Hispanics, blacks, and economically and educationally disadvantaged youth. Rumberger also shows that of the primary reasons why black males dropped out of high school in 1979, disliking school was first (29%), followed by expelled or suspended (18%) and desire to work (12%). Twenty-one percent cited other reasons. For black females, 41% left school because of pregnancy and 18% said they disliked school. Forty-one percent cited other reasons that included home responsibilities (8%), poor performance in school (5%), having been expelled or suspended (5%).[7]

Hispanic male students cited their chief reasons as disliking school (26%), desire to work (16%), home responsibilities (13%), financial difficulties (9%), and suspended or expelled (6%). Hispanic females' reasons for leaving were more evenly distributed among the categories of disliking school, pregnancy and marriage (15% in each category), and other reasons (25%). By way of comparison, white males' primary reasons for leaving school were disliking school (36%), desire to work (15%), and expelled or suspended (9%), White females cited disliking school (27%), marriage (17%), and pregnancy (14%) as their major reasons for leaving.

Rumberger's analyses by race, sex, and ethnicity show that school-related processes and economic reasons are key determinants of dropout behavior. It is extraordinarily ironic and paradoxical that economic reasons are cited as factors influencing the decision by many poor and non-white students to drop out of school, because these young people will find it more difficult to keep jobs throughout their lives given their lack of educational attainment and lower academic skills. Rumberger accentuates this fact by citing the Census Bureau finding, which shows that the difference in expected lifetime earnings from the ages of 18 to 64 between a male high school graduate and a high school dropout in 1979 was more than $250,000.[8]

However, Rumberger makes an incorrect assessment of the impact dropping out or graduating has on blacks' economic consequences. He states that blacks' incomes are not affected as much as that of whites when comparing dropouts and high school graduates' unemployment situations. The percentage comparisons are misleading, however, because more than half (53%) of black high school graduates were unemployed, according to 1982 census unemployment data, when compared to 71% of black high school dropouts. On the other hand, only 19% of white high school graduates were unemployed, compared to 36% of white high school dropouts. Obviously, this data shows that even black high school graduates have a very difficult time securing gainful employment after twelve years of schooling, thus perhaps suggesting that there are fewer economic incentives for non-white students to stay in shcool.

Dropout Prevention Strategies

As dropout rates have increased nationally, a number of national organizations and foundations, as well as local school districts, have allocated funds to schools and cities to identify more precisely the causes of dropping out within their respective communities. As previously mentioned, the National Education Association's National Foundation for the Improvement of Education has developed Operation Rescue with teachers charged to find and implement solutions to the dropout problem. Program approaches include (1) "Information Exchanges" hosted by teachers and in cooperation with all segments of the community, where successful strategies for dropout prevention are identified; and (2) a publication, *A Blueprint for Success,* designed to serve as a guide for local schools, districts, and communities to develop their own dropout prevention programs.[9]

Another national program is the Ford Foundation's Dropout Prevention Collaboratives Program; this includes twenty-one cities that have been asked to initially develop "informed knowledge about what causes particular students to leave school early." The planning phase for this program began in the fall 1986 and covers the entire U.S. Each urban school system works with a technical assistance agency to develop citywide collaboratives to address the prevention of future dropouts in its metropolitan area.[10]

While there are many dropout prevention programs across the country, a 1987 survey of more than one thousand programs by the U.S. General Accounting Office shows that only a slight majority of the students served by these programs are non-white. Approximately 34% of the youth served are black, 17% Hispanic, and 4% from other racial groups, for a total of 58%, while 45% were white. Males constituted about 54% of the students served. About three-quarters (76%) were from poor families, with 67% from urban and 14% from rural areas. Fifty-nine percent were under 16 years of age. This survey also showed that approximately three-fourths of the youth in these programs were potential dropouts and one-fourth had dropped out at some time. Almost half of the programs (47%) were also targeted toward potential dropouts.[11]

With respect to reasons for dropping out, students in the surveyed programs reported, in descending frequency, that they had poor grades or that school was not for them (66% in each category), planned to get married (38%), chose to work or had been offered a job (38%), could not get along with teachers (31%), was pregnant (23%), or had been suspended or expelled (18%). While many of the youth reported more than one reason, which explains the surveyed programs' total of more than 100%, their explanations are very consistent with the earlier analyses of Rumberger.

A LOCAL AFFILIATE'S RESPONSE TO THE PROBLEM

Because every school system does not have the human and financial resources to develop organized dropout prevention programs, Urban League affiliates over the last twenty years have been instrumental in helping school districts combat the alarming rates of black students who have been suspended, or expelled or have dropped out of the educational system. Street academies and other alternative programs have been successful in remedying the situation to some extent, but today's economic and educational problems call for a variety of strategies. The Urban League of Greater New Orleans has instituted a number of programs to confront the problems of dropout and low academic achievement of black youth in the public school system. These activities have enjoyed full cooperation of all segments of the community and the local school system, as well as the assistance of national organizations.

New Orleans Urban League Street Academy

The Urban League of Greater New Orleans has consistently stressed the need for a quality education for all its students for many years. Studies have been conducted, positions taken, and programs designed by this group to address the large numbers of youth dropping out of local public schools. Available data on this problem illustrate the need for more alternative services in other areas of the country.

In the local schools, 50% of the students do not graduate; black youth are disproportionately represented in this number. The 1984-85 school system data indicate that of the 646 students who dropped out of school because of educational problems, 568 (87.9%) of them were black. Of the 293 who dropped out because of adjustment problems, 228 (77.8%) were black, and of the 199 who dropped out because of family problems, 139 (69.8%) were black.

In New Orleans, the Urban League Street Academy, with the cooperation of the New Orleans public schools, has served as the community's most effective response to this problem for the last fourteen years. During this period, the program has provided services to youth who have dropped or been pushed out of public schools. Regardless of the reasons these students left school, all of them have maintained a strong desire for a second chance at an education.

Students are accepted to the street academy either by referral from school personnel or by self-referral. An increasing number have been enrolling as self-referrals or on the recommendations of family members and friends. Thus, the greatest challenge of the staff is to meet the needs of students with appropriate educational strategies, strategies that may be non-traditional. Many of the students who enroll are emotionally insecure about their ability to achieve. Thus, the preeminent philosophy of the program is that all students possess the talent and intellectual capacity to succeed. To help them recognize these talents and skills, academic activities required for the G.E.D. are combined with individual and career counseling.

Studies of the program's curricula indicate that arts and crafts, when properly mixed with academic work, enhance academic achievement and provide a more enriching experience for the students. Years of work and research at the street academy confirm that these activities are not merely luxuries for this population, but rather are fundamental to their need for expression and growth.

The program also attempts to create an environment where peer and adult relationships can be established to support and encourage students' return to a learning environment. Teachers are provided by the local school district and additional staff support is provided by the state. Over the years, these cooperative arrangements have enabled approximately 500 students, who would have otherwise been among the many permanent dropouts, to obtain the G.E.D.

EDUCATION INITIATIVE

A major programmatic thrust of the National Urban League for the next five years is its Education Initiative. This program encourages local affiliates to work with community groups to address the decline in achievement of black youth across the U.S. By significantly increasing the involvement of black adults, churches, businesses, and community groups in activities that help students improve academically and stay in school, success such as that achieved in Rochester will be realized. Thus, both advocacy and services are needed.

Symptoms of the problems in New Orleans suggest that the initiative is the most feasible solution. The following data from the New Orleans Urban League's *State of Black New Orleans* illustrate some of those problems.

The number of families living below the federal poverty rate increased from 16% in 1970 to 27% in 1985.
Almost half of black families live below the federal poverty level.
Unemployment in the black community is approximately 25%; it is above 50% for black teenagers.
Only 9% of black adults are college graduates, compared to 19% of white adults.

Approximately 46% of black adults are high school graduates, compared to 71% of white adults.

In Orleans Parish, teenagers account for the majority of all births.

Approximately 50% of the students in Orleans Parish schools drop out.

Black students represent 84.4% of the total school population but only 26.4% of the gifted/talented enrollment, while white students represent 11.7% of the total school population and 70.1% of the gifted/talented enrollment.

While a number of activities have been developed to address the low levels of achievement and high failure rates of black youth, one of the most successful efforts is the Central City Alliance for Academic Excellence. The purpose of this targeted community effort is to assist those inner-city schools that need the most help. The collaborative efforts of key individuals (parents, teachers, students, and administrators) are designed to enable the systematic monitoring of the students' academic progress. Further, the purpose of the alliance is to develop a model for academic excellence by a concerted community campaign that uses both human and material resources. The ultimate goal is for students who enter first grade in any of the targeted elementary schools to not only graduate from high school but also to pursue their career goals.

With the assistance of businesses, national professional organizations, and local support, programs have also been designed by the local affiliate to address the academic achievement of black students in mathematics and science. Goals include the enhancement of the students' academic achievement and fewer black youth leaving school early because of academic, family, or adjustment problems.

CONCLUSION

While this article has documented the serious problems of black school dropouts and pushouts, it has also indicated that there are many successful programs that have been developed to combat this problem. However, the best strategy is to ensure that black children learn the necessary academic and cognitive skills in school to proceed to the next grade level. These problems are multifaceted, require complex solutions, and demand the total cooperation of the entire community. School dropouts cost this country billions of dollars in lost wages, taxes, and social unrest; these problems also lessen the future productivity of our technological society. This problem will continue to adversely affect us as a nation and as a community unless every segment of society joins together to promote the literacy of the next generation of leaders and professionals.

NOTES

1. See Antoine M. Garibaldi, "Promising Approaches in Elementary and Secondary Education" (Paper commissioned for the National Commission on Excellence in Education, 1983).

2. Children's Defense Fund, *Children Out of School in America,* (Washington, DC: Washington Research Project, 1974).

3. Children's Defense Fund, School Suspensions: Are They Helping Children? (Washington, DC: Washington Research Project, 1975).

4. For more information on in-school suspension programs see the following articles by the author: "In-School Alternatives to Suspension: Trendy Educational Innovations," *Urban Review,* 11, no. 2 (1979), pp. 97-103; "In-school Alternatives to Suspension: A Description of Ten School District Programs," *Urban Review,* 14 (1982), pp. 317-36 (with Richard Chobot); and "In-School Suspension," in Daniel Safer (ed.), Alternative Education Programs for Disruptive Youth, (Baltimore: University Park Press, 1982) pp. 317-36.

5. Rumberger, Russell W. "High School Dropouts: A Review of Issues and Evidence," Review of Educational Research 57 (Summer 1987), pp. 101-21.

6. National Foundation for the Improvement of Education (NFIE), "Operation Rescue" (program brochure), (Washington, DC: NFIE, 1986).

7. Rumberger, Russell W. "Dropping Out of High School: The Influence of Race, Sex and Family Background," American Educational Research Journal 20 (1983), pp. 199-220.

8. U.S. Bureau of the Census, Current Population Reports, Series P-60, no, 142 (February 1984) Table 48.

9. More information on the NEA/NFIE programs can be obtained by writing the National Foundation for the Improvement of Education, 1201 Sixteenth St. N.W., Washington, DC 20036.

10. Specific information on participating programs in the Ford Foundation Dropout Prevention Collaboratives project can be obtained from the foundation at 320 E. 43rd St., New York, 10017).

11. U.S. General Accounting Office, School Dropouts: Survey of Local Programs, (Washington, DC: General Accounting Office, July 1987). Copies of the report (GAO/HRD 87-108) can be obtained from the U.S. General Accounting Office, P.O. Box 6015, Gaithersburg, MD 20877.

22
Black Teenage Pregnancy: A Challenge for Educators

Joyce A. Ladner

No social problem affecting youth has received as much attention in recent times as adolescent pregnancy. Its causes, consequences, and solutions have been debated in the private and public arenas by legislators, policy advocates, social scientists, child welfare experts, educators, and, notably, in the mass media.

The purpose of this article is to analyze the impact of teen pregnancy on the education of black adolescents. The scope of the problem, the social context of black teen pregnancy, and its consequences will be examined. Several effective approaches to teenage pregnancy prevention, including sex/family life education, school-based health clinics, life skills, school retention, and self-esteen enhancement will be discussed.

OVERVIEW OF THE PROBLEM

In 1983, 1.1 million teenagers (of all races) became pregnant; almost 500,000 of them gave birth. Black teens accounted for 142,105, or 24.2% of all births. Roughly one-fifth of all births are to teens.[1] The births to teen-agers rose when the baby boom generation entered the teen years and has since declined. The number of births to married teens has also decreased. The major change has occurred in the increase in out-of-wedlock births to teens. At present, a majority of births to teen-agers are out of wedlock. Minority youths constitute 27% of the teen population in the U.S., but have roughly 40% of the adolescent births and 57% of births to unmarried teens. In 1982, white teens had 362,101 births, 38% of which were out-of-wedlock; black teens had 125,929 births, 87% of which were out-of-wedlock. By their eighteenth birthday, 22% of black females and 8% of white females have become mothers. By the time they are twenty, 41% of black females and 19% of white females have become mothers.[2] Further, an estimated 90% of black teens who give birth keep their babies rather than surrender them for adoption.

Originally published in the *Journal of Negro Education*, Vol. 56, no. 1 (1987). Copyright 1987, Howard University

CAUSAL EXPLANATIONS

Various explanations have been offered as the causes of teen pregnancy. These include an attempt to fulfill emotional needs by having someone to love and call one's own[3] and a feeling of hopelessness and despair toward the future that stems from economic deprivation. In such cases, early childbearing is not necessarily regarded by pregnant teens as a major obstacle to achievement,[4] because these youths experience a severe limitation of achievement opportunities. Teen pregnancy is also thought to result from cultural transmission because some blacks regard the bearing of children as a symbol of having achieved womanhood and manhood, especially in the absence of more traditional and acceptable methods for achieving success.[5]

Teen pregnancy may be symptomatic of widespread alienation from and rebellion against traditional societal norms. According to a study by the Education Commission of the States, conservative estimates indicate that there are 1,250,000 white, 750,000 black, and 375,000 Hispanic 16-to-19-year-olds who are at risk to become "disconnected" from the wider society. These are alienated and economically disadvantaged youths who will not be prepared to participate in the work force unless programs are developed to provide education and jobs for them. Since 1960, teen pregnancy in this age group has increased by 109% for whites and 10% for nonwhites.[6]

The causes of teen pregnancy are sufficiently complex to defy simple, single-factor explanations. The restriction of opportunities to acquire education and training and to access necessary resources is a major cause of too-early childbearing. For black teen parents, most of whom are poor, economic causation offers the best explanation for the increase in the magnitude of the problem. As blacks faced greater economic scarcity, the black family experienced increased fragmentation, which has led to a rapid increase in female-headed households; most of these households are at or below the poverty level. A large percentage of such households are headed by women who became mothers as teenagers. In less than 25 years, black households headed by females more than doubled, increasing from 21% in 1960 to 48% in 1984. This problem is compounded by the weakening of the extended family. Traditionally, this resource served as an indispensable support system to its members, providing child care so the teen mother could complete her education.

SOCIO-HISTORICAL CONTEXT OF BLACK TEEN PREGNANCY

Teen pregnancy among blacks must be placed within the context of changing sexual norms in American society. For over twenty years, since the so-called "sexual revolution," society has experienced the major transformation of sexual mores that has influenced every sector of the population. Teenagers of all races are now experiencing the residual effects of this major shift in cultural values—a shift from the premarital double standard, abstinence, and stigma of out-of-wedlock births to the abolition of the double standard, premarital sexual permissiveness, and a lessening of stigma for such births. Few punitive social sanctions are now leveled against females who have out-of-wedlock births or against children resulting from the nontraditional alliances. The decline of marriage as a means to legitimize birth is one result of this situation.

It is important that the socio-cultural context of pregnancy of black teenagers is explored. Historically, blacks have expressed greater tolerance and acceptance of teen pregnancy than have whites. Black out-of-wedlock pregnancies were expected to result in early marriage in order to legitimize the child's birth and to form an intact family. Usually, the welfare of the child from such a union was very important. Historical accounts of the attitudes of blacks on this subject reflect a consistent and uniform theme.[7] Invariably, the out-of-wedlock birth was regarded as a mistake made by the female, for which she could be rehabilitated. Early marriage was a major method of such rehabilitation.

If marriage did not occur, blacks were generally more accepting of the teen mother and in assisting her efforts to reorganize her life in a productive manner. Failure on her part to utilize the assistance made available by the extended family, including child care, assistance in completing her education, and obtaining employment, resulted in the isolation of the female from the respectable community. The literature is consistent in regard to the treatment of childen born into out-of-wedlock status. For the most part, these children were not assigned negative labels nor given inferior treatment because they were regarded as innocent and, therefore, not held responsible for their own birth status.[8]

Another equally compelling and unique feature of teen pregnancy from an historical perspective is that blacks rarely surrendered their children to agencies for adoption.[9] While the practice of informal adoption occurred with frequency, it almost always involved the rearing of the child by one or more members of the extended family, or by other individuals known to and accepted by the mother. It was a practice referred to as "giving the child" to persons who were expected, because of personal familiarity, to provide adequately for the child. This practice was not one of first choice, but often resulted when it was difficult or impossible for the teen parent(s) to marry or to provide for the child. Agency adoptions were rarely practiced because they catered to a white middle-class clientele and did not place significant numbers of black children in such families.

Today, a small minority of black teenagers place their children for adoption despite the fact that a majority of black teens who become pregnant are also poor and cannot economically support their children. A widespread sentiment among black teen parents is that the economic and other hardships encountered due to the birth of the child are unavoidable realities of life over which they have little control. Indeed, this represents a fatalistic attitude engendered by a lifetime of economic deprivation and a sense of powerlessness to exercise control over one's life. The expectation, enforced by cultural and religious standards among the black poor, is that out-of-wedlock children are to be kept in the family and community regardless of the hardships involved in doing so.

The most serious consequence of too-early childbearing is the truncation of educational attainment,without which teen parents are unable to adequately fill a parenting role. It is estimated that at least 50% of teen mothers drop out of school because of pregnancy. In some cities, the rates are much higher. A study by Card and Wise based on a national sample found that mothers who had given birth before they reached eighteen years of age were half as likely to have graduated from high school as those who postponed childbearing until after their twentieth birthday. These researchers also found that adolescent males who became fathers before age eighteen were 40% less likely to have graduated from high school than were those who waited until after schooling was completed.[10]

Youth who already have a low level of school performance are more likely than those with high performance to become teen parents.[11] Low levels of aspiration and performance place them at greater risk to have children. Early parenthood may symbolize, for many such students, the ability to achieve in at least one area deemed to be important by their peers, even if all others are obstructed. To have a child remains an ancient rite of passage into womanhood and manhood for many of this nation's poor youth. It may also enhance self-esteem, albeit temporarily, and some teens have also reported increased popularity in their peer group. Moreover, poor school performance frequently represents the inability of the youth, due to a variety of internal and external factors, to conceptualize and plan for the future. Teenagers who cannot do this are unlikely to acquire the necessary skills to prepare for future jobs and careers, because conceptualization requires positive role models, resources, and a basic understanding of the way to acquire the skills to achieve goals.

Youth who are at risk educationally are not only more likely to become parents, but also are at risk of becoming unemployed if they drop out of school. In 1985, the unemployment rates for black teenagers were 41.4% for males and 37.9% for females.[12] An obvious repercussion for teen mothers is that at any given time, 60% must rely on Aid to Families with Dependent Children (AFDC) for their livelihood. In 1985, the cost of AFDC, Medicaid and food stamps for teen parents and their children was $18.5 billion.[13]

ISSUES AND APPROACHES TO TEEN PREGNANCY PREVENTION

There is a greater understanding of the causes and consequences of teen pregnancy than of solutions to prevent its occurrence. Society has failed to adopt a prevention model to counter the consequences of early unprotected sexual activity by youth. The traditional approach to solving social problems has been the adoption of the short-term, stop-gap (residual) method of intervention. Such solutions have also included the adoption of a services-delivery model designed to assist individuals in need on a temporary basis with the objective of providing rehabilitation after the fact. The more effective and rarely used alternative approach is the long-term or institutional model that attempts to identify and eradicate root causes. Such a comprehensive type of approach emphasizes prevention.[14]

The Alan Guttmacher Institute found that the U.S. has the highest teen pregnancy rate of any Western nation and is the only major Western country that fails to provide teens with adequate information on family planning. In all other countries surveyed, contraceptives were much more readily available to teens without the traditionally punitive sanctions and double standards practiced here.[15] Another barrier to the adoption of the institutional/prevention model is the reluctance of many adults to sanction contraceptive programs for teens because they feel such designs encourage youths to become sexually active. There are no data to substantiate such a claim.

The most effective approaches to teen pregnancy prevention are those that emphasize a variety of strategies, including education and training, jobs, sex/family life education, life-skills training, peer counseling, and male responsibility counseling, with equal emphasis on the needs of females and males. Effective programs implemented in educational settings, include the Teen Outreach Program and the Choices and Challenges curriculum.

Life Skills Training

An innovative teen pregnancy prevention program, the Teen Outreach Program, was started in St. Louis in 1977 by the Danforth Foundation, the Junior League, and the St. Louis Public Schools. Teen Outreach, which now exists at twenty-four sites in several cities, is an after-school program that works with male and female at-risk youths in middle and high school to reduce teen pregnancy and encourage the completion of high school. The program is conducted by facilitators who instruct the participants in a curriculum that includes such life management skills as sexuality, self-esteem building and career planning, and covers substance and child abuse and teen suicide.

The program also requires that each participant, all of whom are self-selected, volunteer for community services. By helping others, participants derive a stronger sense of self-worth and a sense of mastery over the environment. The Teen Outreach Program was evaluated in 1985 with the use of a comparison group: participants were found to be less likely to get pregnant or to fail courses than were subjects in the control group.[16]

Another program of interest to educators is the Choices and Challenges curriculum, developed by Girls Club of America to assist preadolescent and adolescent males and females to plan their futures and to acquire a more realistic understanding of the social, economic, and emotional implications of teen parenthood. This very popular course is designed to take participants through the maze of experiences they are likely to encounter as adults, using a variety of typical situations. Participants thereby receive a more realistic picture of what parenthood is like and they acquire coping skills. After completion of the Choices and Challenges course, students are less likely to romanticize about becoming parents because they acquire a concrete understanding of the demands parenthood imposes.[17]

Sex Education and School-Based Clinics

The fact that contradictory views exist regarding teen sexuality is evident from the considerable opposition launched against sex/family life education in the schools and school-based clinics that offer family planning services. Critical issues include identifying the content of appropriate sex education, acceptable boundaries (for example, should courses include information on contraceptives, abortion, decision making, and population issues) curriculum control, and the age or grade youth should receive sex education. There is little agreement about such concerns. In a study conducted by Allen and Bender,[18] it was found that responses varied widely on the appropriate forum in which sex education should be taught. The family, school, and church were all regarded as the appropriate institution to teach sex education.

Sex education in the schools is an especially controversial issue today because of the political conservatives' advocacy of the view that parents have the exclusive right to determine the proper forum in which their offspring should receive such information. This thinking presents a serious barrier for youth who come from families where the parents cannot capably discuss sex. Parents may lack an understanding of basic sex education, or they may be reluctant to mention the subject for fear of stimulating the child's interest in it.

Sex/family life education programs in schools vary according to curriculum design, staff, resources, and the extent to which they are regarded as a priority by the school system, parents, and the community. For example, Washington, D.C., is one of only three areas in the nation which have mandated sex/family life education for grades kindergarten through twelve (Maryland and New Jersey are the other two). Yet, even in this area, there is no systematic implementation of the curriculum, nor are there effective teacher training programs and coordination efforts.[19] In an evaluation of fourteen sex education programs in schools and community-based organizations, Kirby found that the most effective programs were those affiliated with a school-based health clinic and those that attempted to facilitate positive parent-child interaction and communication.[20] Unfortunately, most students do not take a sex education course until high school, long after such youths may have become sexually active. More innovative curriculum designs propose teaching sex/family life education in elementary school on a level appropriate to the learning environment of young children.

The type of education and support that schools are able to provide to the prospective teen mother and father is critical to their success. Until recently, efforts were not made to keep pregnant girls in school on a consistent basis. Title IX of the 1972 Education Amendments prohibits the expulsion of pregnant students and requires that they be provided instruction either in the school or elsewhere. Whether the expectant teen mother will remain in school usually depends on the availability of child care, a service most teen parents cannot afford. Grandmothers, who previously provided this service, are more likely to be in the work force or still in their childbearing years, and thus have less time to take care of grandchildren while their daughters return to school.[21]

A few schools offer child care for teen parents; this strategy can be especially effective in promoting secondary prevention (i.e., prevention of additional pregnancies) and providing parent education and quality child care. A recently-completed longitudinal study found that teen mothers who had day care for their children were more likely to complete high school, to obtain post-secondary training, and to become self-supporting. The children benefited intellectually from the programs, scoring significantly higher than control persons on a general cognitive index.[22]

School-Based Comprehensive Health Clinics

The school-based health clinics started in St. Paul, Minnesota twelve years ago are an education-related innovation in teen pregnancy prevention. Since the introduction of the clinics in two St. Paul high schools, there has been a 56% reduction in birthrates and a 35% reduction in the school drop out rate among teen mothers.[23] There are now over seventy clinics nationwide, with over a hundred more in the planning stages. School-based clinics are thought to be very effective because they provide comprehensive health services to a highly under-served population within close proximity to the one institution with which the teenager has the most consistent and sustained involvement outside the family. Clinics are staffed by health practitioners and social service workers known to the teenagers, and provide basic, high quality services at minimal or no cost. Broad, comprehensive health care is provided to teens that includes physical examinations for sports, screening for undiagnosed health problems, family planning counseling, counseling and treatment for sexually transmitted diseases, and other basic health services that teens frequently do not get.

A widely held myth is that the only function of such clinics is to provide contraceptives to teenagers. Critics overlook the fact that this is only one of the many services these facilities provide. In a speech before the Education Writers of America in which he criticized school-based cinics, Secretary of Education William Bennett stated that "clinics legitimate sexual activity and cause an 'abdication of moral authority.'"[24] A widely publicized controversy arose at the DuSable High School in Chicago when protesters picketed the school because a clinic was slated to be introduced in the school. However, parents of DuSable students supported the clinic, and it opened in spring of 1986. The following fall, a group of local black ministers filed suit to have the clinic closed. As of this writing, the case is in litigation. Most clinics have not been so controversial, as evidenced by their rapid growth in school districts across the country. These resource centers promise to continue to be a highly effective method of educating teens about primary health care concerns and for helping to prevent too early childbearing.

CONCLUSION

Although teen pregnancy is a national problem that transcends racial and class boundaries, it takes a far greater toll on the lives of blacks and the poor than on other groups. Over the past fifteen years, the most vulnerable black families have become severely fractured. The impact of a worsened economy has produced the highest rates of chronic male unemployment in history, leading to a drastic increase in the number of female-headed households. As noted, 48% of black families are now headed by women, and 46.5% of black children live in poverty. Such households are under great amounts of stress in almost every area.

In 1971, this author published a study of the impact of race and poverty on the psychosocial development of black female adolescents in a St. Louis housing project.[25] Although these youths were acutely sensitive to racial and class discrimination, they were optimistic about their futures and felt they could overcome the handicaps of race and poverty. The quality of their lives was substantially better than the quality of life experienced by many black adolescents with similar backgrounds today. Another striking qualitative difference between the two groups is the lack of optimism about the future evidenced in today's black youths. A generation ago, the typical pregnant teenager did not suffer the multiple exposures often experienced by many pregnant teens today. In addition to pregnancy, today's pregnant teens are more likely to have health problems, inadequate or nonexistent child care, become school dropouts, and lack job skills and employment opportunities. The erosion of many of the stable institutions in black communities has created a more pervasive configuration of multiple exposures (e.g., crime, drugs, and poverty) to which children and youth are subjected. Hence, the most troubled families are more distressed than ever before, and there has been an increase in the incidence and severity of the problems affecting the poor.

While the problem of adolescent pregnancy for blacks is now receiving widespread attention, there are still far too few effective educational programs to curtail its high incidence. The recent decrease in federal spending for social programs is an indication of the government's lack of commitment to primary prevention. There is, however, an increase in programs undertaken by black organizations, including those sponsored by fraternities, sororities, and civil-rights, advocacy, policy, social welfare, and religious groups. It is clear that blacks, recognizing the magnitude of the problem, have seized the opportunity to provide much of the leadership that will be needed to bring about effective, long-term solutions.

NOTES

1. U.S. Department of Health and Human Services, National Center for Health Statistics, "Advance Report of Final Natality Statistics, 1983," Monthly Vital Statistics (Washington, D.C.: U.S. Government Printing Office, 1985).

2. Kristin Moore, "Fact Sheet on Teenage Pregnancy" (Washington, D.C.: Child Trends, Inc., 1985).

3. Thomas J. Silber, "Adolescent Pregnancy Programs: A Perspective for the Future," *Journal of Sex Education and Therapy*, 8 (1982) pp. 48-50.

4. Joyce A. Ladner, "Teenage Pregnancy: Implications for Black Americans," in James Williams (ed.) *The State of Black America*, (New York: National Urban League, 1986), pp. 65-84.

5. Joyce A. Ladner, *Tomorrow's Tomorrow: The Black Woman* (New York: Doubleday, 1971).

6. Education Commission of the States, "Reconnecting Youth" (Washington, D.C.: Education Commission of the States, 1985).

7. W.E.B. DuBois, *Efforts for Social Betterment among Negro Americans* (New York: Russell and Russell, 1969); Charles S. Johnson, *Shadow of the Plantation* (Chicago: Univ. of Chicago Press, 1934); Hortense Powdermaker, *After Freedom: A Cultural Study in the Deep South* (New York: Viking Press, 1939).

8. Ladner, *Tomorrow's Tomorrow*.

9. Andrew Billingsley, and Jeanne Giovanonni, *Children of the Storm: Black Children and American Child Welfare* (New York: Macmillan, 1972); Joyce A. Ladner, *Mixed Families: Adopting Across Racial Boundaries* (New York: Doubleday, 1977).

10. J.J. Card, and L.L. Wise, "Teenage Mothers and Teenage Fathers: The Impact of Early Childbearing on the Parents' Personal and Professional Lives," *Family Planning Perspectives*, 10 (1978), pp. 199-205.

11. Jerald G. Bachman, S. Green, and I. Wirtanen, Vol. 3 of *Youth in Transition, Dropping Out-Problem or Symptom?* (Ann Arbor: Univ. of Michigan Institute for Social Research, 1971); I. Berkowitz, "Improving the Relevance of

Secondary Education for Adolescent Developmental Needs," in Max Sugar ed. *Adolescent Parenthood*, (New York: S.P. Medical and Scientific Books, 1980); Frank Furstenburg, *Unplanned Parenthood: The Social Consequences of Teenage Childbearing* (New York: The Free Press, 1976).

12. U.S. Bureau of Labor Statistics, "The Employment Situation-Current Population Survey" (Washington, D.C.: USDC, 1985), pp. 85-471.

13. M. Burt, *Estimates of Public Costs for Teenage Childbearing* (Washington, D.C.: Center for Population Options, 1986).

14. Huttman, Elizabeth, *Introduction to Social Policy* (New York: Macmillan, 1981); Alfred Kahn, *Social Policy and Social Services* (New York: Random House, 1979); and Thomas Meenaghan, and Robert O. Washington, *Social Policy and Social Welfare* (New York: Free Press, 1980).

15. Elise Jones, *et. al.*, "Teenage Pregnancy in Developed Countries: Determinism and Policy Implications," *Family Planning Perspectives* 17, (1985), pp. 53-63.

16. Karen Pittman, *Model Programs Preventing Adolescent Pregnancy and Building Youth Self-Sufficiency*, (Washington, D.C.: Children's Defense Fund, 1986).

17. *Choices: A Teen Woman's Journal for Self-Awareness and Personal Planning*, (Santa Barbara: Girls Club of America, 1983); and *Challenges: A Young Man's Journal for Self-Awareness and Personal Planning*, (Santa Barbara: Girls Club of America, 1984).

18. James E. Allen, and Deborah Bender, *Managing Teenage Pregnancy: Access to Abortion, Contraception, and Sex Education* (New York: Praeger Special Studies, 1980).

19. *Preventing Children from Having Children*, (Washington, D.C.: District of Columbia Department of Human Services, 1985).

20. Douglas Kirby, *Sexuality Education: An Evaluation of Programs and Their Effects* (Santa Cruse: Network Publications, 1984).

21. Joyce A. Ladner, and R.M. Gordine, "Intergenerational Teenage Motherhood: Some Preliminary Findings," *SAGE: A Scholarly Journal on Black Women*, 1 (1984), pp. 22-24.

22. Frances A. Campbell, Bonnie Breitmayer, and Craig T. Ramey, "Disadvantaged Single Teenage Mothers and Their Children: Consequences of Free Educational Day Care," *Family Relations* 35, (1986), pp. 63-8.

23. Douglas Kirby, *School-Based Health Clinics: An Emerging Approach to Improving Adolescent Health and Addressing Teenage Pregnancy* (Washington, D.C.: Center for Population Options, 1985).

24. Joyce Ladner, "The Most Basic Health Care," Washington Post, April 27, 1986, p.C8.

25. Ladner, *Tomorrow's Tomorrow*.

ABOUT THE AUTHORS

MARGUERITE ROSS BARNETT, Ph.D., is chancellor, University of Missouri, St. Louis, Mo.

MELINDA BARTLEY, Ph.D., is associate vice chancellor for Academic Affairs at Southern University of New Orleans, La., former vice president of the New Orleans Urban League, and previous acting director of the New Orleans Urban League Street Academy.

DERRICK BELL, J.D., is professor at Harvard University Law School, Cambridge, Ma., former dean of the University of Oregon Law School, former deputy director of the office of Civil Rights in the U.S. Department of Health, Education and Welfare, and former attorney with the NAACP Legal Defense and Educational Fund, Inc.

JAMES E. CHEEK, Ph.D., is president of Howard University, Washington, D.C.

EVA WELLS CHUNN, Ph.D., is senior research associate, National Urban League Research Department, and associate editor of Urban League Review, Washington, D.C.

JAMES P. COMER, M.D., is Maurice Falk Professor of Child Psychiatry and director of the Yale University Child Study Center, and associate dean of the Yale Medical School, New Haven, Conn.

MARY E. DILWORTH, Ph.D., is director of Research and Information Services, American Association of Colleges for Teacher Education, Washington, D.C.

BETTY DWYER, M.A., is manager of the Education Initiative of the Urban League of Rochester, N.Y., Inc.

ANTOINE M. GARIBALDI, Ph.D., is chairman of the Education Department at Xavier University of Louisiana, New Orleans, La., chair of the New Orleans Urban League Education committee, and a former director of the St. Paul (Minn.) Urban League Street Academy.

MURIEL HAMILTON-LEE, Ed.D., is associate research director of the School Development Program at the Yale University Child Study Center, New Haven, Conn.

NORRIS M. HAYNES, Ph.D., is research director of the Schools Development Program of the Yale University Child Study Center, New Haven, Conn.

WILLIE W. HERENTON, Ph.D., is superintendent of the Memphis Public School System, Memphis, Tenn., and member of the board of the National Urban League, Inc.

ASA G. HILLIARD III, Ph.D., is Fuller E. Callaway Professor of Education at Georgia State University, and former dean of Education at San Francisco State University.

JOHN E. JACOB, M.S.W., is president and chief executive officer of the National Urban League, Inc., New York, N.Y.

SYLVIA T. JOHNSON, Ph.D., is professor of Psycho-Educational Studies, School of Education, Howard University, Washington, D.C.

WILLIAM A. JOHNSON, JR., M.A., is president and chief executive officer of the Urban League of Rochester, N.Y.

FAUSTINE C. JONES-WILSON, Ph.D., is editor-in-chief, *Journal of Negro Education*, and graduate professor of Social Foundation of Education, School of Education, Howard University, Washington, D.C.

VALERIE SHAHARIW KUEHNE, M.Ed. is a doctoral student in the School of Education and Social Policy, Northwestern University, Evanston, Il.

JOYCE A. LADNER, Ph.D., is professor of Social Work, Howard University, former chair of the mayor's Blue Ribbon Panel on Teenage Pregnancy Prevention for the District of Columbia, and adjunct fellow at the Joint Center for Political Studies, Washington, D.C.

CHARLES D. MOODY, SR. Ph.D., is vice provost for Minority Affairs, University of Michigan, former Illinois superintendent of schools, and founder of the National Alliance of Black School Superintendents (now the National Alliance of Black School Education).

CHRISTELLA D. MOODY, M.A., is assistant to the dean of Education, Eastern Michigan University, Ypsilanti, Michigan.

JAMES J. PRESTAGE, Ph.D., is former chancellor at Southern University, Baton Rouge, and coordinator of the Louisiana Consent Decree, Baton Rouge, La.

JEWEL L. PRESTAGE, Ph.D., is dean, School of Urban Affairs and Public Policy, Southern University, Baton Rouge, La.

DIANA T. SLAUGHTER, Ph.D., is associate professor of School Education and Social Policy Northwestern University, Evanston, Il.

JOHN W. SMITH, M.Ed., special assistant to Representative Augustus F. Hawkins, chairman of the U.S. House of Representatives committee on Education and Labor, Washington, D.C.

WILLY DEMARCELL SMITH, Ph.D., is former editor of the *Urban League Review* and currently director of faculty research/professor of business communications, School of Business and Public Administration, Howard University, Washington, D.C.

JOAN Z. SPADE, Ph.D., is research associate, Urban League of Rochester N.Y., Inc. and adjunct assistant professor at the State University of New York College at Brockport.

ALVIN THORNTON, Ph.D., is associate professor of Political Science, Howard University, Washington, D.C., chairman of the monitoring committee of the Community Advisory council in Magnet and Compensatory Educational Programs of Prince George's County Public Schools, and vice president of Prince George's County NAACP, Md.

MARY CARTER-WILLIAMS, Ph.D., is coordinator of Continuing Education and Community Service Programs, School of Communications, Howard University, and former senior fellow, Institute for the Study of Educational Policy, Howard University, Washington, D.C.

CHARLES V. WILLIE, Ph.D., is professor of Education and Urban Studies, Graduate School of Education, Harvard University, Cambridge, Mass.